A DANGEROUS FREEDOM

BOOKS BY BRADFORD SMITH

A DANGEROUS FREEDOM

TO THE MOUNTAIN   THIS SOLID FLESH

AMERICAN QUEST   THE ARMS ARE FAIR

THE STORY OF JESUS   AMERICANS FROM JAPAN

BRADFORD OF PLYMOUTH   CAPTAIN JOHN SMITH

A HANDBOOK OF ENGLISH & AMERICAN LITERATURE

FOR YOUNG READERS:

WILLIAM BRADFORD—PILGRIM BOY
DAN WEBSTER—UNION BOY

A DANGEROUS
FREEDOM

By BRADFORD SMITH

J. B. LIPPINCOTT COMPANY
PHILADELPHIA AND NEW YORK

It is by the enjoyment of a dangerous freedom that the Americans learn the art of rendering the dangers of freedom less formidable.—DE TOCQUEVILLE

323.47
564

24499

FOR

JOHN and DOROTHY CANFIELD FISHER

Sturdy champions of the American Way

CONTENTS

A DANGEROUS FREEDOM

I

Home Town

If you could take the roofs off the public buildings of Bennington, Vermont, on a weekday evening, the activity of the human animals thus disclosed would resemble that of a very busy hive. The Y.M.C.A. alone would show a cluster of active cells, including a basketball game in the gym, a meeting of the League of Women Voters upstairs, a Scout troop in the cellar room, and a meeting of the Y's board of directors. A few doors to the west the ladies' group of the Methodist church is listening to a young man recently returned from India, while across School Street to the east the members of the Congregational Men's Club have pushed their chairs back from the supper table to hear the president of Bennington College speak about his recent tour of duty in Germany.

Or in the Georgian Room, upstairs over the Paradise Restaurant, the Lions Club is listening to a report of its treasurer and deciding how much money it will have to raise to support its program of eye tests and glasses for children whose parents cannot afford to give them proper eye care. Up the street the lights are ablaze in the high school where adults who have not lost their zest for learning are busy with classes in typing, world affairs and crafts, while a play rehearsal is going forward in the antiquated auditorium.

Red Cross headquarters is lighted up too. Civilian Defense volunteers are ironing the kinks out of a plan to handle evacuees who might pour into Bennington in case of a disaster. The rooms which house the Family Service Center, upstairs over Joe's Clothing Store, are also alight. The directors are discussing the budget for the coming season. In the town offices a group of taxpayers are meeting with the selectmen and the town manager.

Even if there is no regular meeting, the lights shine from the new Knights of Columbus Building, the Masonic Temple, the ornamented old mansion which is now the headquarters of the Elks. There are always a few of the boys at the American Legion rooms, or in the frame house which accommodates the Veterans of Foreign Wars.

At the College, four miles from town, a group of townspeople, students and staff members are practicing a major work of Bach under the direction of Paul Boepple, a member of the music faculty. Scattered through the town, in homes and offices, half a dozen other groups are meeting voluntarily for a variety of reasons—the Izaak Walton League to tackle the problem of stream pollution, a committee of Rotary to decide how to raise funds for a youth program, the hospital board of directors for its regular monthly meeting. Camera Club, unions and Grange may be in action.

All across the broad face of America a similar activity stirs the people, makes living organisms of the structures of wood and steel and stone which rise out of the quiet earth. To calculate the man-hours of effort involved in these activities on even one evening of the year would be impossible, while the whole year's output of energy voluntarily poured into all these associations is a quantity more appropriate to stellar distances than to the affairs of men.

Well over a hundred years ago Alexis de Tocqueville, that astute observer of things American, could write: "In no country in the world has the principle of association been more successfully used or applied to a great multitude of objects than in America." Yet it has been ignored or misunderstood not only by Americans but by most observers who come to study us and then go home to write their books about us. And because it has been ignored we have built up a myth about ourselves which is damaging our reputation abroad and limiting our behavior at home.

This myth is that the United States is a capitalist-materialist-individualist culture in which the individual, through the mechanism of a free economy, devotes himself to the piling up of material goods and comforts as his sole end and aim in life. The damage being done by this myth is apparent in our foreign relations—in the distrust with which even our friends abroad view us and in the confusion and resentment in our own minds.

We are still thinking of ourselves through outworn slogans and habits of mind. We are vaguely aware that they do not express us, yet they are part of our tradition, and tradition is a hard thing to change or throw off. So we go on, a little nervously and halfheartedly (or what is worse, belligerently because doubtfully) shouting the old cries of free enterprise—when everyone knows enterprise is no longer free and has always depended on governmental protection; and of free-wheeling individualism—when we know that no man is able to live by and for himself, or could endure it if it were possible.

There is some truth in the accusation of foreign observers that we are not a people much given to reflection, or how would we let a caricature of the real America represent us at home as well as abroad? Granted that free-wheeling individualism and unrestricted competition characterized us in the first burst of industrialization, why have we allowed the image to remain when the substance has long faded? Anthropologists have a word for it—they call it "cultural lag." Traditions often hang on when the need for them is dead. Our creed of rugged competition is like tying a Ford to a hitching post.

The American proposition is bigger, always has been bigger, than the tooth-and-claw theory of survival. We are nearer today then we have ever been to a realization of the American dream. But we are also, by a cruel and ironic paradox, closer to annihilation and the collapse of all we have built up through three centuries of hard work. In this dilemma the scared businessman jumps back into the protective briars of free enterprise (which was never so free as to deny him tariffs, subsidies and other forms of protection), the scared intellectual retreats into whatever negativist creed happens to be fashionable, and the average citizen just stays scared.

Much of the uneasiness and indecision in American life today comes from the gap between our behavior—which for the most part sensibly meets and solves problems as they arise—and our value system, which clings to old slogans that never did express the true genius of the American people. If we could square our beliefs with our actions, we would rid ourselves of an unnecessary strain and at the same time affirm a set of values based solidly in the American past which could lead us forward instead of holding us back.

First, let us see what is really going on in some of the towns Americans call home.

* * *

When the schoolhouse burned down in New Sharon, Maine, in 1949, people cried as they watched the volunteer firemen lose their battle against the flames. It was the third time in thirty years that this town of eight hundred people had seen it happen, and they had no idea where they could get the money to build again. Their whole school system—both the grades and high school—was in that building.

Faced with a problem which involved the whole community, New Sharon did what a New England town always does. It called a town meeting.

The school board had already talked with a man from the state's Department of Education. He had told them a new school would cost $80,000. To start with, they had $15,000 fire insurance. State law limited the amount they could borrow. Since the town was already in debt $8,000, they would be allowed to borrow only $10,000 more. That left them with $55,000 to raise. For a town of 761 this was a huge sum.

But the motion to build the school was made, seconded, and passed without a dissenting voice.

A citizen stood up. "I would like to ask for a showing of hands of all those in this hall that would pledge a hundred dollars in money, labor, or material," he said.

The sum of $6,500 was raised in pledges. That left $48,500. Meanwhile school was held wherever space could be found. The Grange Hall kitchen became the science laboratory.

The Grange also volunteered to clear away the debris and prepare the site for the new building. Plans were drawn and approved—this time for a fireproof building. Selectman Harold Gray was put in charge of buying the building materials. Merchants gave wholesale prices. Townspeople who owned trucks brought the materials to the site. Volunteer labor lowered the cost still further. But with every possible saving, New Sharon was still running $20,000 short.

The ladies of the Farm Bureau volunteered to raise money for the school kitchen. They had a food sale and a cowboy show; profit—$103. They had a card party, a candy sale, a paper drive. They sold pencils, pins, cards. These activities brought in $134. They hired two booths at the Skowhegan Fair and sold home-cooked food. All the women helped—not only as cooks but waiting on customers, setting tables, washing dishes. They went on to two other fairs and cleared $3,000.

An ox-pulling contest brought in another thousand. The state legislature made a special appropriation of ten thousand. Still they had six thousand to go. So they held an auction. They went into their attics and barns and hauled out everything they could spare—chairs, tables, old sleighs, dishes, clothing, knickknacks and gewgaws of all kinds, some of them fine old antiques and some just old. They made a lot of money on the auction.

Seven months after the fire, they opened their new school— a school built by the voluntary effort of the citizens.

A remarkable achievement? New Sharon's Dr. Fitch doesn't think so. "I think we're, by and large, just like the people throughout the rest of the country," he said. "We had a big job and we just went at it and did it. That's about all it amounted to."

❀   ❀   ❀

In Arlington, Virginia, the schools were so crowded, because of the influx from near-by Washington, that halls and washrooms were being used for classes. Students had to attend in shifts, and teachers were so worn out by the overcrowding that they left as fast as they could. Where teachers lasted only a few weeks at a time, learning was next to impossible. The school board, resentful of the problem created by the influx of so many new citizens with their children, was interested primarily in keeping taxes down. When parents organized a group to meet with the board, they were treated with a chilly hostility. There was no money for new schools, they were told, and there would be none unless there was a bond issue. Before there could be a bond issue, there had to be a petition with a thousand signatures on it, and then a vote.

The petition was started then and there. Then the parents went on to form the Citizens Committee for School Improvement. They canvassed for members, cranked out publicity on a mimeograph machine, and circulated the bond issue petition for which they rounded up five thousand signatures. Then the school board sidetracked it anyhow.

The older residents of Arlington were afraid that after the bond issue had been voted, the new residents would move out and leave them with a heavy debt. A whispering campaign tried to break down the Citizens Committee. It was said that children of the Committee members would be failed in the schools.

But the Committee wasn't scared. If the board wouldn't present the bond issue to the voters, the voters would get a new board.

Only under Virginia law the school board was not elected; it was appointed by a judge.

That meant a trip to Richmond, and a law to permit election of school boards.

So members of the P.T.A., the League of Women Voters and the Citizens Committee went to Richmond. The trip paid off. They got a law permitting a referendum which would let the

people of Arlington County choose whether to have an elected
or an appointed board.

Now another doorbell campaign was necessary. The children
helped by handing out leaflets. There were speeches on the
radio, and on election day a sound truck cruised through the
streets reminding everyone to vote. There were car pools to
take voters to the polls. Other volunteers saw that new voters
understood how to vote.

The referendum passed, a new board was elected, and
Arlington was now ready to begin improving its schools. But
this did not mean that the volunteer work could stop. Now the
bond issues had to be passed, and this meant more ringing of
doorbells. Between 1948 and 1951 the volunteer workers persuaded voters to authorize issues totaling $11,401,000. Even
then Arlington would have to go on building one schoolroom a
week for eight years in order to catch up with its needs.

The new superintendent, William Early, relied on volunteer
work to keep the program going. He got people who had been
fighting the school program to work on committees. And
Arlington began to have the school system its children needed.

Said one of the students: "When you was in the first or second
grade you only went three hours, now you go six hours and you
can learn a lot more in six hours than you do in three hours. At
least if you don't, you should."

One of the mothers said: "In the midst of all the chaos of this
world, we are building schools like these, beautiful permanent
structures that say to the other parts of the world: we believe in
democracy; we believe in the public school system; we believe
in the education of every child in this way of life."

*   *   *

But even when you have the building and the teachers, a
school needs other things that can be supplied only by voluntary
service. One of these is career guidance. Until very recently, a
high school student was expected to find out what he wanted
to do with his life pretty much on his own, aided by family

pressure which might as easily be wrong as right. Now most high schools have guidance programs. But even aptitude tests and the aid of a trained adviser cannot show a boy or girl what a job is really like.

To fill this need, service clubs throughout the country have been running career clinics in recent years. Men of different trades and professions talk to students, answer their questions, try to make real to them the rewards and hazards of the job.

Career Day has become an annual affair in many high schools. In Goshen, Indiana, the Rotary Club volunteers its services to give the 260 juniors and seniors an idea of the opportunities open to them.

First, a Rotary committee carried out a survey to identify the town's major vocations. They listed a hundred. Each student then selected three from this list. The range ran from agriculture and architecture through dentistry and interior decorating to real estate and veterinary work. Then the Club arranged for sessions at each place of business so that the students could see what the work was like, learn what preparation they would need, how long it would take, what the chances for advancement might be. They visited an electrician in his shop, an accountant in his office. They looked over the equipment of an optometrist, talked with an advertising man, an airline hostess. Some were surer than ever about what they wanted to be; others changed their minds. Most of them felt as if they had taken a tangible step toward a career.

* * *

The teen-agers who in their yearning toward adulthood are looking for careers are also a great reservoir of volunteer energy which is too rarely tapped. In Pascack Valley, New Jersey, they did not wait to be tapped but went to work by themselves.

The Pascack Valley area needed a new hospital. A Hospital Association had been formed by adult volunteers, but fund raising had lagged. The captain of a high school ball team decided to do something about it. With a group of friends, he

organized an association—the Teen-Ager Hospital Auxiliary—
which was soon way out ahead of the adult group. The teen-
agers raised enough to pay for the hospital site. But they did not
stop there. They gave dinners and variety shows. They took on
odd jobs. They placed and serviced contribution boxes in public
places. They gave free concerts to arouse interest in the hospital.

They heard about a directory which was about to be delivered
door to door, and took on the job at five cents a copy for a profit
of several hundred dollars. They noticed a model home in a real
estate development and asked permission to charge a ten-cent
admission fee. Then they went out and rounded up an audience.
They brought six thousand people into the house and $600 into
their treasury. They now have several branches of their organization throughout the hospital area.

Other communities are beginning to use this tremendous
reserve of untapped voluntary manpower. In Baltimore Harry
Bard, assistant director for curriculum of the Board of Education, decided that such a program could be started in the high
schools. He checked first with some of the voluntary service
agencies in town to see if they were interested. They were. Some
of the teachers were skeptical, but Mr. Bard was able to make
a trial start in two schools.

Representatives of the agencies came and talked to the
students about their work. Then the students visited the hospitals, recreation centers, libraries, children's home, and Red Cross
centers where they could watch adult volunteers doing the kind
of work they themselves would be doing. Finally they chose
their activities.

They packed materials for the Red Cross blood program,
made posters, visited hospital patients. They helped set up a
Golden Age Club for oldsters, gave aid and advice on a bicycle
safety program, prepared a booklet on housing, helped with
canvassing. The program has been running successfully for four
years.

In Louisville Catherine Morat, dean of Atherton High, has
been urging her girls to do volunteer work ever since 1926. Now

there are social service courses in eight high schools there. High school girls contributed six thousand hours of volunteer service in 1952, and more than a dozen of Louisville's social agencies were the beneficiaries. Similar programs are raising community standards in Philadelphia, Cleveland, East Orange, Memphis. In New York City the girls of Walton High School have formed the Community Service Corps. Each member promises to give two hours of service each week to civic work.

The teen-ager who is treated like an adult is most likely to act like one. School vandalism has definitely declined where the volunteer program functions. Too often the approach to juvenile delinquency has been to give something to the youngsters, instead of showing them how to give themselves to something. Teen-agers with their idealism and wonderful energy need such a positive outlet. Their response is almost universally positive, and the example they set raises the tone of the whole community.

*   *   *

Lorain, Ohio, was like most other communities after the war; it was suffering from an acute housing shortage. Men who had endured the danger and discomfort of battle came back to find that their dreams of settling down in quiet homes of their own were beyond their grasp. In Lorain there were jobs waiting in the steel mills. But the only place they could live was in a house full of relatives.

"I was living in my dad's home with my husband, my two brothers, and my little boy," said one veteran's wife. "Then my sister and her husband and two children got evicted and they came in with us. That was nine of us in a three-bedroom house."

Of course they thought of building. But costs were so high that $12,000 appeared to be a minimum.

Then Al Lash, an ex-sergeant, read about some miners in Pennsylvania who had built their own homes with the encouragement of the American Friends Service Committee. He and his friend Don Poplar asked their union to stake them to a trip to Penncraft. Impressed with what they saw, they got in touch with Hurford Crosman of the Service Committee. He agreed to come to Lorain and give them his advice.

Encouraged, Lash and Poplar formed the Lorain Veterans Housing Association. Thirty-six of their friends joined. Then each man put up $500—a big sum for most of them—for a tract of land. They agreed to put in twenty hours a week until they had built all thirty-eight homes.

But when they went to the banks for money, they were turned down. Discouraged, many of the men wanted to sell the land. But Al Lash talked them out of it. "If we build one decent house, just to show them we can do it," he said, "maybe they'll change their minds."

None of the men were skilled in the building trades. It was hard work for them, and they had to learn the hard way. But when they had built the first house, they got the loan. They went on to the next house, and the next. Money ran out, but somehow they kept at it. They were building $12,000 houses at a cost of six thousand. Thirty-eight houses represents a lot of effort, especially when it is done by men who have already done a hard day's work. But it is doubtful whether anyone will get more pleasure out of his home than these families in Lorain.

While the Quakers were indirectly responsible for the Lorain project, they were directly behind another self-help building project in Philadelphia where a block of slum dwellings was chosen for an experiment in slum clearance on a voluntary basis. The buildings in the block had once been fine brick homes with handsome marble doorways. Originally twenty-five families had lived in them; now there were 114. Shacks and sheds filled the back yards. Plaster was down, floors rough and splintered, windows broken. The wretched housing was directly responsible for delinquency.

Francis Bosworth of the Friends Neighborhood Guild, a nearby settlement house, wanted to tackle the housing problem. Meanwhile the Friends Service Committee which had guided the Penncraft building project was interested in trying a similar experiment in a city. The two agencies joined forces. Years of patient work were needed to iron out legal problems, but finally a loan was arranged through the Federal Housing Administration.

Now all they needed were residents who wanted clean, decent homes to live in. It was hard to convince people that anything could be made of these slum dwellings. The idea of working eight hundred hours for a stake in the project sounded like a racket. Who wanted to work twenty weeks for nothing?

But those who felt they could trust the Quakers signed up. They went to work demolishing the old sheds, carting out rotten plaster and debris. Then contractors came in to do the basic reconstruction which according to law had to be done by skilled workmen. When they had finished, the self-helpers came back to paint, finish floors, install kitchen cabinets which they had built themselves. Much of the painting was done by the women. One girl became an expert in refinishing doors, another in laying asphalt tile. This self-help aspect of the work, since it has to be done by people who already have full-time jobs, is slow and inefficient. But it produces something more important than efficiency. Working together makes good neighbors. Since the Friends were determined to make the project inter-racial, this was important. It also produces good homemakers. People who have worked so hard to create their own homes are not going to let them go to pot. It is not just the buildings that are being improved. Pride in their achievement is making better people of the group.

Rents are to be no higher than these families had to pay for slum dwellings. And in forty years they will own their homes outright. The city's Redevelopment Authority has agreed to help clean up the surrounding area, and the Friends are already planning to carry their project to three more blocks. They do not pretend that their program is an answer to all slum areas. But they believe in concentrating on the people rather than the real estate.

"To clean up a slum," Francis Bosworth says, "you have to attack the 'slum spirit,' to rouse it from apathy and despair."

And that is not a thing that can be done by government handouts. It calls for an urge within the individual. Then, when individuals with this urge get together, it is hard to stop them. The tradition of the logrolling and the barn-raising—of tackling by joint effort what cannot be accomplished individually—is not dead yet.

*　*　*

The Quaker plan for slum clearance is strong because it rests upon self-help. But throughout the country other attacks are being made on substandard housing, often by voluntary action. In Baltimore a young social worker, horrified by what she saw, sparked the formation of the Citizens Planning Committee, a group of citizens which set out to arouse public opinion and force the city to act. The Committee succeeded in getting a new housing code which established minimum housing conditions. A Division of Housing was set up within the city Health Department, with power to enforce the new rules. When court cases dragged on, a special housing court was established where offenders could be prosecuted promptly—both landlords and tenants. Inspectors not only look for violations, but conduct contests and give prizes for the cleanest yards, thus stimulating further voluntary activity instead of relying only on compulsion.

In Lawton, Oklahoma, it was a group of women, members of the Women's Forum, who discovered slum conditions just outside the city limits. Lawton itself was a pleasant, orderly city of thirty thousand. But Lawton View was a square mile of shacks without water, sewage system, garbage disposal, street lights, fire or police protection—a menace not only to its own health and safety but to Lawton as well.

Shocked, the women determined to do something about it. But Lawton View belonged to no town. Though it came under state and county government, it was a no-man's-land so far as any local services were concerned. In order to provide it with services, the women petitioned the city council to annex it. But the council wanted no part of Lawton View. The women persisted, and in the end they won out.

Now Lawton View would have the services it needed. But the women were not satisfied with that. There was still a good deal that the city would not provide. So they furnished a recreation hall for the youngsters, laid plans for a children's park, a community center and a nursery for working mothers.

Deservedly, the three women's clubs of Lawton who did the work won a state prize in the "Build a Better Community" contest sponsored by the General Federation of Women's Clubs (a voluntary organization) and the Kroger Company of Cincinnati.

Although slums and shortages create the most dramatic housing situations, a sudden expansion of new housing can lead to trouble too.

In 1951 the U.S. Steel Company began to build the most modern integrated steel plant in the world at Morrisville, Pennsylvania, with half a billion dollars earmarked for the project. To be near this source of steel, 285 other plants began to build or expand. Whole cities of new housing would be needed. Levittown alone was to hold seventy thousand. Growth which would normally take twenty to fifty years was being compressed into three or four. The prediction was for an increase of a million within ten to twenty years. A rural area was changing almost overnight into a metropolitan center.

Old residents were fearful and resentful. Some sold out at high prices and escaped. But many of the Quakers in this once-quiet countryside saw an opportunity. Members of fifteen Friends Meetings united to form the Friends Service Association for the Delaware Valley. They wanted to help ease the immense dislocations resulting from this sudden influx.

Problems facing the area included a sudden flood of children into the small rural schools, a lack of health, welfare and recreational services, a shortage of church buildings, and a resistance to change on the part of local government. Of special interest to the Quakers, as always, were the human values—the chance to foster inter-racial understanding, the need of people in a strange environment for friendship and group activity.

An old Quaker Meeting House, built in 1789 on grounds where William Penn once worshiped, was right in the heart of the area. Used only on Sundays in the summer, the building was available for use, if Friends could decide to throw the historic old property open to strangers. They did. The building is now the William Penn Center of the Service Association.

Next, Friends volunteered to call on the hundreds of new families who were moving into the housing projects and trailer parks. They welcomed them to the new community, answered questions about community resources, offered help with any problems the family might be facing.

They soon found that women in the trailer parks were hungry for some kind of community organization but did not know how to go about it or where to find a place to meet. They found a Jewish group having to cancel its meetings because it had grown too large for the homes where it had been meeting. They found a dramatics group about to dissolve for lack of a place to rehearse and build scenery. They found young married people, suddenly cut off from the communities they had lived in and eager for something worth while to do with their leisure time.

To all of these the Friends Service Association ministered. They found space for the trailer women, the Jewish group, the dramatists. They offered an arts program as a means of filling the need for recreation and at the same time bringing all races and religions together. They opened a nursery and arranged week-end work camps, friendship parties for young people and a course in accident control.

Then, because they believe in service as a way of life, they opened up opportunities for the residents to give their time to such projects as surveys and census-taking, collecting clothing for overseas, repairing the William Penn Center, finding space for other community groups, and promoting unrestricted occupancy in housing projects. For young people they established work camps, a unique Quaker method which has been widely used to acquaint young people with the problems of the under-privileged and at the same time to help overcome these problems by working with the occupants of depressed areas to improve their homes or their health and recreational facilities. "By exposure to the needs of others," say the Quakers, "by laboring to meet those needs, by simple co-operative inclusive community living, the work camp gives volunteers a vigorous impetus toward a loving life."

The Quakers appear frequently in the history of voluntary association, perhaps because they have consistently tried to follow the command, "Do unto others as you would have them do unto you." Voluntarism is strongest, among Christian nations, where the Protestant idea of individual responsibility is strongest. It is strongest among Protestants where the responsibility is placed most heavily upon the individual member. Since Friends have no minister, they must do voluntarily the work for which a pastor is usually paid. The result is that though small in numbers they do a large amount of voluntary work. Voluntarism is a paradox: its base is freedom, but its manifestation is service. It requires that we give freely of ourselves; but how can one be free if he must serve? The answer is to be found, at last, only on the plane of religion and in the universal idea of the brother-hood of man. Where all men are brothers, service to one is service to self; there is no mine and thine. Thus we acknowledge the universal creative spirit "whose service is perfect freedom." The roots of voluntarism are fastened deep in the soil of faith. For without faith in the dignity and perfectibility of man and his place in the great universe, such service would have no significance.

* * *

One of these fields of service is to the aged. Thousands of them nowadays live in nursing homes and institutions, in rented rooms or with families which find them a burden. Many of them feel lost, unwanted, friendless. What Syracuse, New York, did for them must serve here as the example for thousands of similar programs throughout the country.

Concerned for the older population of Syracuse, the Council of Social Agencies formed a Council on Aging with a sixty-five-year old psychiatrist, Dr. Harry Steckel, as its head. Dr. Steckel organized seven fact-finding committees, enlisting volunteers to go out and learn what problems oldsters face and how they might be met. They learned that very few men or women above sixty-five were employed, that many were living in lonely, miserable quarters. The first need seemed to be a meeting place where they could find each other and where they would feel at home.

The Corinthian Foundation, a group of civic-minded women, offered to help. They donated the ground floor of a carriage house and named it the Wagon Wheel. With help from the city Recreation Department they furnished it with pianos and games. Volunteers worked to put it in order, donated furniture and rugs and curtains—even a sewing machine. Opening night arrived. A reception committee of charter members was on hand to greet the crowd. But the crowd never turned up. No one had thought to extend the personal invitation that would be needed to attract older people to a new and unknown thing.

But slowly the word spread, and those who were lonely or had time on their hands or wanted to make new friends of their own age began to come and look the place over. On Wednesday and Friday evenings there was dancing, both rounds and squares. There were games of all kinds, hobbies and crafts, or for those who wanted it, just a place to sit and talk.

Director Ibson Potter insisted on letting the members run the program themselves. "You mustn't be doing things for them at all times," he says. "Most people make the big mistake of having these elaborate programs and have them playing games which are children's games that aren't for the mentality of older people."

What do the members think of their club?

"It's wonderful here," Mrs. Mary Vogt remarked. "You feel a little bit lighter because you've been out and you enjoyed yourself, see?"

Said one woman of her father: "He has so many new interests, he's like a different person."

George Siebert said: "I think it's wonderful. Heaven on earth to me, this is, believe me."

The people of Syracuse went on to expand their program for the aging. Nearly every organization in town did something to help. Over a thousand volunteers a month work on the program.

*   *   *

Americans take a peculiar attitude toward politics. They want their governing bodies to be above any suspicion of corruption, yet they expect to find corruption in them. They want good men in politics, yet expect to find them crooked. They think politics dirty, yet instead of going in to clean up they prefer to stay on the outside. They will give hundreds of hours to voluntary agencies, yet shy away from political jobs which would take no more time.

This has been the pattern. But perhaps it is changing. Brookfield, Illinois, supplies an example. This suburb of Chicago, a few years ago, was so badly governed that it was constantly without funds in spite of high taxes, a big debt and public services that were falling apart. Over half the water in the mains, purchased at high rates from Chicago, was being lost through leakage. The leakage of public funds was in a similar state.

So a group of citizens formed the Civic Management Association. They agreed that no contributions higher than $25 would be accepted. They agreed that their Association would remain purely voluntary, with no paid workers. And they voted that no previous candidates for any political offices would be eligible to run on their ticket.

The organization started too late and was politically too innocent to win in the 1945 elections. But in 1947 they were fully prepared. They had canvassed the city in a search for able candidates, selecting Dan Kulie as their choice for council president. Then they went to work to convince voters of the wisdom of a council-manager system. They mailed their leaflets to every voter in town. They made a house-to-house campaign. This time the reform ticket elected the president and five out of six trustees.

The new officers found finances in an almost hopeless state—a town of thirteen thousand people owing more than $738,000, with next to nothing in the bank.

They hired a city manager and went to work. They got every citizen of Brookfield to help locate the costly water leaks. Within a year they had saved $30,000 in water rent.

Tax records were found to be chaotic. Lots still listed as vacant had buildings on them which had never been taxed. So volunteer teams went to work on the assessor's books, checking eleven thousand parcels of land. Seven thousand hours of volunteer work donated by seventy citizens saved $25,000 which would otherwise have been spent on an audit of the town's special assessment records. Thousands in assessable real estate were added to the tax list.

The community was without a recreation program. On the edge of insolvency, Brookfield had no money to start one. Again the citizens' group supplied volunteers—126 of them donating more than 2,400 hours of service.

By 1952 Brookfield had reduced its debt to $264,000, lowered taxes, increased the police force and raised municipal salaries 36 per cent. Its example influenced the Illinois legislature to pass a law permitting cities under half a million to adopt the council-manager form of government.

The National Municipal League (a voluntary organization) chose Brookfield as one of the eleven All-American Cities for 1952. Dan Kulie was on hand to receive the plaque at a ceremony held in the local high school. A good many of Brookfield's citizens were on hand too. The shift from insolvency to leadership had been swift but sound, and they were proud of the recognition it had brought them. Yet they had used no secret formula—only the voluntary power of citizens to conduct their own affairs.

* * *

Corruption was no part of the problem in Tin Top, Texas. Tin Top was an old broken-down store and two churches, only one of which had services and then only once a month. Tin Top had been built on cotton, but when the crop had become unprofitable the cotton gin had moved away, and Tin Top had become almost as primitive as when the Indians had possessed it.

Then Mrs. E. B. Cartwright, a newcomer, decided that the churches ought to be painted. She persuaded her husband to have it done by some painters who were working on the Cartwright property.

The fresh paint on the two churches had an effect on the people of Tin Top. They began to look around for other ways to put the area back on its feet. But they were a scattered community. The only organization they had was a Home Demonstration Club, and it hadn't met in four years. Now some of the old members got together in the freshly painted Baptist church. They had read in one of the farm papers about a contest for rural improvement.

"The first prize is to be a thousand dollars," Mrs. Caraway said. "That would be a goal for us to work for."

"We could band together and get electricity for this community," someone said. "That would help us more than anything."

"And we need our telephones. They're getting them in some sections of the state, so why shouldn't we?"

The men got together too. One of their biggest problems was the bad roads, which prevented them from getting their produce out to market. With good roads, they could go in for truck farming and dairying.

"I think the first thing we need do on these roads is to clean out the brush and dig ditches," Rancher Smuthers said. "We need bulldozers, but we haven't got 'em so we'll just have to do it with our hands and our axes and things."

As the men worked together, they began to feel like a community. So naturally they wanted a place where they could meet. They were spread out all over the countryside, so they built a community center out in the middle of the Texas grasslands. The men dug and built while the women cooked and gave advice. Once the community center was finished, Tin Top came to life. Committees were organized to tackle each important problem. The women studied how to improve health and child care and family life. The whole community put on a play. They got their telephones, and after a lot of work they got electricity. They pushed for bathrooms in every home, starting out with only two. They built two and a half miles of road, practiced delayed grazing, improved their homes, fixed up the churches, conducted rat and safe water campaigns, sent a girl to college, and did a good many lesser things.

Tin Top also won second prize in the rural improvement contest. Much as they appreciated the $400 it brought, the prize was no longer the important thing, but the fact that they had built a community with their own hands.

Mrs. Hodges summed it up in words which have a simple dignity. "We have so much to be thankful for here in Tin Top. We share, in our hearts, the love and joy of our neighbors, the success and failures, the pain and sorrow, which welds us together as a community in which to live."

* * *

Geary, Oklahoma, is a metropolis beside Tin Top, but it is still a small agricultural town of 1,600. The people of Geary wanted a community center, and perhaps they would have been willing to approve a $40,000 bond issue to get it. But L. E. Lyon, owner of the cotton gin, thought they ought to try doing it by voluntary subscription and free labor.

Volunteer money-raising teams visited every home and place of business. It took them nine months to collect $9,000. Then they began to buy their materials, and to call on the free labor that had been promised. When work actually started, more money came in until the total was sixteen thousand. With the women serving noonday meals, the men buckled down to work. When an Oklahoma City company wanted $200 to raise the I-beams for the roof, Farmer Enos Zweiacher brought in his truck and winch, and aided by other volunteers finished the job for nothing. The soil conservation district put $6,000 of its money into offices for its own use, a community kitchen, dining room and rest rooms. The Legion Post, in exchange for use of its building, fitted out the other half and installed the Geary Library in its new quarters. And Geary ended up with an attractive tile and brick building which had added nothing to taxes and given the community two dollars' worth for every dollar it spent.

This was quite an achievement for a town of 1,600 people. But having learned the way, Geary went on to provide other things it needed. Volunteers put up a garage to take care of the school buses. "We have $25,000 invested in school-transportation equipment and no place to work on it or store it," Dwight Peters, member of the school board, explained. "We figure if we want to protect it, we have to put up this building ourselves."

Stimulated by Geary's success with self-help, farmers in the southern end of town began a road project to put an end to the mud they had to drive through. They contributed their trucks and time, and the Chamber of Commerce paid for the gas and oil. For $400 a mile they have been building roads that cost the federal government $5,000.

Geary also wanted night baseball. So sports fans got together to fix up the ball park. A farm-implement dealer gave the use of a machine to dig post holes. Other citizens hauled in used railroad ties for beams. Geary got a $5,000 job for $500.

Three miles northwest of Geary the women wanted a community building. They bought an old schoolhouse for a dollar, and that supplied their lumber. They went out and raised $1,000, and that supplied their capital. They went to work on their husbands, and they supplied the labor. Now they have a building which would have cost them $5,000.

Voluntary co-operation has also started a $22,000 education building at the Methodist church. Other religious groups have used the same method to build a church and a parsonage.

Geary now has $140,000 worth of public property for which it paid only $60,000 in voluntary gifts. But even more important than the money saving is the sense of pride and achievement, the feeling of having created something through common effort, and the strengthened sense of community.

* * *

Clayton Hoff was disgusted with the mess men had made of the once beautiful Brandywine Creek. At Wilmington, Delaware, the Army Engineers had to operate a big dredge to keep the Brandywine's silt from clogging the channel. Each year they spent $300,000 to dredge up millions of dollars' worth of precious topsoil. Thirty-five miles to the northwest the stream was picking up the soil from fertile farmlands. At Coatesville it got a load of rust and pickling acid from a steel plant. At Modena it took the dye from a paper firm. All along its length it received raw sewage and industrial waste until by the time it crossed from Pennsylvania into Delaware it was a stinking, sticky mess. In the spring it flooded towns and bottomlands.

In 1945 Clayton Hoff gave up a top job with the Du Pont Company in order to save the Brandywine Valley. He talked to public-spirited citizens and brought them together in the Brandywine Valley Association. The program was to be bold and inclusive, with projects to reclaim eroding land, control floods, improve farmland, end stream pollution, and restore fish and wild life. Hoff's idea was to achieve all this in the characteristic American way—by voluntary, co-operative effort of the people and institutions concerned.

With about a thousand members and $36,000 a year, Hoff has remade the Brandywine Valley. With two offices and a staff of six he has brought pollution under control, persuaded farmers to cultivate fifteen thousand acres of rolling land in contour strips, turn five thousand acres to pasturage, and plant a million trees for soil conservation and eventual cash crops. Several times a week he and his staff talk to clubs and neighborhood groups. Industries have co-operated by controlling their wastes, sports groups by financing a biological survey of water and land.

Wild life is reviving. Fish are returning to the stream. A marshy section is being turned into an area for duck, geese and musk-rats. Sixty farms have built fish ponds which also supply emergency water in case of fire. The appearance of the valley is changing as the land recovers from the damage men have done it. And the residents have caught Clayton Hoff's vision of prosperity and loveliness achieved through their own efforts.

*　　*　　*

Twelve years ago the people of Kentucky awoke to the fact that their once-progressive state had sunk to forty-seventh place in the nation in length of school term, to fortieth place in teacher salaries, to fifth from the bottom in per capita income among southern states.

Henry Schacter, president of a Louisville department store, decided it was time something was done. But a Democratic legislature was in session under a Republican governor. It seemed a poor time to act. Schacter went ahead anyway. He wrote to all the members of the Merchants Association throughout the state. He got people together and formed The Committee for Kentucky. First of all the Committee went to work collecting the facts about economic and social conditions. Then they published them widely throughout the state, urging the people to take action.

The legislators were not convinced. "Maybe it's true, what you tell us about conditions," they argued. "But who wants to pay the taxes to correct them? People are yelling about taxes being too high already."

"When the people realize the facts," Schacter insisted, "they'll demand action, and they'll be willing to pay for it." Then he showed them the cost of a remedial program as compared with the cost of failure.

Enough people backed up the Committee so that the legislature was convinced. It doubled the budget and launched Kentucky's new deal.

The town and county of Henderson was chosen as the spot for an experimental program. The people there were eager to co-operate in a program of community improvement. They went to work on a health program, developed recreational and social services, and in the process acquired a spirit of self-reliance and successful co-operation which was worth as much as the improvements themselves.

A former G.I. named Robert Hubbard was studying government in Transylvania College. Fed up with the conditions exposed by the Committee, he asked his professor what he could do.

"Get elected to the legislature," the professor told him.

But Hubbard had no political background. And he did not want to get tied up with any group who would try to give him orders. So he ran as an independent Democrat and got elected.

"The things that bothered me as a student are still many of them awaiting action and solution," he says. "But I've seen real progress made."

Some of that progress was made through the efforts of Mrs. Shelby Carr of Richmond, a doctor's wife who was voted president of the women's auxiliary of the State Medical Society. Stimulated by the Committee's revelations, Mrs. Carr took it into her head to look into conditions in the rural schools of her own county. She was shocked by what she found—bad roads, unhealthy drinking water, no medical examinations, and in one case the bullets of feuding mountaineers flying through the school windows!

Mrs. Carr got together an action committee. Now there are five hundred women volunteers who work to improve conditions in rural schools. They test the drinking water, help out with hot lunch programs, arrange for eye and ear examinations, enlist help to improve the roads. Mrs. Carr feels that her Committee is simply following the method of those who pioneered the country. "They believed in using what they had available instead of waiting around hoping for someone else to help them," she says.

* * *

These stories of life in the United States today have been picked almost at random from hundreds and thousands. A book, a dozen books could be filled with them. But these few will have to serve. They exemplify a characteristic American attitude, a habit of mind—a faith in the value of action, in the power of men to help each other through voluntary association, a faith in the dignity of human effort.

But how does a community get started in the right direction?

Often, as these stories have shown, the initial push comes from some energetic citizen who sees something that needs doing and doesn't mind sticking his neck out. If he is able to convince enough people of the need for action, the wheels can begin to turn. But sometimes a community is too sunk in apathy, or too divided into hostile groups to respond. Out in Montana, under the leadership of Ernest O. Melby and Baker Brownell, a method was developed which successfully tackled such situations. The heart of the Montana Study was the formation of self-study groups. Men and women of varying backgrounds grouped together to study their own community. Through a pooling of information they gained new insight into its structure and needs. Then usually they decided to do something about it.

One of the communities which decided to study itself was Conrad, a town of 1,600 in the midst of the wheat fields. Two Conrad teachers, Ruth Robinson and Alicia O'Brien, were responsible for starting the Study Group. They had no trouble gathering members—teachers, ministers, executives, businessmen, farmers. Of diverse religious and political faiths, however, it seemed doubtful that they could discuss vital community problems without flying apart. The group operated with very little assistance from Brownell and his staff. But they had the study guide to help them—a list of searching questions which directed them in their examination of the various aspects of their community life.

As the Conrad group got on with their study, they discovered that one major problem overshadowed all others—community recreation. It was this lack which took the young people away from Conrad. As one girl put it when she set out for San Francisco, "Jeepers, I can't afford to let myself rot!"

But then, as committees reported on various phases of the community life, it became clear that recreation could not be separated from education. For a full and rich community life, Conrad needed a tax-supported, year-round program serving all ages.

Said one member: "Our school ought to be a real community center offering adult education through discussion groups, and recreation for everyone."

No one in Conrad had thought of school as anything but a place where the children got their three R's. Now they were beginning to see that the school was inadequate even for the regular classes. There was a fine collection of books at the high school which was supposed to serve as the town library too, but it was crowded into one end of a study hall where the public could hardly get in. The gym seemed to have been designed for midgets, the stage at one end of it for marionettes.

The Study Group now had to face the fact that what Conrad really needed was a new high school, so designed as to serve also as a civic center. But did they dare tell the citizens that they ought to spend a quarter of a million dollars?

"If we don't spend it for education and recreation we'll be spending it later for insane asylums and penal institutions," said Alicia O'Brien.

"Let's launch a drive for money!"

"Wait a minute," said another. "This is a study group, not an action committee. We'll be in politics if we aren't careful."

The same thing was happening in Conrad that had happened

in other towns where the Montana Study had been tried. Weeks of study had made the group so conscious of their community's needs that they could no longer sit back and do nothing. They decided to call a general meeting so that everyone could learn the facts they had dug out. They announced a date six weeks ahead. They talked to their friends, to members of other groups they belonged to. The newspaper co-operated. A week before the meeting they issued a report of their findings, with an eight-point program for Conrad.

Colonel LeRoy Anderson, one of Conrad's outstanding war heroes and ranchers, presided at the meeting on January 30, 1946. He proposed that the discussion follow three points—recreation, education and taxation. Then he called on Sig Hefty to outline the proposed program. A lively discussion followed. One of the school board members came out for a new high school, and found himself solidly backed up. Another citizen recommended a complete recreation program with a full-time director.

When the discussion had gone on for two and a half hours, Colonel Anderson proposed a recess. When the meeting was resumed, a motion came for the formation of the Conrad Education and Recreation Association. A council was elected, and of the nine members, five were from the original Study Group. Then came more study, legal work, consultation with an architect, and finally a proposal that Conrad float a bond issue for a new high school, to the full extent of the $281,000 that the law allowed. Even at that price Conrad could not have everything it wanted, but there would be a large gym designed to serve also as a community center for adult recreation and education, a library designed for access by the public.

It was a large order for a district with only seven hundred voters. By Montana law 40 per cent of the property owners had to turn out to vote, and of course 21 per cent could defeat the measure. Already the usual cry of "radical" had been raised against those who wanted such an ambitious program for Conrad. But again the volunteers went to work. Seven groups went into action to get out the voters. The bond issue passed by a three-to-one majority.

Shortages held up the building of the school, but the Association went ahead with the other part of its program—improving the facilities of a room in the City Hall which had been set aside for young people, setting up an outdoor recreation program with a full-time director during the summer, installing play equipment in the park, expanding the high school dramatics program, encouraging the development of an outstanding community chorus. Country dancing, a fine arts and crafts program, and an outdoor swimming pool followed. The pool called for another $25,000 which was raised by local businessmen who formed an association for the purpose and located volunteer labor to build it.

Other benefits grew out of the study program. A small industries committee looked into the possibility of new businesses which would encourage returning veterans to stay in town. Eight new industries resulted. Young people were not so anxious to leave home now; the population rose to two thousand—an increase of 25 per cent. Conrad liked the community analysis approach so well that it continued the Study Group as a public forum.

Thus out of a small study group a whole community was revived and turned into a united people determined to make their town a place where anyone would be happy to live.

"This is the heart of Christianity," said the Catholic priest who was one of the original group members. "It is only through groups of this kind that transcend differences among people that we can cure the evils of the world—not by laws and political speeches."

During three years of operation (when it was bitterly opposed by political interests) the Montana Study helped fourteen communities to study their history, resources and needs. Over fifty related projects were carried to completion—home industries established, historical pageants enacted which involved the whole community in their preparation, dying economies revived, the educational and cultural level measurably raised. Twelve other states and five foreign countries have used the Montana Study method in programs of their own. The Montana Study showed people how they could come together even though their views and backgrounds were divergent. It showed them how through an objective study of facts they could forget personal differences and work together for the common good. It provided a technique through which ordinary men and women could co-ordinate the forces of education, religion, government, economics, culture, and democratic neighborliness, and by their own efforts lift the whole level of community life.

* * *

The communities where the stories told in this chapter took place were, if anything, less favored than the average. They were often short of funds and their public facilities were often poor. Yet once the idea took hold, the idea that they could make their community what they wanted it to be by working together, the battle was half won. None of our resources are as valuable as this habit, this skill, this way of working together. This, if anything, is the hallmark of American democracy. Its roots go back to Plymouth.

II

Plymouth Rock—the First Cornerstone

Next to the flag, there is probably no symbol of America more charged with emotion than Plymouth Rock. Its mention brings mental images of the *Mayflower*, bearded, soberly clad Pilgrims (who in fact were neither elderly nor garbed in black), the sickness and hunger of the first year, the first harvest and the first Thanksgiving. Every year a quarter of a million tourists go to Plymouth to stare down at the Rock where it lies surrounded by a pile of memorial masonry, dwarfed and isolated by a well-intentioned effort to do it homage.

Why is it important to so many Americans to see Plymouth Rock with their own eyes? What psychic power does this inconsiderable boulder exert over us?

Well, Plymouth is a beginning, and we are in love with firsts. Yet Jamestown, which was earlier, fails to arouse us this way. There was quite as much danger and far more melodrama at Jamestown, yet the landing there has never acquired the same aura of romance. To be sure, there were women and children at Plymouth and none during the first years at Jamestown. But this cannot be all.

The beginnings at Plymouth are felt to be somehow more American, more representative of what we are, or at least of what we would like to be. The Plymouth settlers were plain folk. They had suffered for their beliefs, and they had chosen America as a haven. They had come to stay. They had burned their bridges, brought their families, taken a chance—and after

41

nearly being wiped out they had prospered in modest fashion. They had established religion and government by consent, by contract. They were Englishmen by birth, but Americans by choice.

This was something new in the world. Every descendant of the Pilgrims—and of all the other immigrants who followed them—thinks of himself as sharing that choice (if he thinks of it at all), and when he makes a pilgrimage to Plymouth Rock it is to the shrine of America as a voluntary community—a nation by choice. When General Patton spoke to his men before the Sicily landings, this was what he stressed—this voluntary nature of Americanism.

What is this heritage of voluntarism we get from the Pilgrims? What has it to do with America today?

*　*　*

About 1606 a handful of obscure country people in the north of England, convinced that a true church must be a voluntary gathering of believers, bound themselves together as a congregation. Their act, though in itself one of great courage since it was opposed to the law of the land, had more than a local significance—even more than a religious. It was one of the foundations on which the American republic was raised.

Leader of the Scrooby group was William Brewster, who had stepped into his father's shoes as royal postmaster and bailiff to the Archbishop of York. But Brewster had not spent all his life in the quiet little village of Scrooby. He had been a student at Cambridge University, he had been a clerk or servant to one of the important men of Queen Elizabeth's court, Sir William Davison, principal secretary of state in charge of foreign affairs. Through this connection he had touched shoulders with the great. He had visited Holland with a royal mission. But then Davison, like many a royal servant, had been broken by his sovereign. Elizabeth had found it convenient to make him the scapegoat for ordering the execution of Mary, Queen of Scots, which she herself had commanded. And Brewster, apparently disillusioned with life at court, had gone home to Scrooby.

Well paid, living in the huge manor house which the Archbishop had not visited in years, and well supplied from the fields and barns of the manor, Brewster might have lived out the rest of his life in quiet ease. His duties were sufficient to prevent idleness, but not heavy enough to be burdensome. The most important man in the town, he could look forward to a life of security, respect and comfort.

Instead of this, he chose the path guaranteed to get him into difficulty.

Perhaps he had first been inoculated with Puritan ideas at Cambridge, the university from which most of the Puritan leaders came. His experience at court may have shaken his faith in the *status quo*. In any case, he had somehow joined the growing group of serious men who were dissatisfied with affairs in the Anglican Church, convinced that it did not meet the standards for a Christian church as found in the New Testament. When a separate congregation formed at Gainsborough, about twelve miles from Scrooby, he became a member. Shortly after, the congregation split into two separate churches in order to accommodate the widely scattered members, the second being set up at Scrooby. Brewster, with the large manor house at his disposal, became host to his brothers (and sisters) in Christ—a generosity which would scarcely have appealed to the absent owner.

To be their pastor, the Scrooby group called Richard Clyfton, minister of near-by Babworth where he had been preaching Puritan doctrine from an Anglican pulpit. According to William Bradford, Clyfton was "a grave and fatherly old man" with a large white beard. Since Clyfton was only fifty at this time, the impression he gave of being a patriarch, a Michelangelo God, must have come as much from within as from the "great white beard." God-like too must have been the strength of his convictions, since he was willing to leave the comfortable security of the Anglican Church and throw in his lot with the despised Separatists.

Another Cambridge man, John Robinson, became Clyfton's assistant and then "teacher" of the group—a post second only to pastor in the Pilgrim Church. One of their most impressionable charges was young William Bradford, an orphan then in his teens who despite the displeasure of his guardian uncles had attached himself to Brewster and the separated congregation. Since Bradford was to become the outstanding leader of the Pilgrims and one of the greatest men of colonial America, the impression made upon him by Brewster, Clyfton and Robinson is important to American history. From them he drank in the conviction that men have a right and a duty to associate voluntarily for religious purposes. Through them he experienced the comfortable mother-warmth of the group bound together by choice rather than by accident or mandate. Here was the origin of the voluntary community which has affected the whole course of American history.

* * *

England, under James the First, was no place for believers in religious liberty. When the Scotch King received Queen Elizabeth's crown, there was at first wide rejoicing among men who had been touched by the spirit of the Reformation and who wanted to worship God according to their own convictions rather than according to formulas devised by the Anglican bishops and the ruling monarch. For in Scotland the Presbyterian form of church government, which the Puritans thought much closer to the primitive pattern of the first Christian churches, gave promise that James would reform the Anglican Church along the same lines.

They were sadly disappointed. James, it seemed, had never cared for Presbyterianism. It savored of too much independence from the royal will and control. James's own religion was built around one simple idea—the divine right of kings. Royalty was a special mark of God's favor to which all men must bow. The

king's will was the earthly expression of God's, and all a man
had to do for his soul was to follow the king's religion.

Under James, therefore, religious reformers continued to be
persecuted as they had been under Elizabeth. And of the reformers, the most depised—because the most feared—were the
Separatists. The Puritans wished merely to purify the Church of
England. But the Separatists insisted on their right to separate
from it entirely. Their founder, Robert Browne (1550–1633)
taught that the civil and religious authorities should be entirely
separate—a shocking idea in a time when as a matter of course
the people followed their king's religion. Even Luther and Calvin, cornerstones of the Reformation, had never thought of
separating state and church. Calvin, in fact, had turned the
tables from state-controlled religion to a religion which controlled the state.

But the Separatists wanted no such connection, no matter
which was tail and which was dog. A true church, they insisted,
was a body of faithful people *voluntarily* united in faith. A
church state or a state church was a contradiction in terms,
since no nation could possibly consist entirely of good people,
worthy to be numbered with the saints. A state church must
necessarily mix in the bad with the good, the sheep with the
goats, and since it forced all to belong to it, good and evil,
believer and non-believer, it was not really a church.

A true church had to be based upon the free choice of its
members, bound together in a covenant with God. Voluntarism
was therefore the imperative of its existence.

It is customary to trace American freedom to John Locke and
the eighteenth-century doctrine of natural rights. On Locke and
natural rights, to be sure, the Massachusetts and Virginia pa-
triots, the Continental Congress and the writers of the Constitution based their justification of independence. But they were
able to work a soil which had long been prepared by an older
tradition of freedom. The struggle for religious freedom had
preceded by a century and a half the fight for political freedom.

When William Bradford, greatest of the men we know as Pilgrims, wrote about the little group in northern England which decided to take the bold step of breaking off from the Church of England, he did so in these significant words:

"They shooke of[f] this yoake of antichristian bondage, and as the Lords free people, joyned them selves (by a covenant of the Lord) into a church estate, in the felowship of the gospell, to walke in all his wayes, made known, or to be made known unto them, according to their best endeavours, whatsoever it should cost them, the Lord assisting them."

It is difficult today to appreciate the revolutionary nature of this decision. But we should try to understand it, for it is the basis of our freedom.

In their defiance of the King, the Separatists sought their defense in the Bible—in the idea of a covenant, a contract between God and men. As God had made a covenant with Noah, with Abraham and with Moses, he would make one with any people who chose to walk in his ways. Any group had a divine right—equivalent to that of kings—to join themselves into a church. They did not need to wait for king or state to permit it, since a covenant with God was beyond the control of civil authority. That the King could interpose his authority between them and God they denied.

To their Old Testament covenant they joined a New Testament form of church government. These earnest readers of the Bible could find there no warrant for bishops, ornate vestments or liturgies. With historical accuracy they observed that what the church of Christ had become was far from what He had founded. They wanted to get back to the pattern of "the first Christian churches, as . . . in the Apostles times."

The apostolic church, they had observed (from I Corinthians xii 28, I Timothy v 17, and Romans xii 6–8), had a simple democratic form of government. The church *was* the people—"one body in Christ, and every one members one of another" (Romans xii 5). The people chose their own pastor, teacher, elders, and a widow to minister to those in need. As his title indicates, the pastor was chiefly responsible for the care of his people, while the teacher dealt chiefly with theology and expounding the holy text. But these leaders were chosen by the people and could be dismissed by the people. The church of the Pilgrims was therefore the cradle of democracy. Whether or not they intended it, the freedom they claimed in religion was inevitably carried over into politics.

The essence of the church community was that it must be voluntary. Through the covenant God Himself recognized the sacred quality of volition, the importance of free choice as the basis of religion. Voluntarism therefore has a religious background in America. We may not be aware of the history, but we know, we feel, the moral imperative which gives muscle tone to our convictions about freedom. And for that we are indebted to the Pilgrims.

* * *

Pursued by officers of the ecclesiastical court, the Scrooby congregation moved to Amsterdam and then to Leyden. But Holland was not wholly satisfactory. Much as they appreciated the haven afforded them to worship as they chose, these Pilgrims still felt that something was lacking. The alien community which surrounded them was having an effect on their children and on themselves. Their children were being tempted away into soldiering and licentiousness. They themselves felt at the mercy of an economy they could not control. As Bradford put it, in his noble and discerning analysis of the causes for their removal to America, "It was not only probably thought, but apparently seen, that within a few years more they would be in danger to scatter, by necessities pressing them, or sinke under their burdens, or both. . . . So they like skillfull & beaten souldiers were fearfull either to be intrapped or surrounded by their enimies, so as they should neither be able to fight nor flie; and therfor thought it better to dislodge betimes to some place of better advantage & less danger, if any such could be found."

It was not only religious freedom they sought, but a way of

life. They had begun to have a vision of a complete community. Bound together in the close and comfortable bonds of their church, they had learned to cherish the life of the group.

"Such was the true pietie, the humble zeale, & fervent love, of this people (whilst they thus lived together) towards God and his waies, and the single hartednes & sinceir affection one towards another, that they came as near the primative patterne of the first churches, as any other church of these later times have done, according to their ranke & qualitie."

In this passage Bradford manages to open up to us the sense of community, of warm togetherness, which the group experienced in Leyden. When the surrounding culture seemed to endanger it, they were willing to risk their lives to establish it on a sound basis in America. Soberly the church members considered all the hazards before them—foundering at sea, change of climate and diet, famine, sickness, torture and death at the hands of the Indians, the lack of sufficient capital, the disastrous failure of many who had tried before them to settle in America.

"It was answered, that all great & honourable actions are accompanied with great difficulties, and must be both enterprised and overcome with answerable courages."

As a group, they made the decision to emigrate. As a group they prepared for what was ahead of them. And though, in the end, not all were able to go, those who did go went as a group. They were joined by others from England who were not members of their church, though some of these became members later. The religious group life remained a dominating force at Plymouth.

There has been a good deal of speculation as to why the Pilgrims settled in New England. But Bradford makes it perfectly clear that before leaving Holland the Pilgrims had decided to go to "northern Virginia" or New England, where they would live "as a distincte body by them selves." * There is the nub of the matter—their desire to be a distinct body, a com-

* For the argument that the Pilgrims had decided to settle in New England rather than in Virginia, see *Bradford of Plymouth,* 108.

munity—not only in religion but in governance and livelihood. The way they achieved this threefold voluntary community by means of the church covenant, the Mayflower Compact and a business contract is important to American history.

The church covenant they already had. It was a contract between the "saints"—the members of the church—and God. But before anyone was permitted to go ashore, another contract —the Mayflower Compact—had to be signed, one which would include all the voting members of the community. Pastor Robinson in his farewell letter had reminded the members of the Leyden congregation that they were to constitute themselves a "body politik." Robinson, like the other Pilgrim leaders, showed a lively interest in the political aspects of human behavior. It was to church government rather than to theology that the Pilgrims made a lasting contribution, for they were interested first of all in creating a Christian community.

How they should go about it must have been a subject for long debate and meditation during the three-month voyage. There was no precedent for what they had to do. To a man of the seventeenth century, complete independence in government was unthinkable. Even the stout Hollanders, when shaking off the Spaniard, had begged foreign potentates to accept the sovereignty, so ingrained was the concept of government from above. The whole fabric of life was held together by feudal allegiance. At this date there was no such thing in England as land held absolutely free.

The Pilgrims therefore thought in terms of this feudal background. Yet they surmounted it. Behind the document which they made the foundation of their colony lay their yeoman yearning for a sound land title, the Dutch adherence to the idea that the sovereign is accountable to his people, and the Congregational way in religion which was the nearest thing to a democratic institution in the European world.

"We doe . . . solemnly & mutualy in the presence of God, and one of another, covenant & combine our selves togeather into a civill body politick, for our better ordering & preserva-

tion & furtherance of the ends aforesaid [advancement of the
faith and honor of King and country]; and by vertue hearof to
enacte, constitute, and frame such just & equall lawes, ordi-
nances, acts, constitutions, & offices, from time to time, as shall
be thought most meete & convenient for the generall good of
the Colonie, unto which we promise all due submission and
obedience."

There is the nub of it—that combining of themselves. Jamestown had been differently established. Newport, Gosnold, Captain John Smith and the rest had come to America as employees
or members of a company of merchants in London which had
drawn up all the rules for them and named their leaders. Important as was the "first representative assembly" which was
finally set up in Virginia twelve years later (in 1619, the year
before the Pilgrims reached America) it was not a self-governing representative assembly at all. Its acts could be annulled
either by the Governor or by the London Company, which kept
a tight hold on its control of the colony.

But Plymouth was a voluntary community, and Americans
still cherish the idea of nationality as an act of will.

If the covenant was a suitable instrument for the relations
between man and God, it was suitable for the relations among
men. Through the Compact, says Gooch in his *History of Democratic Ideas in the Seventeenth Century,* "the democratic
Church had grown into a democratic State." * Every male
passenger on the *Mayflower* known to be of age signed the
Compact, except two seamen who were already bound by a
contract and were not regarded as permanent settlers. The Pilgrims anticipated Locke by seventy years, Rousseau by a century and a half. The accent on government by voluntary association, by a contract freely entered into, has been an American
hallmark ever since. In this respect Tom Paine, Sam Adams and

* While it would be ridiculous to claim that Plymouth was a full democracy
in which all could vote, it is equally false to ignore the fact that the seeds of
democracy were in its institutions of church and colonial self-government. Recent scholars deny democracy to Plymouth because the electorate was restricted
by property or other qualifications. If this is the test, the United States is still not
a democracy.

Thomas Jefferson were claiming ground the Pilgrims had already staked out.

As John Quincy Adams put it, when he rescued it in 1802 from nearly two hundred years of neglect, the Mayflower Compact is "the first example in modern times of a social compact or system of government instituted by voluntary agreement, conformably to the laws of nature, by men of equal rights, and about to establish their community in a new country." None of the recent attempts to depreciate the importance of the Compact can wipe out the fact that it established government by consent, that it set up no hierarchies or privileged groups, and that it laid a sound foundation, probably even beyond the intent of its makers, for democratic government.

The men of Plymouth wanted to be sure about this right of government by voluntary association, so they kept emphasizing it. In 1636 they voted that "no imposicon law or ordnance be made or imposed upon us by ourselves or others at present or to come but such as shall be made or imposed by consent according to the free liberties of the State and Kingdome of England and no otherwise." Governor and council were chosen by the votes of all freemen, without property restrictions, and the Governor was always subject to examination or criticism by a popular assembly of the whole electorate.

This Governor, for most of the time from 1621 until his death in 1657, was William Bradford, who as a boy had thrown in his lot with the Scrooby group and whose qualities of leadership the new world had developed. His influence had a good deal to do with shaping Plymouth. Bradford's vision of the good life was based upon the small, tightly knit community, bound together in Christian brotherhood as firmly almost as a family is bound. Arising in the church, the spirit of brotherhood would also control the operations of government and the getting of a living, and all would prosper under contract—the form of agreement by which man dealt even with God.

Plymouth was built on three contracts—the religious covenant of the congregation, the political compact signed on the

Mayflower, and the business contract with the London merchants who had supplied capital for the voyage. The commercial contract was the source of many difficulties until the Pilgrims finally freed themselves from the merchants, whereupon they made another compact among themselves to cover their business affairs. This arrangement—except for the sharp dealing of Isaac Allerton, one of their own church members—was a success.

In the constant bickering with the London merchants before that contract was ended—at a heavy cost to Plymouth—the Pilgrim point of view is clearly exposed. They hated the contract with the merchants because they felt that they had been forced into it.

While still in Holland, they had been visited by Thomas Weston, a London merchant who had discussed with them the terms on which he would gather capital. Later on, when they sent Robert Cushman over to London to complete arrangements, the merchants backed down on this agreement and forced Cushman to accept several changes.

The Leyden group was furious. Cushman, they said, had exceeded his authority. Even gentle Pastor Robinson called him "most unfitt to deale for other men."

Stung by his critics, Cushman jumped to his own defense. "If I doe such things as I cannot give reasons for," he wrote, "it is like you have sett a foole about your busines, and so turne the reproofe to your selves, & send an other."

Whether or not Cushman intended the irony in that ambiguous "an other," it was true that he had done his best. The merchants had threatened to withdraw their support completely unless the new terms were agreed to.

What were the conditions that raised such a storm in Leyden?

First, the settlers were to retain no ownership in the land they improved or the homes they built, but all was to be equally divided between settlers and merchants after seven years. Second, the settlers must work unremittingly for the common interest, with no time out to work for themselves.

To yeomen like Bradford this meant that they would be losing their status as free men, becoming no better than bond servants. Each share in the joint stock company was rated at ten pounds. Each settler was equally rated. So the London investor who simply put in his ten pounds would gain as much at the end of seven years as the settler who had risked his life and labored unremittingly for the same length of time.

Unable to turn back now, the Pilgrims had to go ahead. But they felt that their contract with the merchants was no longer voluntary. And volition was a sacred thing. It was the essence of their religious lives, it was the germ of the Congregational way. It was even an attribute of God Himself. For the Pilgrim God was not the arbitrary tyrant of Calvin, but a Father who had voluntarily placed Himself under the restraint of a covenant so that all who voluntarily covenanted with Him might be saved.

The Pilgrims believed in a church which was self-governed at the local level; it was therefore natural for them to manage their civil affairs in the same way. The heritage of vigorous local government is still present in New England where town meeting preserves many Pilgrim traditions—even to convening on the first Tuesday in March. The continuing suspicion of "bigness" in America—the distrust of state and federal government—has roots running all the way back to the small, tightly knit, locally autonomous church, court and governor of Plymouth.

The Plymouth idea offered a complete formula for living to those who cared to follow it. It used the instrument of contract or voluntary association to regulate all the relationships of life —God and the church, an earthly government, livelihood, marriage and ownership of the land. The purpose of these contracts was to create a harmonious community, to perfect the human link in the great chain of being which God had forged. God's plan was perfect, but man had failed to fulfill his part. The pattern of that perfection was to be found in the Bible, and in the close-knit voluntary community of the primitive churches. This was the Plymouth way.

For the orphaned Bradford, Brewster and the church had taken the place of father and mother. Brewster had led him through adolescence, had probably taught him languages and introduced him to books. The church community, by wrapping him in its protective, loving and soul-nourishing arms, had taken the place of a mother. So by breath and heartbeat rather than by the colder knowing of the brain, Bradford understood that a community must be the mother of its members and the community's leader their father.

Orphanage had made him know and feel this more keenly than other men. It had shaped his vision—the vision of the community so closely bound that it was to each of its members like an extended personality, an enlargement of self. This was Bradford's greatest gift to his people. Like most visions of worth it was too much for most of them to grasp.

But it is a part of our heritage. There, at the very beginning of the American nation, voluntarism stands forth as the American way.

III

Village Republics

The tightly bound community of Bradford was blown apart by the arrivals in Massachusetts Bay. The Bay settlers within two years were six times as many as those in the Old Colony. Suddenly the men of Plymouth had a market for all the grain, cattle and hay they could raise, and at prices they had never dreamed of—even up to £28 ($2,100) for a beef animal. They insisted on moving out of Plymouth, onto lands where these things could be raised.

"No man thought he could live except he had catle and a great deale of ground to keep them," Bradford wrote. "By which means they were scatered all over the bay, quickly, and the towne, in which they lived compactly till now, was left very thine, and in a short time allmost desolate. And if this had been all, it had been less, thoug to much; but the church must also be devided, and those that had lived so long togeather in Christian & comfortable fellowship must now part and suffer many divissions."

So Duxbury, Marshfield and the Cape Cod towns came to be settled.

For years they were run without any established local government. The General Court at Plymouth remained the governing body, though the towns sent deputies to help make the laws. On the local level the proprietors, to whom the land had been granted, dispensed it to desirable settlers and were responsible for roads, bridges and other public improvements. There was no representative local government until 1651 when Sandwich was granted the right to choose selectmen. Other towns soon followed.

During the long period before the towns were formally organized, the settlers must have learned to handle their own affairs on a voluntary basis, though there is scarcely any record of how they did it. One of the difficulties in writing about voluntary group activity is that people so engaged are generally too busy to write about it themselves. They take it for granted anyway. It does not seem worth writing about. When formal government begins, the need of records is recognized. Minute books come into existence, officers are elected, motions made and recorded. But in the time before, the record is often sparse.

Sometimes the line between voluntary activity and organized government is hard to draw. When the Pilgrims came ashore at Plymouth, they had little but the Mayflower Compact and the Bible to guide them. For several years they kept rather scanty records. They elected a few necessary officials who served without salary. The quality of their community was that of a self-governing, self-sustaining unit far removed in spirit as in space from autocratic England. Governor and General Court constituted a government, but one so small and intimate that no one could have felt detached from it, as men often feel detached from larger units of government whose officials they do not see. The Plymouth settlers were where they were by choice. They had signed an agreement to abide by the laws they should make for their own government. Their officers served without pay. What had to be done for the good and safety of all was done by common effort. That was how the buildings, the fort and the stockade had been raised. For several years food was raised that way too.

So government itself, in its beginnings, had a home-grown, face-to-face, voluntary quality. Its members had to co-operate to survive. When Franklin, nearly 150 years later, counseled the colonists to hang together in order to escape hanging separately, he was giving voice to a conviction many Americans could prove from their own experience.

When the people of Plymouth began to spread out, they did not go as individuals. They went as groups. They formed communities, then towns. The Massachusetts Bay settlers did the same.

From the earliest days, the New England settlers had taken local affairs into their own hands. They met, discussed matters of common concern, decided what action should be taken, and appointed men to carry out their decisions. Government itself was therefore, on the local level, a voluntary association. So much was left up to the initiative of the inhabitants that it is often very difficult to say when an early colonial settlement became a town. "In the minds of the early legislators," as Sly remarks, "it seems that extensive municipal organization was quite possible under simple voluntary association." The Massachusetts General Court seems to have assumed that local communities would take whatever steps were necessary on their own initiative. And they did.

The earliest known town records in the colony of Massachusetts Bay are those of Dorchester in 1632. Yet they begin by providing a sort of steering committee rather than officers empowered to act for the town. No formal act of incorporation took place. Out of this beginning, however, the office of selectman developed.

The New England town was, and at its best still is, a cooperative enterprise, more like a voluntary association than a formal government and with mutual service more conspicuous than self-aggrandizement. There are no plums to be picked from the political tree. Town officials are under the watchful eye of those who put them into office. Anyway, they are first of all farmers or merchants and only in their spare time selectmen or members of the school board. Small-town politics is still managed by amateurs who engage in it by choice or from a sense of public duty.

*　*　*

Within three years of their arrival in America, the men of Dorchester began to look westward. After sending scouts into Connecticut, Pastor John Wareham in October, 1635, led about sixty of his congregation to the place now known as Windsor. Settlers and their cattle went by land, while their goods were sent around by water. Wareham, dissatisfied with Winthrop's rule in the Bay Colony, wanted to get beyond his jurisdiction. Unfortunately for the Plymouth colony, which had already established a trading post on the Connecticut, he chose to settle on its land. Plymouth was never able to persuade him to go elsewhere, and ultimately was forced to give up most of the territory it had pioneered.

What happened to Pastor Wareham's group must have looked to Plymouth like just retribution. They had hardly settled when an early and severe winter attacked them. The river froze over by the middle of November. Snow was knee-deep. The shelter they had hastily built could not keep out the frost and snow. Food was scarce. They could neither feed nor protect their animals. Of those who tried to get back to Massachusetts, six were shipwrecked. Of thirteen who tried to return by land, one fell through the ice and was drowned. The other twelve would have died except for the chance discovery of an Indian wigwam. Seventy men and women struggled down to the river's mouth where they hoped to find the ship bearing their goods. They found her frozen tight. When a lucky rain set her free, the miserable colonists returned to Massachusetts. Of those who remained at Windsor, some died of hunger, while most of their cattle died from exposure or lack of fodder.

Yet they hung on. Reinforcements reached them the following spring, and their toehold on the Connecticut was enlarged into a beachhead for still other settlements.

On May 31, 1636, the Reverend Thomas Hooker set out from Newton (Cambridge) for the Connecticut wilderness with the members of his church—thirty-five men and their wives, children and servants. Altogether they made a party of a little more than a hundred. Driving their flocks and herds before them, they moved slowly through the forest. Mrs. Hooker, too sick to walk, had to be carried on a horse litter. Making about ten miles a day, they slept out in the open each night and reached the Connecticut after two weeks.

Thomas Hooker, one of the great religious leaders of colonial America, had been discontented with his place in Massachusetts Bay. Whether he found that with Cotton there two suns could not shine in one sky, or whether he wanted to live under a more liberal form of government no one can say for certain. Unfortunately he left no such journal as Bradford's for Plymouth or Winthrop's for Massachusetts Bay. But the government set up in the Connecticut river towns was more liberal than that of the Bay. It suggests Plymouth. Whether Hooker was influenced by Plymouth directly or through Roger Williams, the government in which he had an influential hand did not restrict the franchise to church members. Hooker believed that all authority is laid "in the free consent of the people."

The origins of political authority in Connecticut are too complicated to be described in detail, since we are looking rather for instances of voluntary activity than for formally organized government. But the two are hard to separate in early New England. Government often began in a voluntary association. The steps by which the voluntary group became an organized political body are often, because of a lack of records, difficult to trace. But one thing is clear: the voluntary group which was formed by a church covenant was often the seed from which a town later sprang. Having the church discipline to guide and control them, such groups often took their time about organizing as a town. This was the case with Thomas Hooker and his church flock.

Hooker's group came to Connecticut with the approval both of Massachusetts Bay, which had issued a commission to the emigrants, and of John Winthrop, Jr. who had been sent over by Lord Saye and Sele and other English proprietors to establish a plantation at the mouth of the Connecticut and guard their interests in the whole Connecticut territory. By a neat compromise the conflicting claims of Massachusetts and the Winthrop plantation were brought into harmony. The Massachusetts commission gave to eight men the power to make decrees, punish offenders, and convene the inhabitants. But their powers were to last only for one year. The commissioners met at Hartford, April 26, 1636, when they swore in a constable for each of the three river plantations then being established—Hartford, Wethersfield, Windsor.

Community life therefore started with a voluntary religious organization and an appointed law officer.* But after one year the commission expired. No one seemed to be in a hurry to replace it. Meanwhile the settlers had obviously taken many important matters into their own hands. Land had to be apportioned, buildings put up, fields cleared and laid out. Trade with the Indians was established. Yet there is nothing to show that the three towns had drawn up any kind of formal civil agreement either before or after they came into the Connecticut Valley.

"The three settlements were still in the plantation stage and can have had no other organization than the meeting of their inhabitants to take common action in the choice of committees to the general court and the management of their agricultural, military, and prudential obligations." This is what Charles M. Andrews, leading authority on Connecticut history, concludes. It was not until 1639, after the Fundamental Orders had been adopted, that any system of town government was agreed upon.

What held these communities together before that time?

"Whatever government we find the colonists exercising was unofficial, unorganized and unsystematic," says Andrews. "Such government was purely democratic, but it was not the government of an independent town."

What Andrews refers to as "simple democratic self-manage-

---

* The people of Windsor and Hartford had moved as organized churches. But Wethersfield, settled by scattered groups at different times, "gathered" its church after the plantation was organized. As to the commission, the settlers later held that it arose from their own initiative, and from their determination not to remain in a colony with whose spirit they were not in sympathy.

ment" was in fact voluntary association—a working together to carry out group needs and purposes, but without formally organized government.

Yet the settlers managed to set up communities, divide and clear the land, defend themselves against possible attack, build meeting houses and other public works. Some scholars have argued that they must have come as organized towns in order to work together so efficiently. But the fact is that no town organization, no local government, no town officers existed until 1639. It was by voluntary association that America was settled from the very first. Yet little attention has ever been paid to this initial phase of community life. Students of government have been interested only in the later stage of formal organization. The importance of voluntary association in America's formative years has been consistently overlooked.

* * *

When the town of Roxbury, Massachusetts, began to grow crowded, a town meeting was called. The citizens voted that if at least thirty people wanted to settle on new land, they should have the land and a loan of £100. This money was to be used for community purposes—to build a meeting house, a minister's house, a sawmill and bridges.

Plenty of people were ready to go out to the new settlement. So in 1683 the selectmen petitioned the General Court for permission to acquire a tract of land seven miles square. Three years later the first settlers were ready to start out. Thirteen went ahead to examine the piece of land in northeastern Connecticut which is now Woodstock. When they had approved it, the selectmen bought it from Major James Fitch. In August thirty families arrived. The advance party had already set up the sawmill. The settlers divided into three groups in order to settle in three specified areas. Then lots were drawn for the land. The first drawing was for the home lots of ten to twenty acres. Then meadows, uplands and woodlands were distributed. A quarry was set aside for the use of all, and so was a clay deposit which would be used for chimney bricks. Land was reserved for a minister.

At first the settlers had to camp out. Church services were held in the open air. After the first house was finished in November, a grist mill and another sawmill were arranged for.

In the months that followed, the settlers cleared their land, built roads and bridges and set out orchards, making homes where there had been wilderness. Because there was still danger from Indian attack, the houses were built close together in three small clusters. The life of the town, of a gathered people, was still a necessity both for military and social reasons.

Finally in 1690 New Roxbury (Woodstock) was recognized as a town by the General Court. But for four years, during the difficult period of settlement, it had operated by the voluntary co-operation of its people. Conditions required this kind of co-operation. Survival itself depended on families working together. This necessity had a good deal to do with the shaping of American character. And with the strong feeling for local autonomy, the suspicion of bigness and remoteness in government.

New England proved that new communities could be conceived, established and controlled by voluntary association. Nothing was more important among the causes of America's growth. It is only necessary to compare the growth of New England with that of New France to see how important voluntarism was. Canada from the first was tightly controlled by an autocratic church and an autocratic king. When French Protestants, around 1700, begged to be allowed to settle under French sovereignty on the Mississippi, they were rebuffed. "The King has not driven Protestants from France to make a republic for them in America," they were told. While New England was often far from tolerant in matters of religion, it was possible for men like Thomas Hooker or Roger Williams to establish their own colonies. Small, self-governing units were able to split off and settle in the wilderness. The absence of strong central control over the English colonies resulted in strength rather than weakness, as the final contest between France and England in North America made clear.

Having created his church and state, as Henry Commager points out, the American took for granted his capacity to create all lesser institutions and associations. All sorts of organizations sprang up to do good, to influence political decisions, to change and improve the world as it was. The lyceum movement, free libraries, higher education for women—all began in voluntary association.

But voluntary association can flourish only where there is a problem to be met, where people know each other well enough to sense the mutuality of the problem, and where they have a strong enough sense of belonging to want to tackle and solve it.

These conditions were met in New England. A natural result was that men came to think in terms of the small, manageable community. Local autonomy was so firmly established that any larger unit of government came to be looked on with suspicion. During the early years the tiny colonies were left pretty much to themselves. But from the time of the Parliamentary Commission for Plantations (1643) and the Lords of Trade (1660), the hand of the home government came to be more heavily felt—and resented. Provincialism—or its international counterpart isolationism—thus became a corollary of independence, and voluntary association the weapon with which to attack the increasingly heavy hand of royal government.

IV

Sons of Liberty

On the sixth of February, 1765, Isaac Barré who had fought with Wolfe at Quebec rose from his place in the British House of Parliament. He rose to speak against the bill brought in by the ministry for taxing the American colonies.

"They, planted by your care!" he answered Townshend. "No: your oppressions planted them in America. . . . They nourished by your indulgence! They grew by your neglect of them. As soon as you began to care about them, that care was exercised in sending persons to rule them . . . men whose behavior on many occasions has caused the blood of those SONS OF LIBERTY to recoil within them."

He spoke eloquently, but nobody listened. The Stamp Act passed by a vote of 294 to 49 and was promptly approved by the Lords.

Jared Ingersoll of Connecticut was present in the House of Commons. As agent for Connecticut—or lobbyist—he had tried to prevent the bill's passage. He made notes of Barré's speech and sent a report of it back to Connecticut. Barré's words were printed in the *New London Gazette* on May 10, and thereafter throughout the colonies. The phrase, "Sons of Liberty," provided a slogan, a reputation to live up to, a suggestion for an organization to oppose the bitterly hated Stamp Act which was just now being denounced by Patrick Henry in words that made his listeners cry, "Treason! Treason!"

The idea of organizing the Sons of Liberty into action groups seems to have taken hold first in eastern Connecticut where Ingersoll's report of the Barré speech had first appeared. Under the leadership of Israel Putnam of Pomfret it spread quickly throughout the New England hill country and as far northward as New Hampshire.

By a strange coincidence, a liberal group calling itself the "True Sons of Righteous Liberty" had formed a political club in Connecticut ten years before the passage of the Stamp Act to protest rigid "Old Light" orthodoxy and the passage of penal laws in matters of religion. This may help to explain why the Sons caught on so quickly there.

Meanwhile Jared Ingersoll had been offered the post of stamp distributor for Connecticut. He went and talked it over with another colonial agent in London, Benjamin Franklin. Franklin not only advised him to take the job, but had miscalculated the effect of the act in America so badly that he was seeking the Pennsylvania post for a friend. So Ingersoll returned home as stamp master. And there he discovered the Sons of Liberty, whose organization had originated from his own report.

Fleeing from New Haven to Hartford, Ingersoll was pursued by five hundred Sons of Liberty, led by three trumpeters and two militia officers in full uniform. The Sons demanded that he resign his office. To expedite matters, they produced pen and paper.

Ingersoll looked at the sturdy Sons of Liberty, some of them armed with staves, some with muskets.

"The cause is not worth dying for," he said, and signed his name.

He was then asked to swear that he had signed of his own free will.

Ingersoll was prudent, but he was no coward. "No," he said.

The Sons held a brief conference. "Then throw your hat in the air and shout three times, 'Liberty and property, huzzah!'"

Before they were through with him, Ingersoll had to throw his wig in the air too. Thus, four months after his appointment,

Jared Ingersoll went out of business before he had distributed a single stamp.

* * *

The Stamp Act hit Boston on top of a severe slump which had forced a number of the great shipping houses to close their doors, left farmers without markets for their wheat, and thrown thousands out of work. It hit the man of wealth and property even harder than it hit the workman. The well to do and the debtor class, who for years had fought each other in the Assembly, were inadvertently united by an act of Parliament. In their resistance to the Stamp Act they now made common cause. Men like John Hancock of Boston or John Morin Scott and William Livingston of New York were behind the acts of mob defiance which soon stirred the seaports.

Mob scenes were nothing new to these towns. For years there had been brawling in taverns and brothels as hard-muscled sailors or working men followed their own way of having a good time. But on August fourteenth the brawling took on a new dimension at Boston.

Early in the morning an effigy of Andrew Oliver, Secretary of the Province and stamp distributor, was found hanging from an elm opposite Boylston Market. Beside it hung a large boot (for Lord Bute) with a devil peering out of the top. Shortly before dark a mob assembled, cut down the effigy and bore it to the Town House where the governor and council were sitting— Oliver among them. Mob and effigy poured through the building. They went on to the waterfront where they destroyed a building Oliver had recently put up—allegedly as headquarters for his stamp distributing. They marched to his house, broke the windows, smashed furniture, destroyed the garden—and while still on the premises formed a society which they called the Union Club. Later they were to claim that this was the origin of the Sons of Liberty (see page 84).

This was no mob of brawling sailors and working men. It had been led by forty or fifty well-dressed citizens. Describing the event, the *Boston Gazette* quoted Barré's praise of the American sons of liberty. Liberty and property! If Parliament would not respect American property, taxing it in a fashion Americans considered robbery, then they would not respect the property of those who acted for Parliament. They had tried petition and protest, to no effect. Now they would see what action could do. On August twenty-sixth the mob burned the records of the vice-admiralty court and looted the beautiful home of Governor Hutchinson.

Acknowledged leader of the mob was Ebenezer Mackintosh. Behind him was a group calling itself the Loyall Nine which had formed either in the spring or about the time of the August riots. These nine men were merchants—distillers, braziers and the like—respectable businessmen. Since they are the men John Adams mentioned when he visited the headquarters of the Sons a few months later, it seems clear that they were responsible for establishing the Sons of Liberty in Boston.

On the eleventh of September Boston, with appropriate ceremony, affixed a copper plate to the tree where Oliver had been hanged in effigy. The Liberty Tree, they called it now. It was the first of many. Sooner or later every self-respecting town in the colonies either raised a Liberty Pole or dedicated a Liberty Tree. And usually it was the Sons who did it. Only the Liberty Boys of Plymouth (though not until 1774) deviated from the pattern. They tried to haul a large boulder from the shore up into the center of town. The rock split and most of it fell back into the hole. But the top was carted away. It was not reunited with its other half until 1880. The Plymouth boys have been vindicated by time. For while the Liberty poles and trees have long since disappeared, Plymouth Rock—now back in its original location—attracts a quarter of a million Pilgrims every year.

✿ ✿ ✿

In June James Otis had proposed to the Massachusetts Assembly that all the colonies be invited to send delegates to a meeting to make common cause against the Stamp Act. The mo-

tion passed, a circular letter was sent to each of the colonial
assemblies calling for a congress to be held in New York, and on
October seventh the Stamp Act Congress convened with representatives from nine of the thirteen colonies. On October nineteenth the Congress brought out its Declaration of Rights and
Grievances with its claim that taxation without representation
was a violation of the rights of British subjects, and that the
colonists could not legally be taxed except by their own legislatures. Petitions for repeal were sent to the King, the House of
Commons and the House of Lords. Then the delegates went
home.

On October seventeenth John Lamb, Isaac Sears and other
New York radical leaders had formed an association to oppose
the Stamp Act. On October thirty-first, the day before the act
was to go into effect, a meeting was held in Burns' Coffee House.
It resolved to oppose the distribution of the stamps. It resolved
to stop importing British goods until the act was repealed. It
proposed a committee to correspond with other colonies and
draw up articles of confederacy which would make the opposition to the act effective.

But when it came to naming the committee, no one would
serve. Opposition to royal authority could, after all, be dangerous. Finally Sears, Lamb, Gershom Mott, William Wiley and
Thomas Robinson volunteered to tackle the job.

The next day there was rioting. A mob broke into the Governor's coach house, hoisted an effigy aboard and then dragged
the coach through town and back to the fort.

"Here they come, by God," said Major James from the wall.

Having pulled down the gallows, the mob placed it up against
the fort gate and then beat upon the gate with clubs, daring
Major James to give the order to fire. The Major, credited with
having said he would bring New York under control with five
hundred men, was the particular object of their ire.

It was now decided to burn both coach and effigy on the
Bowling Green, before the eyes of the soldiers.

"They told M. James as soon as the Coatch was burnt they

would knock down his house . . . and if he was A Man he should Go and defend it. . . . In Less than 10 Minutes they had the windows and dores the Looking Glasses Mehogany Tables Silk Curtains . . . drank 3 or 4 Pipes of wine . . . and at last burnt the whole." This was New York's welcome to the Stamp Act.

November first was marked in Boston by the tolling of bells and blowing of conch shells at daybreak. Little business was done. Many shops were shut. Ships in the harbor flew their flags at half mast. Crowds came to the Royal Elm before noon, some of them with weeds (crape) in their hats. At three o'clock the effigy of Grenville which had been hoisted onto the Liberty Tree was cut down and carried to the gallows on Boston Neck, where it was hanged, torn apart and thrown into the water. The crowd carried no weapons. There was no brawling or vandalism. This behavior, remarked the *New York Gazette,* is to be expected as the Sons of Liberty have agreed to unite as brethren in preventing disorder. Was this an ironic comment on Boston's August riots, or an attempt to encourage moderation in the future?

No group calling itself the Sons of Liberty had yet appeared in New York. But Livingston speaks of a "secret party." A few weeks later, when the Sons began to be spoken of, it was Lamb, Sears and John Morin Scott who led them. When the Governor, Sir Henry Moore, arrived in New York from England early in November, their influence was already strong enough so that he declared he would not compel the issuance of the stamps. He also ordered an end to the work begun on the forts and batteries by acting Governor Cadwallader Colden. The Sons sent him a congratulatory letter. The next day a large meeting was held in the fields, pyramids were erected in the Governor's honor, and a magnificent bonfire was lighted in the evening.

When Peter Delancey arrived from England near the end of November, a committee of the Sons persuaded him to resign his commission as stamp distributor.

But when Zachariah Hood, the stamp distributor for Maryland, had to flee his own state and arrived in New York, the local Sons found real sport. Hood apparently expected that he could remain anonymous in the city. But the Sons found him out. When he sought refuge in Flushing they chased him there too, and on November twenty-eighth they forced him to resign his commission.

"Our Society," the Baltimore Sons wrote to New York, "order us in a particular manner to return thanks to your Sons of Liberty for obliging our fugitive Stamp Master to resign his Odious Office, he having fled from the just Resentment of his injured Countrymen."

A brig came into port bearing the hated stamps. The Sons seized the stamps and burned them in the shipyards.

Lewis Pintard, a merchant, made use of two documents on stamped paper, a bond and a Mediterranean pass. The Sons demanded the papers, destroyed them, and got his oath that he did not know the papers were stamped.

Finally on December fifth the *New York Gazette or Weekly Post-Boy* published its first account of the proceedings of the Sons of Liberty. Zachariah Hood's story was told, as well as the success of the Sons in relieving Simon Metcalf of his inspectorship of stamps. James McEvers had also been persuaded to swear that he would distribute no more stamps. Captain John Montresor, a British officer stationed in New York, wrote in his Journal for December eighth that the Sons of Liberty "as they term themselves" were openly defying all established authority and were the sole rulers of the city.

A few days before Christmas a large band of armed men boarded the *Minerva,* demanding the stamped paper for Connecticut which she was said to have aboard. Assured that the paper had been taken ashore to Fort George, the men searched the ship anyway, found nothing, and went peaceably ashore without doing any damage.

From New York in late December, 1765, agents went into New England to propose an association of Liberty Boys. The terms of association included mutual defense against British officials (the course of events would indicate that it was the officials who needed aid!), vigilance against use of the stamps, and the defense of officials who agreed not to enforce the act.

At last on January 7, 1766, the New York Sons of Liberty held an open meeting at the house of William Howard. A large number assembled, affirmed their loyalty to Great Britain and declared that the Stamp Act encroached upon their rights as free men.

"We will go to the last extremity and venture our lives and fortunes effectively to prevent the said Stamp-Act from ever taking place in this city and province," they promised.

The Sons of Liberty, it seemed, meant business.

* * *

Organizations are made by men. Who were the men who made the Sons of Liberty? Why did they do it and where did they get their support?

New York politics had long been polarized by a struggle for power between the conservative Delanceys and the more liberal or Whiggish Livingstons. The Stamp Act united Whig merchants and the working and artisan classes and opened the way for the appearance of popular leaders like John Lamb and Isaac Sears.

Lamb, the son of a celebrated optician who as a youth had barely escaped the gallows in England as an accomplice of the notorious Jack Sheppard, was thirty years old at the time of the Stamp Act, and in business for himself as a wine merchant. He was known to be turbulent and high-tempered. Sears, of Pilgrim stock, had made a small fortune as a privateer before becoming a merchant. He was to be the leader of nearly every demonstration of mob violence in the years ahead. Like Alexander McDougall, Marinus Willett and Joseph Allicocke, Lamb and Sears were practical-minded merchants with an understanding of popular psychology and an ability to appeal to the working man. The Whig leaders, Livingston and Scott and William Smith, Jr., saw in them the means of getting wider support.

Because the Stamp Act bore down on merchants and workers alike (or at the least appeared to do so), it provided the stimulus any voluntary association must have. An irritating cause, a growing sense of need or discomfort, and leadership—any association needs these. New York had them all now, in full measure. As a result, the Sons of Liberty were able to act with a firmness which many a royal officer thought treasonable. And they were able to commit themselves to bringing about nothing less than the act's repeal.

Throughout the early months of 1766 the *New York Gazette* reports meetings of the Sons and reprints some of their correspondence, while Captain Montresor continues to lament their power. They control the press, he confides to his Journal. They have declared they will fight up to their knees in blood rather than let the act operate. They daily threaten the life of Lieutenant Governor Colden. They had even taken it on themselves to decide whether to permit the "strollers" to put on a play which General Gage had already approved. When the play went on, they pulled down the playhouse at the beginning of the second act, stealing, throwing brickbats, and crying "Liberty."

When the Sons at their meeting of February 4 appointed a committee to correspond with Sons in near-by colonies, they started something that was to have an important influence on the future.

From manuscripts in the New-York and Massachusetts Historical Societies it is possible to trace a part at least of this network of letter exchanges which now began to take place among the colonies. For by this time there were Sons of Liberty—or Liberty Boys as they were also called—in many towns and most of the colonies.

New York is in touch with New Jersey, Pennsylvania and Maryland to the south, and through them with the southern colonies. To the north, it is in touch with Connecticut, Rhode Island and Massachusetts, and through Massachusetts with New Hampshire. It also corresponds with other towns in its own colony. From Oyster Bay, for instance, it receives a set of resolutions typical of those being passed by Sons throughout the country—to defend their right to be taxed by their own representatives; to oppose and suppress the arbitrary and unconstitutional Stamp Act with their utmost power.

Directly or indirectly, all the provincial capitals were in touch with each other. Each of them served as a center of information for the towns of its own colony. It encouraged the towns to act, it sent them news from other colonies, and in some cases it summoned them to meetings. Boston was informal headquarters for eastern and northern New England. Philadelphia and Baltimore passed southward the news they received from New York. But New York was the nerve center. Partly because of its central location, partly perhaps because the Stamp Act Congress had sat there, but largely because of the energy and enthusiasm of Lamb, Sears and a few others, who sent their long-hand epistles north and south, it soon became unofficial headquarters for all the Sons of Liberty. Nothing less than a firm bond of all the colonies from Georgia to New Hampshire was what they aimed at. Resistance to the Stamp Act in every possible way was the program, but chiefly by transacting legal and commercial business while ignoring the stamps. And, of course, repeal of the act. The New York Sons even had a representative in London, Nicholas Ray, with whom they exchanged information.

In Boston as in New York the Sons of Liberty gained prestige and power. They expressed the feelings of the people. They were a voice for feelings in search of an outlet. They provided a program. They offered a wedge with which the common people could split open the old aristocratic front. They gave shape and substance to the popular hostility to arbitrary rule.

The juries were packed with them. The justices favored them. No one opposed them. They terrified the customs officials into opening the port without stamped clearances. They compelled the courts to transact business as if the act had been nullified.

Deacon Cushing of Hingham well expressed the current of feeling when, toward the end of November, he drove two large oxen into Boston bearing the inscription "King George and Pitt forever! Liberty and Property and no stamps!"

John Adams records in his Diary how the Sons of Liberty, on December seventeenth, forced Andrew Oliver to come to the Liberty Tree and there give his oath that he had never taken any measures to act as distributor of stamps and never would directly or indirectly enforce the Stamp Act. Justice Richard Dana was on hand to see that the oath was properly administered, with no legal loopholes.

On Wednesday evening, January 15, 1766, Adams was invited to Hanover Square where, near the Liberty Tree, the Sons had their own apartment. He found there John Avery—whom he describes as "distiller or merchant, of a liberal education," "John Smith the brazier, Thomas Crafts, the painter, Edes, the printer, Stephen Cleverly, the brazier, Chase, the distiller, Joseph Field, master of a vessel, Henry Bass, [and] George Trott, jeweller." Adams was "very civilly and respectfully treated by all present."

"We had punch, wine, pipes and tobacco, biscuit and cheese, &c.," he confided to his Diary. "I heard nothing but such as passes at all clubs, among gentlemen, about the times. No plots, no machinations." But the Sons were already planning to celebrate the repeal of the Stamp Act. "I wish they may not be disappointed," wrote John Adams.

In February the Boston Sons were seeking his advice on sentiment in Braintree and asking him to write inscriptions in connection with a big event they were planning—the ceremonious burning of the detested stamped paper. On February twentieth effigies of Grenville and Bute in full court dress were pulled through the streets in a cart and burnt together with the stamped paper. A manuscript letter from the Boston Sons (apparently to Portsmouth) brings the celebration into sharp focus.

"Enclosed you'l find a Portion of that detestable Paper mark'd with America's Oppression it being half that we obtained of [our] Brother Sons from another Colony [New York] which we intend to exhibit with Chains &c. next Thursday in a Publick Manner on Liberty Tree. . . . It will be taken down at 12 OClock by a Common Executioner and burnt—Let us show as

much abhorence as possible—After which we propose to have
the following Toasts drunk—George the Third, our gracious
rightfull and Lawfull Sovereign—Succession [*sic*] to the Royal
House of Hanover—Confusion to its Enemies—Success to the
Foes of the Stamp Act—A perpetual Itching without the Benefit
of Scratching to the Friends of the same—Long Life Health &
Prosperity to all the Sons of Liberty on the Continent—We are,
Gentlemen, with the greatest Esteem—

> Yours &c. The Sons of Liberty"

A few days later the Sons held another bonfire when a ship
captain arrived from Jamaica (where the Stamp Act had been
accepted) with his clearance on stamped paper.

Meanwhile the New York Sons had not been idle. On the
eighteenth of March Captain Montresor reports:

The Sons of Liberty preparing to have a procession, with Sir Jeffry
Amherst's effigy, afterwards to burn it, as they say he proposed to
augment the military forces in America, towards the more effectual
forcing the Stamp act. Also propose, erecting a Statue of Mr. Pitt (as
a friend) in the Bowling Green, on the Identical Spot where the
Lieut. Governor's Chariot was burned and to name that Green—
"Liberty Green" for ever. Many declaring that they will oppose the
landing of any troops from Great Britain.

The next day he reported that the Sons "insolently sent Mr.
Allecocke and Sears, two of their Representatives on board the
Garland Ship of War to demand the Lieut. of his Majesty's Ship,
for having said that the Printer of the Thursday's Gazette, one
Holt, was he in England would be hanged for the licentiousness
of his Paper." The Lieutenant ordered them ashore. On the following day the Sons assembled, says Montresor, to attack the
vessel, when General Thomas Gage, Commander in Chief of
the British forces in America, sent a message to the vessel that
he would give whatever assistance they needed. The Sons thereupon determined to call on General Gage and ask why he had
sent such a message and why he had ordered troops to New
York.

The Albany Sons, not to be outdone by their brothers down the river, pursued Henry Van Schaack to his home, finding it necessary to destroy a balcony, furniture, a sleigh and other assorted property before getting his oath that he would never be a stamp master.

Montresor thought the Sons the worst sort of rabble. But it is clear that they were remarkably successful in thinking up ways to maintain a continuous agitation against the Stamp Act. They crystallized public opinion against it. They proved that a voluntary association cleverly managed was more than a match for his Majesty's government backed by his army and navy.

* * *

One of the most remarkable things about the Sons of Liberty was the way they sprang up throughout the colonies. In Charleston, South Carolina, they stormed the fort, where they found one private awake and the rest of the garrison of twelve asleep. In 1766 the Sons became a mechanic's association and in effect a political party which in 1768 put Christopher Gadsden into office. In North Carolina five hundred heavily armed Sons besieged Fort Johnson. They were met by a garrison of two. In Georgia, the southernmost colony, the Sons had begun to meet in October, 1765. Many had signed an association to prevent the use of stamps and to prevent the act from taking effect.

Philadelphia failed to build up steam as promptly as Boston or New York. But a small group including Charles Thomson, the printer William Bradford and Robert Morris got together to oppose the Stamp Act. Lamb went down from New York to help oust the last stamp collector in America, which he succeeded in doing with the help of the Heart-and-Hand Fire Company. Apparently there was no effective association of Sons there at that time. But a letter from the Philadelphia to the New York Sons on February 15, 1766, shows that they were by then in existence.

"Our Body in this City is not declared Numerous," they confessed, "as unfortunate Dissentions in Provincial Politicks keeps us rather a divided People, but when the Grand Cause calls on us, you may be assured we shall universally stand forth and appear what we really are,

Sons of Liberty in Philadelphia."

In Maryland Samuel Chase and William Paca, well-known leaders, undertook to organize the Sons in Annapolis and Baltimore. On the first of March, 1766, the Sons of Baltimore and Anne Arundel counties met in the Courthouse at Annapolis. A few days later the Baltimore Sons, through their Committee of Correspondence (Thomas Chase, William Lux, D. Chamler, Robert Alexander and Robert Adair) informed New York that they were trying to bring about a union of all the counties in the province. "From our Intelligence since rece'd we find it succeeds as we could wish as the whole Province seem unanimous in prosecuting the same design."

New Jersey also worked out a colony-wide plan. "Each town was to elect delegates to a county convention, which was to appoint a committee of correspondence. From the county committees delegates were to be sent to a provincial convention, and it in turn was to appoint a committee for the colony," says Philip Davidson in *Propaganda and the American Revolution*. Since this was the plan followed when the Revolution came, it forms an important link between the Sons and the coming of independence.

Connecticut, where the Sons had first started, called a convention of all the towns which had Sons. A great majority of these assembled at Hartford on the twenty-fifth of March and passed the usual resolutions. Thanks to Britain, Americans were learning how to co-operate. The self-sufficient towns were learning to act together as a team. The colonies, with their long-standing grudges and jealousies, were pulling together.

On the fifth of February, for example, the Boston Sons informed John Adams that New York and Connecticut had signed an agreement of mutual defense. They were ready "to march with all despatch, at their own costs and expense, on the first proper notice, with their whole force (if required) to the relief of those who shall or may be in danger from the Stamp Act or its abettors." Boston circulated the proposal for union throughout its area. When its letter addressed to the New Hampshire Sons reached Portsmouth, the Superior Court was in session. Taking advantage therefore of the presence of men from other towns, the Portsmouth Sons posted a notice in the most frequented parts of town, calling for a meeting to consider the proposal. Drums were sent through the principal streets just before the hour of meeting. When the people had assembled on the parade, the proposals were read out. Then an answer (written apparently by the Portsmouth leaders) was read.

"They were desired to manifest their Approbation by holding up their Hatts, which was immediately done by the whole body. The affair concluded with Three Hearty Cheers."

A letter of March third from Norwich, Connecticut, congratulated the Portsmouth Sons on their stand for liberty. Eleven days later Boston informed New Hampshire that New York had sent a circular letter to all the provinces as far as South Carolina, and that as a result a united body from there to New Hampshire was in prospect. An assembly is looked for, and the prospects are for "the happy Union of the Colonies which seems to bid fair for an everlasting One."

The assembly, or congress, did not come off, though it no doubt would have if the act had not been repealed.

The device which bound the Sons together was the committee of correspondence. Nearly every local group of Sons had one. Shrewd Sam Adams noted how successful they were in creating public opinion and drawing the colonies together. He was for continuing them even if the act should be repealed. At a later time he revived them, and their activity brought on the Revolution.

* * *

The Sons of Liberty came to life in response to a need. The irritating cause had to come first. There had to be widespread feeling over it. There had to be men of initiative, willing to risk punishment, who could offer to the people an association through which they could express their resentment. But there also had to be in the surrounding culture a habit of forming into voluntary groups. This, we know, was present. It may be no accident that New York's leader, Isaac Sears, was of Plymouth stock. As for Boston, the habits of local independence and forming into groups were firmly seated. Societies to promote trade, humaneness, music and whatnot are frequently mentioned in the newspapers of the Stamp Act period.

In fact, the existence of such organizations gave the Sons something to hook on to. The Loyall Nine in Boston were all members of the Caucus Club which had been meeting for years. The Ancient and Honorable Mechanical Company had been formed in Baltimore in 1763 as a voice for tradesman and the artisan group. It became the Sons of Liberty in 1765. In Philadelphia it was the Heart-and-Hand Fire Company from which the Sons of Liberty sprang. The desire of the less affluent to share political power was a great help to the speedy formation of the Sons of Liberty.

As in any organization, most of the work was done by a few people. A small group of men in each town steered the formation and activity of the Sons—men like Mackintosh of Boston and Isaac Sears of New York who already had the status of leaders with a large number of their friends, business acquaintances and neighbors. Through them the plans and ideas of the steering group could be communicated to the membership.

The method of operation is well described by a contemporary, William Gordon, though he is speaking of Boston a few years later, about the time of the Massacre.

The prime managers were about six in number; each of whom when separate, headed a division; the several individuals of which, collected and led distinct subdivisions. In this manner the political engine has been constructed. . . . When any important transaction is to be brought forward, it is thoroughly considered by the prime managers. If they approve, each communicates it to his own division;

from thence, if adopted, it passes to the several subdivisions, which form a general meeting in order to canvass the business. The prime managers . . . if they observe that the collected body is in general strongly against the measure they wish to have carried . . . declare it to be improper: is it opposed by great numbers, but not warmly, they advise reconsideration at another meeting.

Sometimes men calling themselves Sons of Liberty used the current unrest as an excuse for private pillage. Then it became necessary for the "True-Born Sons of Liberty" to disown their "Bastard-kin."

Despite these impediments, the Sons in 1766 were a remarkable organization, loosely affiliated from colony to colony but remarkably effective in unifying public sentiment and in directing the whole opposition to the Stamp Act. Unheard of a year before, they had in a few short months stolen the show. They drove out the stamp masters or forced them to resign, burned stamps, usurped much of the real power of government, prevented the act from taking effect, forced the courts to operate without stamps and newspapers to publish without regard to stamped paper. They passed resolutions condemning the Stamp Act and binding themselves to ignore its provisions. By their concerted actions they did in effect nullify the act before Parliament repealed it. Ben Franklin was right in saying that if troops were sent over to enforce the act, they would not find a rebellion but they would make one.

When persuasion was ineffective, the Sons were quite willing to resort to intimidation, as in the case of the Maryland stamp master or the few merchants who handled stamped paper.

By exchanging news amongst themselves, the Sons of the various colonies brought about a unanimity of feeling which prepared the ground for revolution. Exchange of ideas also led to fuller use of effective propaganda devices such as the symbolic burial of Liberty in several towns on the day the act went into effect.

The Sons even formed military alliances, to be ready in case the British used troops to beat down their opposition. When the New York and Connecticut Sons signed their agreement, Connecticut was said to have ten thousand men armed and ready to march under the command of Colonel Israel Putnam, veteran of the French and Indian War.

A New York Son who visited Boston "was admitted in their most Honourable Privy Council." He was informed "that they can at Two Hours Notice Bring 3000 Men under the Tree of Liberty who would go any where for the preservation of the Constitution & that there is above 40000 in that Province & New Hampshire who are determined to take up Arms for the same Purpose if necessary." It was said that the Boston Sons had laid plans to cut off a British army before it could reach Boston overland. Clearly, the Sons were ready to push their voluntary association to the point of replacing British rule, if that should prove necessary.

Not to be outdistanced by the men, the women were soon associating as Daughters of Liberty. Eighteen young ladies of Providence met on March 16, 1766, at the home of Dr. Ephraim Bowen. They spent the day spinning as a means of encouraging the use of local products over British goods. They resolved to buy no British goods until the Stamp Act was repealed. They omitted tea from their dinner. The association grew so rapidly that their next meeting had to be held in the courthouse, where they spun a handsome piece of linen as a prize to be given the largest flax grower. It was reported that one group of patriotic daughters had voted not to marry any man who proposed to use a stamped license.

*　*　*

Repeal (passed on March 18, to take effect May 1, 1766) brought an end to all this activity, but not until the Sons had celebrated with "such illuminations, bonfires, pyramids, obelisks, such grand exhibitions and such fire-works as were never before seen in America," according to John Adams.

The Sons of Exeter, New Hampshire, held their joyful celebration at the place they had named Liberty Square. There was ringing of bells, firing of cannon, a pennant displayed, and in the evening illuminations and drinking the King's health. Bumpers flowed freely throughout the colonies. Twenty-five toasts were drunk by a crowd in Faneuil Hall, leading one anonymous writer to complain that it would have been better to impart to the poor rather than to get men drunk.

In New York the *Gazette* dropped from its masthead after May eighth the slogan "Liberty, Property and No Stamps" which had appeared there every week since the passage of the act. On May twentieth, when certain news of the repeal arrived, there was a great din of bells, and boys ran through the streets carrying poles with handkerchiefs or papers stuck on them. At one o'clock the next day a twenty-one-gun salute was fired. Captain Montresor sourly observes that it was intended "to Salute General Allicocke," one of the Sons, though it was obviously for the King. Two large bonfires were constructed, one for the Sons, a holiday was declared, and at night there was a grand illumination. "Night ended," says the Captain, "in Drunkenness, throwing of Squibbs, Crackers, firing of muskets and pistols, breaking some windows and forcing off the Knockers off the Doors. A large Mob of the Sons of Liberty went to the Fort to congratulate the Governor, three of which, drunk as they were, had admittance."

The Sons of New York promptly dissolved their association. When Nicholas Ray wrote to them from London, suggesting that they commemorate repeal on March eighteenth or May first "forever," they promised to arrange an annual celebration but said there were "difficulties" in the way of establishing a permanent club. Montresor happily noted in July that there were no meetings of Sons since the arrival of additional British troops in New York, and that not even the name was mentioned. But he was mentioning their name again himself in less than a month.

This time the trouble arose out of the Quartering Act. Back in 1765, just before the passage of the Stamp Act, General Thomas Gage as commander of the British forces in America

had asked the home government for an act which would require
the colonies to provide barracks and supplies for his troops.
The act went into effect on March 24, and Gage's request to
carry out its provisions had reached the New York Assembly at
the height of the furor stirred up by the Stamp Act. The Assembly had complained that the act fell most heavily on New York
since Gage had his headquarters there. It failed to comply fully
with his request. Bad feeling between the troops and the citizens
of New York therefore continued even after the Stamp Act
was rescinded, and in the late summer of 1766 it soured completely.

On the tenth of August some soldiers cut down the Liberty
Pole. The next day two or three thousand Sons of Liberty
assembled in protest. Red-coated soldiers with bayonets moved
in to break up the meeting. A scuffle resulted and Isaac Sears
was wounded. The Sons of Liberty, who had dissolved their
association and whom Montresor had thought defunct, continued squabbling with the soldiers throughout August. They
tried to prevent the markets from selling to men in uniform.
They wanted Gage to prevent his men from wearing side arms
when off duty. The Sons might be dissolved, but the solution
still had a lot of acid in it.

As a matter of fact, the old New York leaders had banded together again to see to it that March 18, 1767, the anniversary of
repeal, was appropriately celebrated. They assembled at Bar-
din's, where they dined and drank their toasts. That same night
the soldiers again cut down the pole. The next day another was
erected, so reinforced with iron bands that it would be no easy
job for the troops to fell it. The soldiers went to work on it with
gunpowder but failed to upset it. The Sons saw to it that a guard
was left on duty so that when the soldiers turned up the following night they would find it well defended. But the night after
that the soldiers returned with loaded muskets which they fired
in the direction of the house where the Sons had drunk their
toasts. The officers apparently decided that this was going too

far, for when the troops made another attack on the pole, they were ordered back to their barracks. Squabbles over the pole, sometimes with serious results, continued until in 1770 the Sons bought a piece of land and moved the pole to it.

Boston chose to celebrate August 14, "the day of the *Union* and firmly combined *association* of the TRUE SONS OF LIBERTY." In 1768 the celebration began at dawn with the firing of fourteen salutes. Two effigies were found hanging on Liberty Tree—this time the customs inspector and the head of the customs board. At noon a crowd gathered around the tree to sing a popular song beginning:

> Come, join hand in hand, brave AMERICANS all,
> And rouse your bold hearts at fair LIBERTY'S call.

Thereupon, according to the *Boston Evening Post*, "The fair Daughters of Liberty showed themselves at the neighboring windows with Smiles of Satisfaction." There was toasting, a flourish of French horns, more booming of cannon, a banquet and a parade.

In 1769 the celebration was even more sumptuous.

"Dined with three hundred and fifty Sons of Liberty, at Robinson's, the sign of Liberty Tree, in Dorchester," John Adams wrote in his Diary on Monday, August fourteenth. "We had two tables laid in the open field, by the barn, with between three and four hundred plates, and an awning of sailcloth over head, and should have spent a most agreeable day, had not the rain made some abatement in our pleasure. . . . We had also the Liberty Song—that by the farmer [John Dickinson], and that by Dr. Church, and the whole company joined in the chorus. This is cultivating the sensations of freedom. There was a large collection of good company. Otis and Adams are politic in promoting these festivals; for they tinge the minds of the people; they impregnate them with the sentiments of liberty, they render the people fond of their leaders in the cause, and averse and bitter against all opposers. To the honor of the Sons, I did not see one person intoxicated, or near it."

John Adams' testimony to the importance of this voluntary association is worth noting.

❖ ❖ ❖

The Sons of Liberty never regained the strength and importance of the Stamp Act days. But here and there, and in one cause or another, they did continue until the Revolution made every American either a Son of Liberty or a Tory.

In 1767 the Townshend duties again set Boston "on boiling." Although the taxes they imposed were all external—import duties on glass, lead, paints, paper and tea—one of the provisions was for a Board of Commissioners of the Customs at Boston, responsible directly to the British Treasury Board. Sam Adams planned to seize the commissioners on their arrival and make them resign, but the plan did not come off. A Boston town meeting drew up a list of British goods for boycotting, however, and once again the colonists began a campaign of nonimportation. The Boston Sons strengthened their alliance with New York, and when news came that British troops were being sent to Boston, the Sons held a meeting. The local Tories were sure they were planning to rouse the country and take Castle William. In the summer of 1768 a Boston mob prevented a customs officer from inspecting a ship of John Hancock's and carried off a supply of Madeira under his nose.

"The Sons of Liberty have declared open war," one observer wrote. They called a mass meeting and asserted they would obey no laws made by a body in which they were unrepresented. Yet they found time, too, to serenade John Adams with "sweet songs, violins and flutes" under his window.

The New York Sons, meanwhile, had split into two factions. But by 1769 they had managed to patch up the quarrel in order to unite in supporting the nonimportation agreement directed against the Townshend Act. Governor Moore, writing to the Earl of Hillsborough early in the year, complained that "the remains of that licentious Rabble who during our late disorders, called themselves the Sons of Liberty, had formed a design . . .

to disturb the tranquility of the City by carrying the effigies of certain persons thro' the Town in procession." In December John Lamb spoke to a crowd of fourteen hundred which had been assembled by means of a handbill signed "A Son of Liberty." The crowd disapproved the action of the Assembly in voting money for the support of British troops.

As Philanthropos pointed out in the *New-York Journal,* the Sons of Liberty had two kinds of meetings. A small group of leaders did the important business, and a larger group was called out to draw public opinion toward issues on which the Sons wanted support.

But by 1770 the Sons of New York were hopelessly split again into two factions. The merchant group was for importing any British goods not taxed, the radical group for complete nonimportation until all duties were repealed. Each group held a dinner on the anniversary of the Stamp Act repeal, and each party claimed to be the true Sons of Liberty. New York continued to be troubled by this split until the eve of the Revolution.

When all the Townshend duties except that on tea were canceled in 1770, nonimportation was abandoned. But Alexander McDougall, a leading Son in New York, found a way to keep the pot boiling. In a broadside "To the Betrayed Inhabitants of the City and Colony of New York" he attacked the decision of the Assembly to grant British troops £2,000 worth of supplies. The usual events followed—the Liberty Pole was cut down, the Sons of Liberty came out in force, and a serious riot took place in which thirty or forty soldiers fought citizens armed with swords and clubs. McDougall was arrested, charged with having written the broadside, and thrown in jail where he was so thronged with visitors that he had to give out appointments. His trial never took place, though he was later imprisoned by the Assembly for contempt.

While all this was taking place in New York, clashes in Boston built up to the so-called Massacre of March fifth. If Lieutenant Governor Hutchinson had not withdrawn the troops from the city when Sam Adams demanded it, the Revolution might have begun five years earlier.

By 1771 the conflict had simmered down to a boycott on tea, the only item still subject to duty. Two years later, however, in order to save the East India Company from bankruptcy, Parliament gave the Company what amounted to a monopoly on the sale of tea to America. The tea was consigned to a picked group of merchants in each of the main ports.

The Tea Act gave the radical leaders what they needed. In New York they prepared a document which they called "The Association of the Sons of Liberty of New York." It repudiated the action of Parliament. It provided for the reorganization of the Sons "to transmit to posterity those blessings of freedom which our ancestors have handed down to us." It branded as enemies any merchants who agreed to become consignees. Harbor pilots were warned against guiding any tea ship into port.

But the tea reached Boston before it reached New York, the first of three ships arriving on November 27, 1773. Two great mass meetings were held, demanding that the tea be returned to England. But Hutchinson refused to let the ship depart until the duty had been paid.

Though the Sons of Liberty were not openly identified with the events which followed, it was the same old crowd which operated behind the scenes.

On the evening of December sixteenth, eight thousand people crowded Old South Church and the area around it. According to law, the tea aboard the *Dartmouth* would be liable to seizure the next day for nonpayment of duty. This meant that it would be brought ashore and offered for sale. A committee had been chosen to visit the Governor and see whether he would take any measures to satisfy the people. He had promised an answer by five, but had left town when the committee returned. Sam Adams, chairman of the huge meeting, asked Captain Rotch of the *Dartmouth* whether Hutchinson was willing to let his ship sail—with the tea. Rotch said the Governor had refused.

"Let every man do his duty," shouted the meeting. Then there was a "general huzza" for Griffin's Wharf. "There appeared to be an understanding that each individual should volunteer his services," wrote one of the participants, "keep his own secret, and risk the consequences for himself." Working throughout the night, the group of men disguised as Indians dumped 342 chests of tea into the harbor.

The next day the Sons of Liberty held a mass meeting in New York at which letters were read from Boston and Philadelphia, though of course the news of the Boston Tea Party did not arrive until Paul Revere came galloping in with it several days later. John Lamb was made chairman of a new committee of correspondence. Then the meeting turned its attention to a proposal of the Governor that when any tea arrived, it should be put in the fort.

"Gentlemen, is this satisfactory to you?" asked the Mayor.

"No! No! No!" yelled the crowd.

"Is it your opinion, gentlemen," said the chairman, "that the tea should be landed under any circumstances?"

"No!" Again three times.

Once again the Sons were in the saddle. But no tea arrived.

Finally on the eighteenth of April, 1774, the *Nancy* arrived off Sandy Hook with the first shipment of East India tea for New York. Captain Lockyer left his ship and came ashore to see what the prospects were. He was met by the Committee of Fifteen who escorted him to the home of Henry White, one of the merchants to whom the tea had been consigned. He refused to accept the tea, whereupon Lockyer was told to leave as soon as his ship could be provisioned.

Meanwhile the *London*, Captain Chambers, arrived in the harbor. Two members of the Committee of Inspection boarded her. Chambers swore he had no tea, but word had come from the Sons of Liberty in Philadelphia that he had. His ship was searched, the tea found. At eight o'clock in the evening of April twenty-second a small group of Sons led by Sears and dressed as Indians boarded the ship, seized the tea, and dumped it into the harbor. They knew that the port of Boston had been closed in punishment for its tea party, but they went ahead anyway.

At the same time the Sons of Wallingford, Connecticut, were busy erecting a Liberty Pole, the Portsmouth Sons were parading with drum and fife and announcing their intention of taking over the fort, and a "respectable body of Sons of Liberty" in Georgia tarred and feathered Thomas Brown and drummed William Davis three times around the Liberty Tree.

Throughout the first half of 1774 Parliament kept passing punitive legislation—closing up the port of Boston, freeing royal officers of any dependence upon colonial legislatures and finally in effect annulling the charter of Massachusetts. Unkindest cut of all was the prohibition against town meetings—the very core of New England life.

Lieutenant Governor Colden of New York writing to the Earl of Dartmouth in June, 1774, was still complaining about the hot-headed radicals known as the Sons of Liberty. But when the New Yorkers met to consider what steps to take in support of Boston, the more conservative group got control. A Committee of Fifty-One was elected in which the Sons were a minority. This committee managed to sidestep Boston's plea for nonimportation and as a compromise measure came out for a Continental Congress which duly met at Philadelphia in the fall, condemned the various coercive acts, advised the people of Massachusetts to form their own government, and recommended economic sanctions against Great Britain.

Early in 1775 the Massachusetts Provincial Congress under the leadership of John Hancock and Joseph Warren prepared for war. In March Patrick Henry made his famous speech asking for liberty or death. On April sixth the New York Sons met again at the Liberty Pole on the common with Lamb and Willett as chairmen. Sears was there, urging an attack on a hardware merchant named Ustick who had violated the nonimportation agreement. But the meeting ended in nothing worse than a demonstration. The Sons were busy in the outlying counties, making sure that when the convention met on April 20 to choose delegates to a new Continental Congress, it would pick their candidates.

But on the day before the convention Major John Pitcairn had led his troops into Lexington, the unexplained shot had been fired, and war had begun.

When the news of Lexington reached New York, Lamb, Sears and Willett led a crowd which sacked the arsenal, seized six hundred muskets, paraded the streets, forced the customs house to close, put the loyalist leaders to flight and took over the public stores. When Gage the next month sent for the troops at New York to join him at Boston where he had been hemmed in by the provincials, Marinus Willett stopped their commander, demanded that he leave behind the extra arms he was carrying off, and appealed to the soldiers to desert. The one soldier who responded was triumphantly borne off by the crowd. From this time until Washington's army arrived, "King" Sears and his friends ruled the city.

＊　＊　＊

The Revolution, when it came, was largely the result of the activities of the Sons of Liberty during the previous decade. They almost alone had directed the campaign against the Stamp Act throughout the colonies. They had kept the spirit of resistance alive with their annual celebrations. They had proposed the nonimportation agreements in protest against the Townshend Acts. They were behind the tea parties. They began the coercing of public officials which was later taken over by the committees of inspection or safety. If their acts were often impetuous and sometimes violent, it must be remembered that their organization came into being on the wave of a growing discontent with the taxes imposed by Parliament and after the futility of petitions had been demonstrated. They were ripe for action, and their excesses inevitably stand out while their quieter achievements tend to fade into the background. But their effectiveness as a voluntary, intercolonial association is far more important than the fact that in their determination to get results they also got tough.

The Sons were also responsible for assembling the Continental Congress of 1774. This, their last achievement, was a byproduct of the contest in New York between liberals and conservatives. But it was a real triumph, since one of the main objectives of the Sons for over a decade had been to assemble such a body.

They created committees of correspondence which tied the towns and colonies together, providing a method of communication and of influencing public opinion which bore revolutionary fruit under the sponsorship of Sam Adams.

Even Governor Hutchinson failed to see what a weapon these later committees were to become, though he might have foreseen it easily enough if he had thought about the committees the Sons had fathered. "It is such a foolish scheme," he wrote to England, "that the faction must necessarily make themselves ridiculous." But the committees soon proved themselves to be nothing less than a voluntary system of self-government which could operate without royal sanction and which in time exerted more power than government itself. John Adams remarked that these later committees "embodied the whole Revolution." As the provincial governments were prorogued the committees actually took over some of the responsibilities of government— another remarkable example of the way Americans improvise government out of voluntary associations.

For ten years the Sons had been talking the language which was to appear in the Declaration of Independence.

"When Tyrannic and oppressive Measures make their Approaches upon the subject of civil Government," wrote the Providence Sons of Liberty to their brothers in New York, "it becomes not only suitable, but even indispensible Duty, resolutely to combine for the Defense of their Rights. . . . If those, who have in Trust the delegated Powers of the People, should turn their authority against the Good of their Constitents . . . in such Cases an Appeal to Heaven, that is a plain Opposition to the unjust Force & Usurpation, is justifiable & exceeding honorable." Though this has not the force of Jefferson, the words and the feeling are there. The colonies had been listening to this sort of thing from the Sons of Liberty for ten years. Since any great movement of men must find its language before it can learn to respond, one of the great services of the Sons was that they provided the language, the *emotional culture*, without which the Revolution could not have taken place.

The language of the Declaration, echoing what the Sons had been saying for ten years, is full of the idea of voluntarism—of government as a contract freely entered into. Governments derive their just powers from the consent of the governed. It is the right of the people to alter or abolish any government which fails to assure to its people life, liberty and the pursuit of happiness.

Behind this point of view stands the Pilgrim idea of contract and covenant. But also there stands behind it the decade of activity by the Sons of Liberty—practical politicians who organized voluntarily to protest a tax and ended by creating a nation.

V

Frontier Communities

George Washington, having retired to private life at Mount
Vernon, in 1784 issued a handbill offering for lease a tract of
thirty thousand acres on the Ohio. The beginning of the great
westward movement was at hand.

In 1786 two Revolutionary officers, Rufus Putnam and Benjamin Tupper, followed the lead of their Commander in Chief
by forming an association for settling the Ohio country. Putnam,
a self-educated farm boy from Massachusetts, had become a
general at the end of the Revolutionary War after service with
the engineers. Washington characterized him as strong-minded,
discreet and firm, but with nothing "conspicuous" in his character. Conspicuous or not, Putnam became one of the leaders in
settling the West. Six feet tall, sturdily built, and with a peculiar
look about him caused by an eye injury in his youth, he was a
man other men looked to as a leader.

Tupper was also a Massachusetts man who had served
throughout the Revolution and been retired as a brigadier general. He was one of the officers who signed the Newburgh Petition of 1783, requesting Congress to provide in Ohio the land
bounties that had been promised to soldiers. Since Putnam was
chairman of this group, it is clear that their interest in settling
Ohio had been active for at least three years before they set out
to form an association.

The way they went about it is a matter of the first importance.
They did not form a closed corporation with officers elected

from among their own number. Rather they issued a handbill requesting all interested citizens to meet at designated places, to choose their own delegates, and to send them to the Bunch of Grapes Tavern in Boston.

These delegates met in Boston on March 1, 1786, and arranged to sell shares of stock at a thousand dollars each, but payable in the certificates issued to Revolutionary troops. When they met again a year later, 250 shares had been sold. They thereupon formed the Ohio Company of Associates.

In July the Reverend Manasseh Cutler, one of the active Associates, succeeded in contracting with Congress for a large piece of land which at first was to be a million and a half acres but ultimately was about a million. The famous Ordinance for the government of the Northwest Territory was passed at the same time.

Congress might have set up a bureau to handle these western lands. It might have insisted on keeping them under its direct control, in which case the West would have become another colonial area which in time might have had to fight for its independence as did the original colonies. Instead, Congress made provision for the new lands to become states in time, and handed over the settling of the lands to private associations such as the Ohio Company. The company had the right to resell its land to other colonizing groups and individuals.

So on a November morning in 1787 an advance party paraded before Dr. Cutler's church in Ipswich, fired a salute, and headed for Danvers. Leading the procession was a large wagon with the words FOR THE OHIO splashed across its black canvas cover in large white letters. The slogan had been painted there by Cutler himself, who went with the wagon train as far as Danvers. Here he said farewell to the company, which headed west under the lead of Major Haffield White. A second group set out from Hartford. The two parties, having met and built their boats, sailed down the Muskingum under the command of General Rufus Putnam and reached the Ohio on April 7, 1788.

Two years earlier Fort Harmar had been built on the west

bank of the Muskingum where it joins the Ohio, but the settlement built by Putnam and his forty-seven associates was the first permanent civilian one in Ohio. The pioneers, most of them Revolutionary veterans, with a strangely unrevolutionary sentiment named the place Marietta after Queen Marie Antoinette.

By the end of the year 132 men had arrived, but only fifteen families. Benjamin Tupper brought the first family groups on August ninth—his own, his son-in-law's, and two others. A stockade had been built, to which the classical and imposing name Campus Martius had been applied. Within were houses sufficient to take care of forty or fifty families.

Like the Pilgrims off Cape Cod, the settlers at Marietta found themselves outside the bounds of organized government. The directors responded by drawing up a set of regulations which they posted on a large beech tree. It was not until 1790 that Marietta became a town.

The *Records of the Original Proceedings of the Ohio Company* show the company running its affairs with no need of formal government—dividing the land, naming the streets, encouraging iron and flour mills, making preparations for defense, and later providing for schools, roads and the poor. The square which had been set off in the middle of town is leased to Captain Jonathan Heart with the understanding that he is to make and keep sufficient drains. The inhabitants are to finish digging a well in Campus Martius, but the company will bear half the expense. Already the company is taking on the attributes of a welfare association as it votes to care for the sick in need of relief and, when Indian attacks began later on, to cover the expense of moving inhabitants into the stockade.

Already, too, a community life was taking shape. Mutual aid was a necessity in the frontier settlements. In the early stages, help was too valuable a thing to be bought; it could only be exchanged. The log raising was such an exchange. There was no other way for a man to get his cabin built. And every cabin raised was a monument to voluntary association. The building of frontier homes was accomplished neither by private enterprise nor by government, but by a kind of private—or civic, or voluntary —socialism. The plain American word is teamwork.

Building a frontier cabin by community effort was more than a matter of mere necessity. It was also a social event. It brought people together. Where they were new to each other, it helped to forge the social bonds a community needs in order to have a sense of its own identity. For human groups, as much as individuals, have to build up self-knowledge and self-respect in order to function well.

So it was not merely the workmen but the whole neighborhood which came together at a log raising. The men divided the work. Some felled trees and cut them to length. Some hauled them to the site. Others split clapboard for the roof or made puncheons for the floor. These were logs split in half and smoothed with a broad ax.

These preparations usually took up a whole day. On the following day the logs were notched and fitted into place. Holes were left for door, window and chimney. Chimneys were often built of wood too, with a lining of stone or clay.

When the cabin was finished, the owner was expected to give a house warming, with feasting, music and dancing. Like systole and diastole, the shared work and the shared pleasure pumped life into the new community.

After the log raising came the clearing of land, also often a matter of teamwork, then the husking bee, the barn-raising, the jamboree. While the building of cabins and the clearing of land were matters of necessity, no actual need dictated the husking bee. This was a social affair, but with a practical result highly satisfying to the Yankee mind. If need dictated the log raising, a hankering for social warmth and togetherness originated the husking bee.

Before the guests came, the corn had been heaped up in the barnyard in a long pile four or five feet high. When evening came, the neighbors arrived. Two captains chose sides, a rail was laid across the middle of the pile which was then divided into two equal parts. Then the husking began, each captain urging his team on. The party which finished first caught their captain up on their shoulders and bore him around in triumph. Then the corn was stowed safely away and the husks carried to the fodder house.

Meanwhile the women had prepared a feast. After the feast there was dancing to the fiddle. Even the dancing had a quality of mutuality about it. For the square dance is no aimless meandering. It has pattern. The eight people in a square have to know what they are doing. They have to act together or there is chaos. Square dancing belongs to a people who like to share their play as well as their work.

And of course there were the red ears. Every young man who produced one could claim a kiss from the girl of his choice.

Though customs differed according to time and place, the husking bee in essence was the same. The principle was the same. Work itself became play when it was shared. The life of the group enriched the life of the individual. In fact, the two were not separate things, but aspects of one life. The more work and play were shared in the group, the richer was the individual. Individualism itself was enhanced, because the group life gave depth and extent to the life of all its members.

That fine ability to combine useful work with group fun—to increase the pleasures of life by sharing them with the group—turns up also in the quilting party and the apple-paring bee. Thomas Low Nichols, born in Orford, New Hampshire, in 1815, described them this way:

When the orchards have grown, then come the "apple-paring bees." They did come, at least, before ingenious Yankees invented paring machines. The apples were pared with sharp knives and rapid hands, quartered, cored, strung on twine, and hung up to dry in festoons over the kitchen ceiling. The paring bee was a milder kind of evening party than the husking, and ended with the same festivities.

The quilting is mostly a feminine arrangement. Its ostensible object is the manufacture of a bed-quilt. This involves a social gathering—talk, tea, probably a little gossip and scandal, and in the evening the accession of masculinity, with more or less of fun and frolic. The

upper surface of the quilt is that marvellous result of feminine industry—patchwork; the lower stratum is more modest calico; the interior cotton or wool; and the whole is united by quiltings in elaborate
figures, composed of a vast number of stitches, made by as many old
and young ladies as can sit around the frame, beginning on the
borders, and, as the frame is rolled up, gradually working towards
the centre. The reasons for making this a social undertaking are obvious. When the quilt is in the frame it occupies a large space. It
would take a long time for one or two persons to do it, and would be
a long time in the way. Finally, it is an excuse for a social gathering.

Mrs. Anna Foster, an early resident of Batavia in Genesee
County, New York, remembered the co-operative nature of those
early days. "We used to have ox-sled rides," she recalled. "Some
of our earliest parties were got up by first designating the log
house of some settler, and each one contributing to the entertainment; one would carry some flour, another some sugar, another some eggs, another some butter, and so on; the aggregate
making up a rustic feast. These parties would alternate from
house to house. Frolics in the evening would uniformly attend
husking bees, raisings, quiltings, and pumpkin pearings [sic].
All were social, friendly, obliging—there was little of aristocracy
in those primitive days."

A society which could originate the quilting party, the husking bee, the jamboree, the apple paring is far from rugged individualism. Its goals are clearly communal or mutual or co-
operative.

So Marietta, repeating many of the features of its parent communities back East, reinforced the American heritage of mutual
aid on a voluntary basis. The Marietta settlers were there by
choice. They were a voluntary association, and they organized
their social and community activities on the same pattern.

While some New Englanders were transferring their homes
to the Ohio, others were moving into western New York, into the
great tracts of land purchased by Oliver Phelps and Nathaniel
Gorham for a land syndicate, or into the Holland Purchase.
These areas were laid out in towns six miles square. Into them

the land-hungry Yankees poured as if a dam had burst.

Here too the land was settled by men who clubbed together instead of trying to do everything alone.

Levi Talmadge of Wolcott, New Hampshire, tells how James Wadsworth visited the town, called a meeting of the inhabitants, and urged emigration to the Genesee country, describing the flat, fertile farming land and the rich crops it produced.

"Thomas Wiard, Benni Bishop,—Stebbins, Seymour Welton and Abel Curtis, with their families, and Ashbel Atkins, John Curtis, and myself, unmarried men, formed an emigrant party," Talmadge told Orsamus Turner. "There were thirty-eight persons in all. . . . We came with seven wagons, forming a considerable cavalcade; were twenty-one days on the road."

An emigrant party—how typical of American life! From Jamestown and Plymouth to the wagon trains and the dust bowl migrants from Oklahoma, Americans have been on the move. They have tended to move, to settle and to work in groups. The group was no social luxury. It was often necessary for survival.

Settlers moving west often had to stop for hours to build temporary bridges. "It was also necessary that they should travel in considerable companies for the purpose of mutual assistance in crossing streams, passing swamps, and rising hills, such was the state of the road when the settlement of the country commenced," says James Hotchkin.

William Cooper, father of James Fenimore, left Burlington, New Jersey, to found Cooperstown on Lake Otsego in New York. "I had no funds of my own sufficient for the opening of new roads," he recalled in *A Guide in the Wilderness*, "but I collected the people at convenient seasons, and by joint efforts we were able to throw bridges over the deep streams, and to make, in the cheapest manner, such roads as suited our then humble purposes."

Once the land had been cleared, houses raised, and crops put in, other needs were felt, and again voluntary association had to supply them. Oliver Culver of Brighton in Monroe County remembered how "in 1802 there was no school nearer than

Pittsford. We clubbed together, built a log school house, and hired a young man by the name of Turner, who was clerk in Tryon and Adams' store, to open a school."

The nearest post office to the settlement of Angelica in Allegany County was at Bath, forty miles away. "The citizens clubbed, and contracted with William Barney to make the trip."

Stephen Durfee, a Quaker settler in Wayne County, remembered that "all were friendly; mutual dependence made us so; and struggling with the hardships of pioneer life, there was a fellow feeling, a sympathy for each other's misfortunes, but little of which exists now."

Elihu Church emigrated from Berkshire County in Massachusetts, settling first in Ontario County in 1796. Ten years later he moved on to Churchville, having contracted for a house before moving his family. But when they reached the place, the house was unbuilt. The Churches moved in with three other families who had just arrived, which put twenty-eight people in one small cabin. Three residents of the area, hearing that he was homeless, came and helped him put up the body of a cabin in one day. The floor was of split wood, the roof of cedar shingles. There were no boards and few nails. But it was a home. The Churches were able to move in on the fourth day.

From the hundreds of settlements in western New York, two or three will have to serve as samples of voluntary group activity.

East Bloomfield was one of the earliest, having begun at the same time with Canandaigua where Phelps and Gorham planned to settle themselves. A whole town-site, a six-mile square, was purchased, like so many others, by men from Berkshire County, Massachusetts. Deacon John Adams was the first of the purchasers to settle. He took with him his wife, five sons, three daughters with their husbands, three unmarried daughters, and a brother-in-law accompanied by his family. Eight other men joined the party.

Early in 1789, as soon as the Mohawk River was navigable, the group set out from Schenectady. Some of the men took the household furniture and supplies by water. The rest of the party went on pack horses, following the Indian trails. In May five more men came out to join them. A log house thirty by forty feet was raised, but the party was so large that berths had to be built one above the other all the way around the walls. Here was voluntary association in earnest! While there is no point in idealizing association at such close quarters, it is obvious that the settlement of the American continent was hardly the accomplishment of rugged individualists. Men and women who built up a nation through this sort of clubbing together had goals that were wider than individual. They brought with them from New England a well-established tradition of group life, and they passed it on to descendants who, though in ways that changed constantly to meet the needs of new times, kept on with that tradition.

In February, 1790, Nathan Comstock started out from Adams, Massachusetts, by ox team with his family and two other men. Another party followed the next day. They were soon joined by still other neighbors, most of whom were Quakers. Their goal was the town in western New York which came to be called Farmington. For a large part of the journey they had to sleep in the woods, under whatever temporary shelter they could devise —and this in the month of March. Whole families plodded through snow and mud for days and weeks, slept on the ground, and listened to the wolves howling just beyond the light of their fires.

The Friends Meeting at Adams had not favored the departure of its members to the Genesee country. Those who left were consequently disowned by the Meeting.* Through the inter-

---

* Orsamus Turner asserts that these members were disowned by their Meeting, an assertion repeated in Alexander Stewart's "Sesquicentennial of Farmington, New York, 1789–1939," *Bulletin of the Friends' Historical Association*, vol. 29–30 (1940–41), 37–43. Yet a search of the original records of East Hoosuck (Adams) Meeting fails to produce any proof. The only relevant item occurs much later, under date 4th, Fourth Month, 1799. A letter to Saratoga Monthly Meeting reports that the few Friends at the Genesee, having conferred with part of the Yearly Meeting's committee, ask to be recommended to the care of the Saratoga Meeting. Nathan and Mary Comstock are among those mentioned. (Transcript of original records in the Pittsfield Athenaeum, Pittsfield, Mass. Certificates of East Hoosuck, p. 43 [p. 318 of typescript.])

cession of the Philadelphia Yearly Meeting four years later, they were restored to membership and a Meeting was organized at Farmington. But it was another ten years before a meeting house was built. Farmington, settled mostly from Adams, became a prosperous community, famous for its fine apples at a time when few of the western towns had orchards. In this prosperity the discipline and example of the Society of Friends played a part. For Friends had always laid stress upon the power of group action. Perfect democrats, they insisted upon the right of each individual to find religious truth according to the light within. But with this privilege went the responsibility of sharing with the group. The absence of preachers emphasized the responsibility each member had for the life of the group. Their meetings, whether for worship or for business, came as close as any group has come to a merging of individual minds and spirits into a corporate mind which all could share.

In a Friends Meeting there is no altar, no ritual, no priest or pastor and no sermon. If anything is said, it will be said by the members of the group, as they feel moved to share with the rest. Each of these speakings will come from within an individual. Yet the triumph of the Friends' way is that from these separate speakings will come a sense of group participation, in which what each individual has said becomes a part of the group consciousness—is shared and assimilated. This is what Friends mean by a "gathered meeting," when all who are there feel that in their coming together they have become greater than the sum of their separate entities.

*   *   *

In 1831 a delicate young man from Vermont arrived in the frontier town of Elyria in the Western Reserve. Born on the edge of New York state and educated at Pawlet Academy in Vermont and Cambridge, New York, John Jay Shipherd had once made the mistake of taking saltpetre instead of Epsom salts —an error which had left him in delicate health.

In order to provide some work which John could do in spite

of impaired eyesight, his father, Zebulon Shipherd, set up a marble factory at Vergennes. The factory failed. But John had meanwhile become interested in the ministry. Whatever frailties might be attributed to the saltpetre, Shipherd was a man of determination, and one not easily dissuaded. He became General Agent of the Vermont Sabbath School Union—one more of the voluntary associations with which Yankeedom was tightly knit together. And then, deciding that the West was in greater need of spiritual guidance than New England, he set out for Ohio. On the second day of February, 1831, he settled as missionary pastor in Elyria.

But Shipherd was not satisfied with the results of his preaching. His soul demanded a wider effort. He wanted to do something which would influence the whole West.

When the house that was being built for him was finished, he took three students in to live with him. Two of these soon left, but the third, Philo Penfield Stewart, remained. Stewart was also a Vermonter. He had been at Pawlet Academy with Shipherd and had been a missionary to the Choctaw Indians in Mississippi until his wife's health had forced him to leave.

Studying and praying together, the two Vermonters talked of a Christian community to be composed of selected, dedicated people. Each member of the community would consider himself a "steward of the Lord," hold only as much property as he could manage for the Lord, practice simplicity of dress and diet and hoard nothing. "As members of one body," the colonists would promise mutually to provide for their widowed and needy as well as for themselves. Schools would be established to care for every age from infancy to the educating of pastors. The academy was to have a farm and workshop "where, with four hours labor per day, students shall defray their entire expense." If this seemed impossible, Shipherd said, they only had to follow his own example of plain eating and dressing.

In addition to educating the children of the colony itself, Shipherd proposed "to educate School Teachers & Ministers from the four winds; for on our plan we can instruct multitudes."

Women as well as men students were to be taken in, and they too would earn their education by labor.

Because Stewart and Shipherd had been greatly influenced by the example of Pastor Oberlin, who had transformed the area around Ban-de-la-Roche on the border of Alsace-Lorraine, they named their colony after him.

The colony was still only a dream. But the two young men began to look around in the woods for a place to settle. When they found it, Shipherd went back East and persuaded the owners of the land to donate five hundred acres to the colony. He also persuaded them to sell another five thousand acres to settlers at a dollar and a half an acre.

Shipherd also scoured New England for teachers, colonists and funds. He talked to groups wherever he could assemble them, taking pledges or—when he could get it—cash. In August, 1833, with his wife and children he started back for Ohio in an open buggy, the youngest child lying in a willow cradle between its parents' feet.

While Shipherd was away Stewart began work on the new settlement, aided by Eliphalet Redington and others from neighboring communities who had decided to join the Christian colony. Plans for the town were drawn, clearing was begun and Peter Pindar Pease, the first colonist, put up the first house—a log cabin which was nothing but a shed. By June ten heads of families had come. Work was begun on the combination boarding hall and schoolhouse.

A Congregationalist with roots going back to Plymouth, Shipherd required all his colonists to sign a covenant which bound them to "as perfect a community of interest as though we held a community of property." All surpluses above basic living costs were to be appropriated for the spread of the Gospel. Children were to be thoroughly educated and everyone was expected to help support the Oberlin Institute, as it was then called.

Clearly the school was the center of the community. Thirty-five by forty-four feet, it housed the Shipherd and Stewart families, the boarding pupils, dining room, schoolroom and office. Round about it stood the rude log cabins of the colonists. Tree stumps, rough roads and the encroaching forest gave the little colony the familiar frontier look.

But Oberlin was different from its neighbors. It had its covenant, by which the colonists voluntarily bound themselves together "for the express purpose of glorifying God and doing good to men."

The covenant said nothing about government. Perhaps Shipherd was too much occupied with thoughts of education and religion to think of that. During the first year the colonists met together to decide matters of common interest without any written documents or established laws to guide them. They didn't need them anyway. They acted on the familiar basis of voluntary association—surveying the land, clearing it, building roads, forming a school district, petitioning for a post office.

It is true that they were concerned about the legality of their acts. What rights and obligations did they have under Ohio law? To make sure, they appointed a committee to get the facts and to petition for an act of incorporation for Oberlin Colony. But it was not until 1846 that the village was incorporated and came under the same plan of government as other Ohio towns.

Meanwhile, they had the covenant. They were to have the first coeducational college and one of the first where Negroes and whites could study together. When the need came for the Underground Railroad, Oberlin had one of the stations. By that time there were enough Oberlin students scattered around to set up stations in many towns. Skill in voluntary association was expected of those who had been trained the Oberlin way. For Oberlin was built upon voluntary association. The tone of moral earnestness and co-operative endeavor still remains.

*　*　*

Sylvester Cochrane was a muscular young man of sturdy frame from East Poultney, Vermont where he served the community as minister of the Congregational Church. In the fall of 1835 he went to Michigan with the idea of settling there.

Michigan, not yet a state, was still frontier country. As a proper New Englander, Cochrane was disappointed to see the settlers so scattered that little education or religious life was possible.

On the long way back to Vermont he thought about the problem and decided to found a colony. Around the end of the year, after visiting several Vermont towns to talk with possible emigrants, men who yearned for level fields and pastures free of rocks, he called a meeting at East Poultney. After several meetings had been held, a constitution was drawn up and signed at Castleton on March 27, 1836. The signers formed themselves into an association or colony to be settled somewhere in the West. They agreed to live together in a community so as to enjoy the social and religious privileges they were leaving behind them, to educate their children, and to use no liquor except for medicinal purposes.

"As we must necessarily endure many of those trials and privations which are incident to a settlement in a new country, we agree that we will do all in our power to befriend each other," they promised. "We will esteem it not only a duty, but a privilege to sympathize with each other under all our trials, to do good and lend, hoping for nothing again, and to assist each other on all necessary occasions."

Then to make sure that they would be close enough to help each other, they voted the usual New England arrangement of lots—ten acres each in the village, with outlying farm lots.

Forty-two men signed the agreement, but of these only twenty-two became settlers. Five were from Bennington, the others from half-a-dozen Vermont towns.

A committee was next sent out to locate a suitable place. The instructions given them were specific. They were to find a site with good water, rich soil interspersed with wood and prairie, a waterfall, prospects of being speedily settled, proximity to a good market, a location where a railroad or canal seemed likely to go through, and last of all, navigable water. They did the best they could, but there was no waterfall, no railway or canal, no market. The nearest store and post office were fourteen miles away, but most of the trading had to be done at Marshall which was twice that distance.

Trees were felled, the village was laid out around a square, and settlers began to arrive—by canal to Buffalo, then by lake to Detroit, and finally by ox-team. By late spring the usual log houses had been raised, as well as a colony house to take care of new arrivals until they could build. More settlers arrived in the two years following. Cochrane was able to organize his church early in 1837, though with only sixteen members. The next year there was a school. By the time Michigan became a state in 1837, Vermontville had 145 residents.

The colony lived up to its agreement for mutual aid, though not always in ways that had been anticipated back in East Poultney. Cochrane himself wrote an account of one of these occasions for the newspaper at Marshall.

"For a number of days during the month of October [1839], the inhabitants of Vermontville were annoyed by the visits of a bear. Almost every day he had the presumption to come out of the forest and present himself in the streets, and in one or two instances he even took the liberty to parade himself in an erect position in front of the houses, as if desirous to see what was going on within." Worse still, he usually carried a pig away with him.

All the men, dogs and guns that could be collected formed an association for the liquidation of the bear. They encircled the territory where they knew he was hiding, chased him out and killed him.

But death did not end the uses of the bear for purposes of association. His meat was divided to all the families of the village, while his hide was sold and the proceeds used "to replenish the Sabbath School library"!

On the same principle bee trees were robbed of their honey. With sweetening at a premium, these bee hunts were important events in the community.

"At its inception," wrote the son of one of the first settlers, "Vermontville was a co-operative colony in religion and education, as well as by purchase. For many years voluntary and cheerful aid and assistance of others was the rule."

Though one of the most interesting examples of a community founded by voluntary association around a church, Vermontville was by no means unique. The history of Beloit, Wisconsin, is similar. Granville, Ohio, was settled by people from the Massachusetts town of the same name who transplanted church, pastor, deacons and all. "We do hereby agree to form ourselves into an association." "We do by these presents covenant with each other, jointly and severally." One after another the settlements drew up their agreements of association in language resembling that of the Mayflower Compact. When conditions changed, the instrument was adapted to meet them. But it remained the same instrument. So the "Squatters' Union" of Lake County, Indiana, feeling in 1836 "the strong present necessity of their becoming united in such a manner as to guard against speculation upon our rights, have met and united together to maintain and support each other." Later on the Claims Club of Iowa organized in the same way.

The problem is not to find examples, but to select from hundreds the few cases which best tell the story. The New Englanders who went west into New York, Ohio, Michigan, Wisconsin, and later into Kansas and Nebraska and finally all the way to the Pacific—these New Englanders were the offspring of Englishmen who had brought the idea of a covenant with them to the wilderness. The covenant itself was an instrument of voluntary association, but the hardships of pioneering strengthened the need for this kind of working together. For over two hundred years, from Plymouth in 1620 until the Pacific Coast was reached, voluntary association was the essential instrument by which the American continent was settled.

As the communities grew larger, formal government took the place of covenants and associations. But the habit of association did not die. It merely stepped over into new fields, accepted new challenges. Thus Oberlin in the forties organized to oppose slavery. A century later it established an Oberlin in China. Once the basic local needs had been satisfied, other goals opened up. The American assumption has always been that no matter how good a thing is, it can be made better. So the barn-raising gives way to founding a college, establishing a lyceum, starting a social welfare service, and finally reaching a neighborly hand to men and women half the world away.

But first the continent had to be settled. Before the wagon trains could begin to roll, voluntary association had to be adjusted to a new demand.

VI

Voluntary Association on the Hoof

It was in 1841 that overland immigration to the West Coast really began. As early as 1826 Jed Smith had found his way across the mountains to California, and thereafter hunters and trappers began to probe the rivers and mountain passes, searching out the best routes. But until 1841 there were no parties of settlers.

Once the current set in, however, it bore hundreds and then thousands with it. The crossing of the plains duplicated in many ways the earlier crossing of the Atlantic when America was first settled. The men and women who joined the wagon trains were facing unknown hazards in an untested land. They staked their lives and property on the move. They had to rely on the gathered wisdom of the group to see them through. They had to forge their own social controls, and when they reached their destination they would have to build communities without benefit of any established law.

The men of Plymouth had been able to wait until they were off Cape Cod before forming their "body politik" since the ship's captain represented the law at sea. The settlers of New York and Ohio had needed only an informal or rudimentary organization on their westward route since the distance and the hazards were, by comparison, only moderate. But the settlers who proposed to cross the Great Plains and the Rockies had to have an instrument which would hold them together as a community while they traveled—while they traveled through a country without law, often without adequate forage or water, and filled with potentially hostile Indian tribes. Ignorance of the route, bad weather, hazardous fordings and the failure of supplies were other dangers.

The people who made up a wagon train were often strangers to each other, yet they must risk mortal danger together. In wealth, place of birth and upbringing, religion and every other social distinction they were diverse. Was there anything that could hold them together, any way of preventing chaos as their heavy wagons dragged across the endless plains, the high mountains?

* * *

In 1840 a young man who had just lost the land he had staked out for himself in Platte County, Missouri, heard of California. John Bidwell had been forced to leave his claim for a short time. When he got back, he found that it had been jumped by a squatter who refused to move. Bidwell, still below legal age, could not oust him. But there would be plenty of land in California, he decided. Why not go there? Born in New York, moving with his parents to Pennsylvania and Ohio, and then alone to Iowa and Missouri, Bidwell was used to pulling up stakes. As for enterprise, he had walked three hundred miles at the age of sixteen to enter an academy, and the next year became its principal!

But how did you get to California?

Young Bidwell's method of getting there was characteristically American. He formed a voluntary association. He spoke to a few friends and acquaintances. Quickly the word got around. A meeting was held, a corresponding secretary elected and a committee chosen to report on a plan of organization. A pledge was drawn up which obligated each member to buy a suitable outfit and to rendezvous at Sapling Grove (now in Kansas) in May, 1841.

The Western Emigration Society "took like wildfire," as Bidwell himself reported. In a month five hundred names were on the society's roster. Not one of the five hundred had the slightest notion of the route to California. Frémont, the western explorer, had not yet made his exploring trip to the Columbia, and the only available maps were full of errors.

While John Bidwell was getting ready for the journey, rumors began to circulate against California, fed by an article widely copied from a New York paper. One by one the five hundred members of the Western Emigration Society dropped out. Bidwell was the only one of them all who bought a wagon and prepared his outfit. Then the partner who was to have furnished the horses quit. Bidwell had his wagon, but no money to buy animals to pull it across the continent.

At the last moment a man with a fine horse appeared. Bidwell persuaded him to trade the horse for a yoke of oxen and a one-eyed mule. Then two more men decided to join him, and the foursome set out for the rendezvous. They found only one other wagon there on the appointed date of May ninth, but after starting along the Kansas River six or eight more wagons joined them. The emigrants elected a captain and John Bidwell was chosen secretary, but none of them knew where to go next. Fortunately the Catholic mission party of Father De Smet turned up with the famous guide "Broken Hand"—Thomas Fitzpatrick. The two groups agreed to join until they reached Soda Springs (Idaho) where the Catholic party would turn north for Oregon. Five teamsters, three hunters, a Methodist missionary and two men on a pleasure trip were added to the company, which completed its organization on May 18 and the next day began its march with a total population of sixty-nine.*

Though John Bartleson had been elected captain, Broken Hand was the real leader because of his knowledge of the route. That route was one already beaten out by trappers—up the north fork of the Platte, then up the Sweetwater through the South Pass, along branches of the Green River to Bear River Valley near the Great Salt Lake. The only catastrophes on this part of the route were one death and two marriages.

* Bidwell himself gives this figure, the *Dictionary of American Biography* sixty-three.

Near Soda Springs on Bear River the company separated on August 11, the Oregon party heading for Fort Hall. With them went a dozen of the men (some with families) who had originally intended to head for California.

Bidwell's group (still with Bartleson for captain) had a vague idea that they must find the Mary River and then follow it. They had been told that failing to find it would mean perishing in deserts to the south or impenetrable mountains to the north. Thirty-two men, one woman and a child now headed into this perilous adventure.

For ten days they marched down Bear River, turned westward before it emptied into Great Salt Lake, and by August 27 were camped at a spring in the mountains. Bartleson and one other man set out in search of the Mary River. The rest of the party remained in camp until September 5. Moving slowly forward, they met Bartleson on the ninth. A week later they had to abandon their wagons and pack what they could on mules, horses and oxen in order to get across the mountains. Crossing what appears to have been the east Humboldt Range, they finally reached the south fork of the Mary River on the twenty-third. After following it for two weeks, they finally reached the Walker River.

By this time their buffalo meat had given out and they were killing oxen for food. With an apparently impassable mountain barrier in front of them, they had only three oxen left. For two weeks they struggled to get through that barrier. Their food gave out. Three times Bartleson left the rest of the party and with his own group tried to hurry on ahead.

On the last day of October they were in despair. They were half-starved, their horses had given out or been stolen, three of the company had been missing for more than a week, and they were still lost in the grip of a mountain system which was crushing the life out of them. Then suddenly they saw through the trees a valley which looked like paradise to them, though it had been baked dry by the sun and blackened by fire. But there was game in it. They had reached the Stanislaus Valley.

Four days later they reached the ranch of an American named John Marsh whose letters to friends in Missouri had helped bring on the emigration. The lost members reappeared. Bidwell, a few years later, was the first to find gold on the Feather River. He acquired a 22,000-acre estate near Sacramento and became a noted agriculturist and prominent citizen. The Western Emigration Society had carried him across the continent and launched him on a career.

*   *   *

Interest in the West Coast was on the rise. Two years before John Bidwell had set out, ten emigrating societies had been organized in New England, New York and the prairie states. The economic historian could point out that this interest coincided exactly with a period of declining prices. When the bottom fell out of the market for agricultural products in the rich Mississippi Valley, hundreds of disappointed farmers began to think of the Pacific Coast as a solution and the Pacific Ocean as a highway which could carry their goods to markets now denied them. Floods, malaria and cholera also encouraged the movement.

So when Dr. Elijah White prepared in 1842 to return to the Methodist mission established several years before in Oregon, he found a quick response to his campaign for settlers. Crowds of people came to hear him when he lectured at churches on his way west. From the frontier colonies of Illinois, Arkansas and Missouri he soon gathered a hundred people for the trip across the plains.

By the middle of May 160 * had reached the rendezvous at Elm Grove, southwest of Independence, Missouri. About half of these were males old enough to bear arms. White says his heart sank when, looking at this large group with its many women and children, he fully realized what he had undertaken.

But there were no doubts in the mind of one of the emigrants, Lansford Hastings. "On the 16th day of May," he wrote, "in the

* There is conflicting evidence regarding the exact number.

year 1842, all as one man, united in interest, united in feeling, we were, *en route,* for the long desired *El Dorado* of the West.

"Now, all was high glee, jocular hilarity, and happy anticipation," he continued. "The harmony of feeling, the sameness of purpose, and the identity of interest, which here existed, seemed to indicate nothing but continued order, harmony and peace."

The group had organized, voted a set of resolutions, and elected Dr. White captain for a month. They also chose a pilot, a secretary, a blacksmith, a wagonmaker and a scientific corps of three who were to keep a record of everything that might be of service to the government or to future emigrants.

But trouble soon broke out. "All appeared to be determined to govern, but not to be governed." Dr. White suggested that the eighteen wagons come to a halt so that a code of laws could be enacted. But when a committee was appointed to draw up such a code, they returned with the decision that "no code of laws was requisite, other than the moral code, enacted by the Creator of the universe, and which is found recorded in the breast of every man."

It soon developed, however, that the law etched into the human breast was far from uniform. Soon after turning off from the Santa Fe trail, Dr. White announced that it would be necessary to kill all the dogs in the party since they might go mad during the crossing of the arid plains, or their barking bring hostile Indians against the caravan. To frontier people, killing their dog was as obscene a proposal as killing their wife. A vote was taken, a decree passed and a few dogs killed. But some owners stood firm.

"If any man kills these dogs, we'll kill him, regardless of consequences," they announced.

Both sides were armed. To avert a crisis, Dr. White called his company together again. The "dog decree" was rescinded. But the officers never regained the confidence of the company. When their month's term had run out, Hastings replaced White as captain. Those who did not like Hastings separated themselves into a detached column, but were united again at Fort Laramie where the man in charge of the post convinced them that they would need their full strength while passing through the hostile tribes.

"Perfect unanimity of feeling and purpose, now having been fully restored," says Hastings, "we passed on very agreeably, and with little or no interruption, until we arrived at Sweetwater, near Independence rock." Though two divisions of the party later took place, all sections safely reached Oregon. The Hastings party reached the Willamette Valley on October fifth. Near the falls they founded Oregon City. The American Occupation of Oregon had now begun in earnest.

* * *

The emigration of 1842 was nothing to that of the following year. The western fever, fed by hard times, had become epidemic. As spring came on in 1843 the covered wagons lumbered westward from Iowa and Illinois and Missouri, from Arkansas and Tennessee, heading for Council Bluffs or Independence. Many of the wagon covers were crudely painted with the words "FOR OREGON" on their sides. Youngsters sat on the high seat looking out over the two or three yoke of oxen hitched to the stout wagon, or peered from the rear where the cover was gathered like a bonnet, while a grown son herded the milk cattle, prodding them along when they stayed too long grazing.

When Peter Burnett of Platte County, Missouri, rolled into camp twelve miles west of Independence on May seventeenth, he found sixty wagons already there at the traditional meeting place, with a thousand head of cattle grazing near by. At night fifty campfires were lighted, and out of the darkness came the sweet notes of a violin, a chorus of singing voices, the laughter of girls.

Burnett, thirty-six at this time, had a wife and six children with him. Tall and spare of frame, he had a rugged constitution and a cheerful disposition. He was going to need both.

Born in Tennessee, Burnett was familiar with frontier living. When he was ten years old, his father had moved the family into Missouri. They spent the first winter in a one-room cabin, whites and blacks together, with nothing but a dirt floor beneath them and a hole in the roof to let out the smoke of their fire. Among these simple backwoods people Peter Burnett grew up. He worked as a hotel clerk and store clerk. He met Harriet Rogers and began to keep company with her. One day when he was leaving her home, he suddenly realized that it was dark. Meeting her father in the yard, he asked what had become of the sun.

"It has gone down, Mr. Burnett," said Mr. Rogers. The unexplained disappearance of the sun revealed to Peter that he was in love. He studied law, married Harriet, went into business and lost money, returned to the law, became a district attorney, moved to Platte City, but still saw no prospect of paying his debts. That was when he "set to work most vigorously," as he says, "to organize a wagon company." He succeeded beyond his expectations.

The day after his arrival, Peter Burnett visited around among the wagons. A meeting was called, and a committee was appointed to call on the famous Dr. Marcus Whitman who had returned from the Methodist mission in Oregon the previous October and was now on his way back there. Whitman, a minister as well as a doctor, knew the road. If only he could be persuaded to travel with the train, they would feel safe.

A committee of seven was also chosen to inspect the wagons, and a committee of five to draw up rules and regulations. The organization of the wagon train had got under way without delay. Once these essential items of business were attended to, the meeting adjourned to meet at Big Springs two days later.

Dr. Whitman was present at the meeting on May twentieth and agreed to cross the plains with the Burnett party. Another committee was appointed at this meeting for the purpose of hiring John Gantt, once a companion of Kit Carson, as guide. May twenty-second was set as the time when the wagons would roll.

On that day the party, increased by new arrivals, set out for

Elm Grove, the wagons with their white tops making a bright picture as they moved across the fresh green prairies, pulled and followed by fine-looking cattle. The word "grove" proved over-generous. For Elm Grove, when they reached it, had only two elms in the midst of a dogwood swamp. The larger of the two had already lost its branches to emigrants in need of firewood.

Still the election of officers and adoption of bylaws had not taken place. By the time they reached the Kansas River on May twenty-sixth the confusion was terrible. By now the party consisted of well over a hundred wagons, a thousand people, and five thousand animals. The smell of the cattle got into everything. The dust their feet stirred up settled in the food. Their loose hair blew into the wagons. No regular system of herding them had been worked out. No arrangements had been made to post guards at night.

Many of the separate groups had voted their own rules and elected their own officers before leaving home. Such a group, for example, was the Oregon Emigration Society of Iowa Territory, whose constitution begins with echoes of the preamble to that of the United States. In spirit and purpose its laws were like those of the colonies moving from New England into western New York and Ohio sixty years before.

At last, on the first of June, the men (numbering about 260) met together to organize their company. In addition to Burnett, there were others who had come as group leaders. Jesse Applegate with his brothers had brought a party from St. Clair County, Missouri. Somewhat dictatorial in spirit, Applegate was nonetheless a capable leader—thin, wiry, resilient, with a Roman-looking nose and a background of some culture.

T. D. Kaiser had come from North Carolina by way of Tennessee and Arkansas, where he had lived for nine years before deciding to move to Oregon. In 1842 he had sold his slaves and started out, only to be delayed by sickness in his big family of five sons and five daughters. But now he was on his way, with two four-yoke wagons, a two-horse carriage, twenty-two horses, and a large herd of cattle.

Young James W. Nesmith, though he did not arrive as a leader, was soon to become one. Of middle height, sturdily built and with a dark complexion and wavy black hair, Nesmith was only twenty-three years old. Born in Maine, he had lost his parents while still a boy and had wandered about the country until the notion took him of going to South America. Thinking that he could catch a whaler at the mouth of the Columbia River, he had attached himself to the wagon train as a hunter. But the emigrants thought him worthy of a more important post. Whether his strong mouth and chin assured them of his dependable character, or his broad humor and pungent wit had made him popular, he was chosen orderly sergeant when Burnett was elected captain. Nine other men were chosen as a council.

The company was not lacking in personalities. There was "Doc" Sutton whom Nesmith remembered thirty-five years later as always good for a laugh. Once, when his gun went off in the dark by mistake, he killed a mule and apparently struck down an old horse as well. "Great God," he wailed, "I have killed all the cattle in this emigration." Then there was John Ricord who, according to Nesmith, crossed the plains in a swallow-tail coat and a high plug hat. John McClane remembered him as tall, fine looking and well educated. Ricord did not stay long in Oregon, but went on to Hawaii where he became a trusted and valuable counselor to King Kamehameha III. J. M. Ware was another funny man whose stories had such a reputation for humor that people began to laugh as soon as they saw him coming.

If the *New Orleans Picayune* is to be believed, the manner in which the captain was elected was more in keeping with Ware's buffoonery than Ricord's dignity.

The candidates stood up in a row behind the constituents, and at a given signal they wheeled about and marched off, while the general mass broke after them "lickety-split," each man forming behind his favorite, so that every candidate flourished a sort of tail of his own, and the man with the longest tail was elected. . . . These men were running about the prairie, in long strings; the leaders, in sport and for the purpose of puzzling the judges, doubling and winding in the drollest fashion; so that the all important business of forming a government seemed very much like the merry schoolboy game of "snapping the whip."

Provided at last with rules and officers, the caravan moved slowly across the prairie. Young Pleasant Kaiser found the trip one long holiday. The prairie with its green grass spotted with the colors of larkspur, verbena and geranium was beautiful to him. He drove the ox team, herded cattle, and liked best of all the times when they had to ford a river and he could swim across. But the women who rode in the wagons—sometimes converted by buffalo skin coverings into boats or sometimes ferried across on canoes—the women felt differently.

So, apparently, did most of the grownups. Nesmith remarked years later that no one crossed the plains "but what was more or less out of humor." Some of the men who had failed to get elected criticized Burnett. Those who had no cattle objected to taking their turn with the animals. Heavy showers drenched the emigrants. Their tents blew down in a storm of wind. Though they were never in any great peril, "there were ten thousand little vexations continually recurring," as Burnett acutely observed, "which could not be foreseen before they occurred, nor fully remembered when past, but were keenly felt while passing." Cattle were always straying off, there was competition each night for the best camp site, and then for the limited supplies of wood and water on which life depended.

Burnett manfully tried to keep the crowd in order, but whenever he tried to enforce the rules he found so much opposition that he came to doubt whether such a large group could ever be kept together on such a journey. After only a week in office, he resigned on the eighth of June and was replaced by William Martin.

Now the company was split into two columns,* a Light Col-

* James W. Nesmith, in his "Diary," *Oregon Historical Society Quarterly,* VII (1906) 329–59, says that on June 9 the company was divided into four divisions, with a captain and orderly for each.

umn under Martin which included all those traveling without herds of cattle, and a Cow Column under Jesse Applegate, a firm and respected leader. Applegate had sixty wagons in his party which he divided into fifteen divisions of four wagons each. The divisions took turns at the head of the procession. That way every man got an equal share of the grit and dust stirred up by the column.

At night the wagons formed in a great circle a hundred yards deep which provided a defense in case of Indian attack. Guards were posted with watches throughout the night. All the men were divided into three companies, and each company into four watches. In this way every man had two hours of night duty every third night. At 4 A.M. breakfast fires were kindled and the grazing animals rounded up. At dawn the canvas village broke up again, and to the sound of a trumpet formed a column with pilot and guards on horseback. The wagoners soon learned to form and break the circle with military precision.

Once under way, the wagons formed a line three-quarters of a mile long. Some of the teamsters rode at the front of their wagons, others walked beside their teams. Along the line groups of women gathered bouquets as they walked for exercise. Children scampered back and forth while the family dog kept a watchful eye on them. The spare horses followed with little need of herding. But the horned cattle had to be constantly prodded and whipped into motion. For the cow drivers there was not a moment of relaxation. Keeping that vast herd in some kind of order and movement was enough to sour the sweetest temper. Yet it had to be done over a course two thousand miles long.

"No other race of men with means at their command would undertake so great a journey," wrote Jesse Applegate in "A Day with the Cow Column." "The way lies over trackless wastes, wide and deep rivers, rugged and lofty mountains, and is beset with hostile savages. Yet . . . they are always found ready and equal to the occasions, and always conquerors."

To govern this town on wheels, the council met whenever

necessary, though its regular meetings were held on days when the caravan was resting. It exercised both legislative and judicial powers, and according to Jesse Applegate "it was a senate composed of the ablest and most respected fathers of the emigration . . . its laws and decisions proved it equal and worthy of the high trust reposed in it." It considered the state of the little commonwealth, revised or repealed any rules that had proved defective, and made new ones as they were needed.

Then it resolved itself into a court to settle private disputes. Offender and aggrieved told their stories, witnesses were examined, a verdict given. Since the judges were not hampered by technicalities or written law, they decided all cases according to their merits. Government by voluntary association has some advantages over formal government.

Yet there were differences which could not be settled, and the company continued to divide. Nesmith wrote in his diary on July twenty-eighth, "The Oregon Emigration Company has been strangely divided, and no doubt the dividend will be again divided. The materials it is formed of cannot be controlled." He was referring, apparently, to the group from Iowa who had drawn up the impressive constitution. Also Kaiser, dissatisfied with the slow progress of the column, left it at the Green River with many followers. The smaller groups appear to have been more effective. In the shakedown and division into smaller companies, men could group together according to their own preferences. The smaller face-to-face groups could interact without the loss of direct contact which led to misunderstanding in the larger grouping. Friendships were formed which lasted throughout life. Burnett and Applegate, when they met in San Francisco twenty years later, embraced each other with tears.

The farther west they went, the more dependent they became on one another. After reaching the Dalles in Oregon the most dangerous part of the journey was still ahead of them, for there was no road over the mountains into the Willamette Valley and no boats. Nine hundred people (some had turned back or gone to California) with their cattle and household goods had to be transported. It was too late to build a road. So the men cut pine trees and made rafts twenty feet long. The wagons were taken apart and placed with their loads aboard the rafts. At least one child was born on one of these rafts as it floated down the river toward the Cascades. When the Cascades were reached, it took two weeks to build a wagon road around them.

Most of the emigrants reached the Willamette Valley nearly destitute, and with little prospect of being able to replenish their supplies, or to pay for them if they had been available. Yet those who remained at Oregon City exhausted as they were by the journey, arriving too late to select their land before winter, and facing real privation, did a thing which symbolizes all that is best in the American way. They clubbed together and formed a circulating library of all the books which had been brought across the plains.

Mutual aid had got them over the plains and through the mountains, even if there was bickering and division. With a grim winter staring them in the face, they aimed to keep their spirits up with mutual aid too.

* * *

Peter Burnett took an active part in organizing a provisional government for the Oregon territory—another fine example of voluntary association leading to formal government. He was later elected Judge of the Supreme Court. But when news of the California gold reached Oregon in the summer of 1848, Burnett was ready to move on. He talked it over with his wife, who gave her consent. He then talked with Dr. McLoughlin of the Hudson's Bay Company, who encouraged him to make the first try with wagons.

"I at once went into the streets of Oregon City," Burnett says, "and proposed the immediate organization of a wagon-company." Whatever the hardships five years before, Burnett was still committed to voluntary association as the only way of doing business. Within eight days he had a company of 150 robust men with fifty wagons and as captain of the company set out on a journey which was to end by getting him out of debt and ultimately making him Governor of California.

* * *

Gold!

From Maine to the Missouri the California fever was running high. In Cutler on the coast of Maine near New Brunswick, Captain George Kimball went into the woods alone and began to cut timber for a vessel which would carry him around the Horn to the gold fields. Before long friends and neighbors were joining him, helping to move the logs to the mill, the timbers down to the water's edge. Shipwrights and joiners, attracted by his pluck, offered to help him out. When the ship was built, farmers contributed cattle and provisions for the voyage. Contributions were paid for by shares in the vessel.

At her launching on November 29, 1849, the vessel was christened the *California Packet*. She was 144 feet long, with a house on deck divided into twelve staterooms and officers' quarters. Between decks thirty-six tiers of berths had been built. When she set sail for California, there were a hundred in the company—all of them shareholders. Ten wives, sixteen unmarried women and fifteen children were aboard—sure sign that this was to be no grab-and-run project, but a permanent settlement.

Meanwhile emigrant societies had been forming all over New England. A few young men would begin to talk about California. Someone would propose forming a company. An unused room over a store would be turned into a meeting place. Then a constitution was drawn up and officers chosen. Soon the members were appearing about town in slouch hats, high boots and a careless manner of dress which somehow suggested the Far West and great expectations.

The Sagamore and Sacramento Company of Lynn, Massachusetts, organized along military lines. Fifty-two young men set out on March 29, 1849, for Independence and California, first attending church in a body and then marching off in their smart gray uniforms trimmed with silver braid. Each man carried a rifle, a revolver, a sabre and a sheath knife. A band played at the head of the procession and the four horses harnessed to each of the wagons wore silver trappings. When the company reached New York they impressed even that city with their smartness, and with their seven-foot leader, Francis Dixon.

The first of the Gold Rush vessels to sail from Boston with a regularly organized company was the *Edward Everett*. She carried 150 members of the Boston and California Joint Stock Mining and Trading Company. No company had ever been so fully organized as this one, with its own minister, four doctors, eight whaling captains, a mineralogist, a geologist, fifteen other professional men and seventy-six mechanics. At least 124 organized companies left Massachusetts alone in 1849.

Though New England, true to its ancient tradition of voluntary association, was organizing for the westward trek, it was not alone. Down in Charlestown, Virginia (later West Virginia), a few men got together in the law office of Benjamin F. Washington early in January to organize a company. Their announcement of a public meeting for January twenty-second brought out a crowd and produced more than the sixty members they wanted. They finally took seventy-five. On February tenth officers were elected and a constitution was adopted. Each member was to pay $300 into the treasury, and the profits from gold digging were to be shared equally.

While many companies broke up before they reached California, the Charlestown company kept together. "It is a matter of note," one of them wrote back home, "that ours was the largest company that ever crossed the plains, although many, when they started, were fully as large, but by reason of the difficulties of the trip, were induced to separate."

Quarrels and dissensions often did break out in the oversize wagon trains. But the need of forage for several hundred animals would have made separation necessary anyway. "We conclude to divide our party into three divisions or separate trains," one of the emigrants explained, "not because of any ill feeling or misunderstanding among us, but for the simple reason that we have now reached a section of the country where stock feed is becoming scarcer all the time."

While the New England Argonauts were pouring westward by ship and wagon, the western states were also in ferment. Few men in forty-nine escaped the California fever altogether. Of the thousands who did pull up stakes and go, Henry Page of Woodburn, Illinois, is as good an example as any. Raised in Rutland, Vermont, where he grew up in the atmosphere of New England town meeting, he graduated from Middlebury College and with his family's backing went west in search of opportunity. Settling in Woodburn, tall young Henry Page went to store-keeping and, before long, to courting a dainty and charming young lady named Mary Rider. On winter evenings he took to calling at the Rider farm, where there were always apples to roast or corn to pop at the fireplace. Sometimes Henry Burton, a broad-shouldered and resourceful young carpenter, went along with him. Or well-to-do Tom Van Dorn or Henry Tappan, nick-named "Judge" because his frolicsome temper least resembled judicial solemnity.

In the spring of 1841 all these young people took part in an important community activity. The Baptists had decided to build a church. There was little money in town, but there were plenty of able hands. The men cut trees and hauled the logs to the sawmill. They raised the frame, nailed up clapboards and shingled the roof. Meanwhile the girls and women cooked for the hungry workers, and community meals finished off each day of labor. Working voluntarily whenever they could spare the time from farm tasks, the members finished their church by fall. Mary and Henry were married on the last day of June the following year.

Three years later Henry's partner absconded with all the assets of the business, and he became estranged from Tom Van Dorn when he tried to collect a debt due him. He tried farming without success. He and Mary began to quarrel.

Then, in the fall of 1848, came news of gold in California. The desperate young man saw in California's gold the only solution to his problems. Though Mary was terrified at the suggestion, he insisted. The rift grew wider. But before he left, Mother Rider brought about a reconciliation, and they parted with renewed love when the time came. With Henry went Hank Burton and Tom Van Dorn.

The three friends reached St. Joseph with their wagon in April, 1849, and camped with part of the Peoria Company on the bluffs behind the city. From the high clay bluffs Henry could see the timber-marked course of streams making their slow way to the Missouri, whose muddy waters looked "like a well-traveled wagon road after a rain." Villages of white tents and white-covered wagons, usually arranged in circles and with a flag of thirty stars at the center, had sprung up everywhere.

While Henry Page and his friends waited for the grass to grow in order to make their start, "Judge" Tappan turned up and was easily persuaded to join their wagon mess. They were still looking around for a wagon company that appealed to them. Finally they chose the Green and Jersey County Company from Illinois. This group had drawn up a constitution and bylaws before leaving home. "After we have crossed the river," Henry wrote to Mary, "a company will then be formed & officers elected." It was usual to wait until they had passed beyond the jurisdiction of state law before taking this step.

On May ninth the constitution and bylaws were adopted. Five officers were chosen—the captain and his assistant to serve for twenty days, the treasurer and secretary for four months, the officer of the guard for a day. The sixteen wagons were divided into messes of four each, a mess being moved from front to rear of the train three times each day.

Several changes took place as the company moved west, so that by the time they reached the South Pass there were fifty-two men and fifteen wagons.

Henry and his friends reached California without accident, and when the rest of the company split up, the four men stayed together to begin prospecting. After working together through the winter, they separated the following spring. The irony of Henry's trek was that gold was waiting for him, not in California, but back home where his father had died, leaving him $10,000.

*   *   *

Writers looking for the individual drama, the economic motives or the political forces in our history have left us with a very inadequate idea of the importance of voluntary association in the settlement of the West. It is a simple fact that without the emigrating companies and the wagon trains the development of the West would have stopped at the fur trading and exploring stage. Individual initiative explored the land, but group effort peopled it.

"The most interesting feature of the whole movement [westward]," as James Christy Bell noted in his study of the Oregon movement, "is the organization and reorganization of the companies." That co-operation in the companies was anything but effortless and smooth is true enough. Voluntary association does not cancel out the shortcomings of human nature. It has to work with them. But through it men triumph over their individual weaknesses and, through the power of the group as a directing organism, achieve a result larger than the sum of the associated parts. In the long run what is positive and creative gains the victory when men freely associate. The proof of this fact is perhaps the noblest contribution of American history to human achievement.

Because the emigrating companies were composed of human materials, they were affected by their passions and inadequacies. But they succeeded where individual effort would have failed.

Joel Palmer, who crossed the Rockies with his family in 1847, tells how a spirit of dissatisfaction followed the election of officers, when disappointed candidates were unwilling to submit to the will of the majority. He also describes how the problem was handled.

"It was mutually agreed upon, to form, from the *whole* body, three companies; and that, while each company should select its own officers and manage its internal affairs, the pilot, and Captain Welsh . . . should retain their posts." The companies then took turns at traveling in advance with the pilot or guide. Later on, as forage became scarce, they divided up into still smaller parties. Still later, while crossing the mountains, they divided into three functional groups—one to open the road, one to pack provisions across, one to take charge of the camp.

In spite of friction, no one thought of giving up the principle of voluntary association. The fact that it contained within itself the ability to survive change and to adjust to new conditions was one of its strongest attributes. A rigid, authoritarian system could not have survived.

The settlement of Oregon and California in the forties was followed by the trek to Kansas in the fifties. Again the old principle of moving out as a united body was followed. Lawrence, Kansas, clearly repeated the story of western New York, Ohio and Illinois. Church, school and town were transplanted by means of associations similar to those of Oberlin and Vermontville—a story repeated over and over again in the New England towns of Kansas.

As late as 1873 a group of families in Indianapolis decided to move to California. They sent out a committee to choose the land, just as American settlers had been doing ever since 1620. They drew up articles of association. And they became the first settlers of Pasadena.

Meanwhile the old familiar principle had been put to work by the Forty-niners for a new purpose. San Francisco, under the pressure of the Gold Rush, was lawless and crime-swept. Murder and robbery went unchecked. No man's life or property was safe.

The leading men—most of whom had reached California as members of emigrating companies—got together. They considered how the situation could be handled. And what was their conclusion? Why, to "unite themselves into an association for the maintenance of the peace and good order of Society and the preservation of the lives and property of the Citizens of San Francisco." They did not petition the corrupt city government and then await results. They acted. And San Francisco had law and order.

Similarly, each of the mining towns set up its own government before formal government could be organized. When General Bennett Riley was sent out from Washington in 1849, he reported that the local officers elected by the miners were preserving order almost everywhere even though no formal law backed up the powers they had assumed. Bayard Taylor noted that "when a new placer was discovered, the first thing done was to elect officers."

Gold Hill Camp in western Nevada County provides a fair example. In the spring of 1850 a group of prospectors found gold there, and within a week fifteen or twenty men were working in the gravelly bed of the creek. Each miner had his own working space. As their piles of dirt began to touch each other, some kind of organization became necessary. When the circles of two miners overlapped a dispute arose.

By now the population had grown to fifty. A miners' meeting was called, a temporary chairman was installed, a permanent chairman elected. The bounds of Gold Hill were defined, regulation of the size of claims was agreed to, and the meeting adjourned. Thereafter the miners met whenever a problem arose, passing whatever regulations were required or trying criminal cases like a court.

Despite the impression which has been created by Western movies and magazines, criminal trials in the mining camps were serious affairs, drawing on whatever legal talent was available. Few camps in California during the Gold Rush period were without lawyers who, along with men of every other occupation, had come in search of a quick fortune. When a culprit was caught, the whole community was called together, the chairman took charge of proceedings, and evidence was heard. A murderer or horse thief would pretty certainly be hanged. Flogging, banishment and fines were imposed for lesser crimes. The whole meeting acted as a jury and then saw that their sentence was carried out.

In 1851 Congress took up the question of police regulations for the mining country. Thomas Hart Benton and William H. Seward were wise enough to see that the miners would be better off if they were allowed to make their own rules. A year later the home-made law of the mining camps had justified itself so completely that Congress hesitated to set it aside. Finally in 1866 Congress passed an act recognizing the force and legality of the miners' meetings. In later acts which dealt with mining law the experience and procedure of the mining camps was deferred to, and thus what had begun by voluntary association wound up on the statute books.

De Tocqueville in his astute way put the essence of it into this paragraph:

The citizen of the United States is taught from his earliest infancy to rely upon his own exertions in order to resist the evils and difficulties of life; he looks upon social authority with an eye of mistrust and anxiety, and he only claims its assistance when he is quite unable to shift without it. . . . The same spirit pervades every act of social life. If a stoppage occurs in a thoroughfare, and the circulation of the public is hindered, the neighbors immediately constitute a deliberative body; and this extemporaneous assembly gives rise to an executive power which remedies the inconvenience before anybody has thought of recurring to an authority superior to that of the persons immediately concerned. . . . Associations are established to promote public order, commerce, industry, morality and religion; for there is no end which the human will, seconded by the collective exertions of individuals, despairs of attaining.

De Tocqueville fails to mention one of the greater blessings of voluntary association. When the need for it is over, it dissolves. It does not, like a bureaucracy, go on forever. So long as it fills a need, it lives. When the need is gone it dies, as in the case of the emigrating companies. When need arises again, the time-tested mechanism is there to be used, as in the case of the San Francisco Committee of Vigilance.

The experience of America has been that this energy for association, this readiness to organize to meet a need, lies waiting like water in a tap—quiet until it is needed, then flowing with an endless, life-giving sparkle.

❋ ❋ ❋

The essays which make up Frederick Jackson Turner's famous book, *The Frontier in American History*, first appeared during a period of twenty-five years, from 1893 to 1918. It is interesting to observe that Turner was so influenced by his emphasis on the importance of individualism that it was not until 1918 that he recognized the importance of voluntary association as a leading dynamic factor of frontier settlement and life.

It is difficult to see why Turner once seemed revolutionary, his comments on the influence of the frontier now appear so self-evident. Yet it is his achievement to have seen the obvious and to have described it so expertly as to have brought about a permanent marriage between his own name and the idea of the American frontier.

To read Turner nowadays, however, is to realize that in his emphasis on the obvious fact that America moved westward into vacant lands, he failed somewhat in his analysis of the human results. It was his tendency to make broad generalizations about the effect of the frontier on human behavior rather than to examine typical case histories closely and analytically. His generalizations usually took the form of crediting the frontier with making individualists of us.

"The frontier is productive of individualism," he writes. "The tendency is anti-social. It produces antipathy to control." As a result of his great influence upon scholars of the last fifty years, the importance of group activity in frontier life has been overlooked. Because he thought in terms of broad movements, of forces rather than of people, and because individualism for him as for his era was the magic word, he succeeded in giving us only one side of pioneer life.

He did come to recognize that individual activity could not explain the remarkable phenomenon of American pioneering, but this recognition came slowly. It never came in time to be thoroughly incorporated into his description of the frontier. And as a result our own understanding of the frontier has been restricted. By 1903 Turner had noted that in the arid sections of the West some form of co-operation was necessary if farmers were to irrigate their lands. And he concludes that "the physiographic province itself decreed that the destiny of this new frontier should be social rather than individual." But this was to disregard the more important fact that the westward settlement had been "social" from the very moment when fur traders and explorers were followed by settlers. In 1908 he noted that the stream of migration from New England was communal, while that from the South was individual. But he did not carry this insight further.

Finally in 1918, and under stress of wartime conditions when there is a natural desire to look for the things that unite us, he spoke of the capacity for voluntary association as De Tocqueville had described it. "This was natural enough," he remarked. But he does not tell us why the French in Canada or the Spanish in Central and South America did not "naturally" develop in the same way. Nor does he tell us why Southerners settled individually while New Englanders went in organized groups. The frontier of itself does not account for these facts. Turner tended to disregard the cultural background of those who settled the frontier. If the frontier makes men, men also make the frontier.

In his final essay, Turner accepts "the power of spontaneous association" as an element in the frontier as well as "individualistic competition." He recognizes in the logrolling, the husking bee, the squatters' association something he had not pulled into his picture before. And in the America of the first World War he discovered "the pioneer principle of association" in the voluntary agencies organized to back up the war effort on the home front. So on the last full page of his book he gives voluntary association a place in his frontier. But it comes too late to be integrated.

Voluntary association played a vital, indispensable part in settling the frontier. But the seed of it was in the hearts of the men who first settled New England. Frontier conditions gave it earth to grow in and watered it. But the seed was there.

VII

Underground Railroad

William Lloyd Garrison had a gift for irritating people. The time would come when irritation grew so strong that a mob tried to throw him out of a second-story window, and when that failed, pulled him through the streets of Boston at the end of a rope.

He began irritating people as a very young man. A newspaperman since the age of thirteen, he was an editor at twenty-one. At twenty-three he was called to Bennington, Vermont, from Boston to establish and edit *The Journal of the Times*. The backers wanted a strong anti-Jackson journal to combat the pro-Jackson paper in town, and they had seen enough of Garrison's work to know that he would do a thorough job on his opponents.

Garrison accepted the offer on the condition that he also be allowed to write against slavery and in favor of temperance, peace and moral reform.

In the very first number of the *Journal* he proposed the formation of anti-slavery societies in Vermont. This was on October 3, 1828. Four weeks later he succeeded in bringing the citizens of Bennington together at the local academy. A petition to Congress requesting that slavery be ended in the District of Columbia was read and adopted. Copies were sent to several other Vermont towns with a request for signatures. The petition had 2,352 names on it when it went to Washington. And William Lloyd Garrison had launched a crusade which was to occupy his whole life.

The rival editor found himself irritated by Garrison and said so in print. But Garrison thrived on abuse—was shrewd enough to know that the more he enraged people, the more they talked about him; and the more they talked about him, the more the cause was advanced.

It was fitting that he should have launched his crusade from Bennington, for Vermont had been the first of all the states to abolish slavery. It had done so in the constitution of 1777 by which it set itself up as an independent state fourteen years before joining the Union.

Garrison was not the beginner of the fight against slavery. Quakers had long before felt that the keeping of slaves was inconsistent with the Christian religion and with their belief that men of all races were equal in the sight of God. John Woolman (1720–1772) had as a young man refused to write a conveyance of a slave, and had thereafter traveled through the colonies on foot, testifying against slavery. In time Quaker meetings became a refuge for those moved to testify against slavery. Under the influence of a Quaker community, the first anti-slavery society had been formed at Philadelphia in 1775 on April fourteenth, five days before the other struggle for freedom began at Lexington and Concord. It continued on through the Revolution, was reorganized in 1784, and incorporated in 1789 as the Pennsylvania Society for Promoting the Abolition of Slavery. From the beginning one of its main concerns was relieving free Negroes who were unlawfully held as slaves—a germ of the Underground Railroad which was still in the future.

In 1790 Benjamin Franklin, as President of the Society, signed a petition which was presented to the first Congress. Franklin, an indefatigable promoter of voluntary associations, had already established a circulating library, a volunteer fire company, an association for establishing an academy (which ultimately became the University of Pennsylvania), and had played an important part in founding a hospital and the American Philosophical Society. His proposal of a colonial union at the Albany Convention of 1754, an outgrowth of the old New England

Confederation in the seventeenth century, carried the idea of voluntary association into government. The principle of federalism is in fact the carrying over of voluntary association to the sphere of government. The American instinct for states' rights as opposed to centralism is but another aspect of the voluntarism on which our way of life is based, since the states regard themselves as the voluntary creators of the union instead of its creatures.

Other states followed Pennsylvania's lead in forming abolition societies. The New York Society for Promoting the Manumission of Slaves in 1788 made Lafayette an honorary member. New Jersey and Delaware organized before 1810. Even the slaveholding states had societies during the early years, though a few years later a man's life would have been in danger if he had tried to start one. Kentucky had a society by 1808, North Carolina in 1816, Maryland in 1817 and Virginia in 1823. In the twenties over a hundred societies were busily holding meetings, publishing arguments against slavery, sending petitions to Congress and the state legislatures, and protecting Negroes.

These organizations were drawn together in 1794 through a central body which after 1818 was known as The American Convention for Promoting the Abolition of Slavery and Improving the Condition of the African Race. It met periodically to hear reports, pass resolutions, issue anti-slavery literature and petition Congress. It worked for the education of the slaves so that they might safely be set free. It worked to abolish slavery in the District of Columbia. It kept people aware of the need to do something about slavery.

By 1829, however, when its last meeting was held, only seven societies sent delegates. The introduction of the cotton gin had made cotton-growing profitable and slaves indispensable. Public sentiment, faced with this economic fact, seemed to be wilting.

The abolitionists also had to fight the program of the American Colonization Society. This group, organized in 1816 though the idea it represented was much older, wanted to ship all free

Negroes to Africa. The program gained popular support when a free Negro of Charleston, South Carolina, nearly succeeded in a plot to escape in seized ships, and to massacre any whites who stood in the way. In 1822 Liberia was established. But in ten years the society was able to settle only about a thousand Negroes, most of whom soon died.

Levi Coffin, the Underground Railroad operator, joined an abolition society at New Garden, North Carolina, in the early twenties. Slaveholders were included among the members, he says, and they agreed with the society's plan for gradual emancipation. One slaveholder even loaned his new barn to be used as a convention hall. But gradually the idea prevailed that freed Negroes must be sent to a colony in Africa. Most of the New Garden members eventually went west in order to live in a free state.

By 1829, then, the anti-slavery movement seemed worn out. The churches no longer protested. The abolitionist societies were dying. Only William Slade of Vermont represented the voice of abolition in Congress.

At this point Benjamin Lundy, a staunch Quaker who had founded an abolitionist sheet which he called *The Genius of Universal Emancipation,* took his staff in his hand and walked four hundred miles from Baltimore to Bennington to recruit Garrison for his paper. Born in New Jersey in 1789, Lundy had moved to West Virginia while still in his teens and had there grown to hate the suffering caused by slavery. Moving into Ohio, he formed the Union Humane Society to grapple with the evil. Soon he had several hundred members. Thereafter, moved by his Quaker "concern," he devoted himself to traveling and lecturing. A man without wealth or any special qualifications except moral earnestness, lacking even a robust body, he nevertheless undertook singlehanded the task of putting an end to slavery. The instrument he used was the voluntary association. He organized no one knows how many anti-slavery groups, many of them in the South.

Then in 1828 he met Garrison in Boston. The young man appeared to be the sort of helper he needed. So the next year he walked up to Bennington.

"His heart is of a gigantic size," Garrison had written of him after their first meeting. "Within a few months he has travelled about twenty-four hundred miles, of which upwards of sixteen hundred were performed *on foot!* during which time he has held nearly fifty public meetings."

Lundy told young Garrison that he wanted to publish the *Genius* weekly instead of monthly. He also wanted to devote himself to traveling entirely. If Garrison would come to Baltimore as editor, both these things could be done.

Garrison, recognizing in Lundy the same fire and moral earnestness he felt within himself, agreed to go. In less than a year, thanks to his irritative capacities, his writing landed him in jail on a charge of libel. When friends paid his fine he went to Boston and started the *Liberator,* most famous of all abolition papers. Without a dollar of capital, with no place to sleep but the floor of his small shop, Garrison launched the movement for immediate, total abolition.

But Garrison knew that an obscure publication could not win the battle alone. In November, 1831, he brought together a group of men who were willing to form an association "if the apostolic number of twelve should be found ready to unite." The group split on the issue of immediacy versus gradualism. A month later another meeting was held and a committee was appointed to draft a constitution. On the following New Year's Day the committee reported, the constitution was adopted and the New England Anti-Slavery Society was born.

"We declare that we will not operate on the existing relations of society by other than peaceful and lawful means," the preamble ended, "and that we will give no countenance to violence or insurrection."

It was not long before the opponents of the Society were providing the violence.

In 1833 Garrison went to England to make contact with the anti-slavery organizations there. He returned just as a society was being formed in New York. When the news leaked out that a mob was planning to break up the meeting, the abolitionists quietly transferred the session to another place and had just succeeded in forming their organization and voting on a constitution when the mob found them. The members left one end of the building as the mob came in the other. Garrison, now hated as if he had been a hardened criminal, managed to escape.

Soon after Garrison's return to Boston a call was issued for a meeting to be held in Philadelphia which would create a national organization. In November Garrison wrote to a young editor-poet named John Greenleaf Whittier of Haverhill that the Boston Young Men's Association wanted him to go to the convention as its delegate.

The two men had first met seven years before, when Whittier was only nineteen but already a poet. At that time Garrison was editing the *Newburyport Free Press,* the paper which was read in the Whittier home. Mary Whittier, the poet's sister, sent one of his poems in to the editor by the post rider who delivered the papers. Garrison liked the poem, printed it, and rode fourteen miles out to the Whittier farm in order to meet the poet.

When he arrived, young John Greenleaf was crawling under the barn after a hen. Mary came running out to announce the visitor and Whittier stole in by the back door in order to change his clothes before meeting the editor—who was only two years older than himself and equally self-taught. In his excitement he put on a pair of pants much too short for him, so that his appearance was not greatly improved by the change.

These two young men, one just under twenty and the other just over, both of them lovers of peace, were to become the principal forces in a voluntary movement which was to gain its object only at the cost of frightful bloodshed.

In 1833, when Garrison asked him to go to Philadelphia, Whittier was in no condition to accept. He had been through a couple of disastrous love affairs. He had tried to support his mother and sisters by editorial work but had been forced by ill health to give up and return to the family farm from which he was now trying to wrest a living.

But Garrison would not listen to a refusal. When he arranged for Samuel Sewall, a Boston lawyer, to cover the expenses of the journey, Whittier gave in.

On the river boat which bore many of the abolitionists down the Delaware to Philadelphia, a passenger got into an argument with one of them. Gradually he was led around to abolitionist views.

"If all Abolitionists were like you," he said, "there would be much less opposition to your enterprise. But sir, depend upon it, that hair-brained [*sic*], reckless, violent fanatic, Garrison, will damage, if he does not shipwreck, any case."

Samuel May, another abolitionist, happened to be standing near by.

"Allow me, sir," he said, "to introduce you to Mr. Garrison, of whom you entertain so bad an opinion. The gentleman you have been talking with is he."

Between fifty and sixty delegates from ten of the twelve free states came together at Philadelphia. But when they tried to find a chairman from Philadelphia whose known character would help to calm the public sentiment which was rising against them, none of the men they chose would accept.

"If there is not timber amongst ourselves big enough to make a president of," said Beriah Green of New York, "let us get along without one, or go home and stay there until we have grown up to be men."

The delegates were met with abusive language as they walked to their meeting place at Adelphi Hall. Police guarded the building to prevent violence. The doors were kept locked. Their efforts ended in the formation of the American Anti-Slavery Society.

A few women, including the Quaker Lucretia Mott, attended but were not allowed to vote. Though Quakers had for two hundred years given women an equal share with men in conducting their affairs, the men who were agitated over Negro slavery were still not ready to give up the slavery of women. To the credit of the abolitionists, however, it must be said that their movement gave impetus to another great chapter in voluntary association—the suffrage movement.

Although women were not admitted as voting members of the regular abolitionist societies, they formed groups of their own. In the West, the women were better organized than the men. In Indiana the "library associations," made up mostly of women, were really anti-slavery societies. Other groups calling themselves reading circles, sewing societies and women's clubs also served the cause, exchanging visits between towns and benefiting from the ideas they picked up from each other.

The formation of the national society gave a great forward thrust to the whole movement. Local societies began to spring up all over the country until by 1840 there were two thousand, with a membership approaching 200,000.

Whittier returned to Haverhill in high spirits. "I set a higher value on my name as appended to the Anti-Slavery Declaration of 1833 than on the title page of any book," he remarked when he was old and famous, known throughout the English-speaking world for his poems of rural life.

"Whittier, enlist!" Garrison had written to him before the convention. Whittier had enlisted indeed. Appointed an agent for his county, he now began the life of an agitator. He became corresponding secretary for the society which organized at Haverhill. He attended conventions, drew up reports, traveled up and down through northern New England. The New England Society put him on a committee to draft "An Address to the People of the United States" demanding an end to slavery in the District of Columbia and to slave traffic between the states.

In 1837 he succeeded by his own efforts in turning the Massachusetts legislature to abolition. Though he suffered increasingly from an illness which appears to have been psychosomatic, he jumped into the middle of the fight, arranging anti-slavery lectures, serving on committees, and even being mobbed and plastered with "decayed eggs, sticks and light missiles," from which he was forced to retreat at "an undignified trot."

After service in New York at the headquarters of the national society, Whittier went in March, 1839, to Philadelphia to become editor of Benjamin Lundy's *The National Enquirer* when it was taken over by the Pennsylvania society and renamed *The Pennsylvania Freeman*. From 1833 onward he was publishing anti-slavery poems full of zeal and fervor. His service to the cause continued until war came. Though abolition was an unpopular cause, and though Whittier had to give up his political ambitions when he embraced it, the young Quaker poet stuck it out.

Meanwhile Garrison was irritating more people and sharpening the struggle between abolitionists and nonabolitionists until in 1835 a Boston mob broke in upon a meeting of the Female Anti-Slavery Society, pursued Garrison as he retreated and tore most of the clothes from his body. Restrained from throwing him out a window, they pulled him through the streets at the end of a rope. He went with face uplifted, the smile of a martyr lighting his long, bony face. Constables charged the mob and bore Garrison off to the City Hall and then, for safekeeping, to jail.

* * *

Garrison had always insisted that moral force alone must bring an end to slavery. His hostility to political action led, in 1839, to a split in the ranks. Abolitionists believing in political action formed a new national society. In 1840 they founded the Liberty Party and named James Gillespie Birney as their candidate for the presidency.

Birney, born in 1792 into a wealthy slaveholding family of Kentucky, had freed his own slaves in 1834, had tried to persuade his friend Henry Clay to come out for gradual emancipation, and after 1835 gave his full time to the cause of abolition. In 1836 he started to publish *The Philanthropist* in Cincinnati.

His office was mobbed and looted, but though his life was in danger he did not suffer the fate of Elijah P. Lovejoy, the abolitionist editor of Alton, Illinois, whose print shop was three times destroyed before he himself was murdered in 1837.

Unlike Garrison, Birney was moderate in his speech and temperate in his behavior. A defender of the Union, he believed that slavery was destroying freedom for whites as well as blacks. Free speech and freedom of the press had been destroyed in the South, he felt, and in the North. Twenty-three years before Lincoln said that a nation cannot endure half slave and half free, Birney had remarked that "liberty and slavery cannot both live in juxtaposition."

He drew only seven thousand votes in the election of 1840, but in 1844 he polled more than sixty thousand. In 1848 the anti-slavery party became the Free-Soilers, in 1852 the Free Democrats. Finally in 1856 the political action wing of the abolition movement brought about the fusion of Whigs and anti-slavery Democrats which formed the new Republican Party. It was the fate of this new political association to form the government which was to steer the country through civil war to emancipation.

* * *

In spite of Garrison's gift for stirring people up, the most dramatic aspect of the anti-slavery movement was the Underground Railroad. As early as 1786 organized help was available to fugitive slaves, according to no less an authority than George Washington. In a letter of May twelfth he speaks of a society of Quakers in Philadelphia which had formed for that purpose. The Quakers were active everywhere, but especially in southeastern Pennsylvania and New Jersey where their numbers were large. By 1815 fugitives were crossing the Western Reserve in Ohio on their way to Canada and freedom, aided by regular stations of the Underground Railroad. From then until the Civil War the Railroad spread throughout the North.

Because it was illegal to help or harbor escaping slaves, the

Railroad had no formal organization. Yet every free state was involved. Thousands of miles of interconnecting routes stretched northward. Hundreds of station agents gave freely of their time, arising at midnight to take in passengers, providing food, shelter, clothing, protection, transportation. The agent rarely knew anyone except in the stations from which he received fugitives and to which he sent them. There was no central office, no roll of members, no one to co-ordinate activities. Secrecy, courage and ingenuity were essential.

No one even knows for sure where the name first came into use. R. C. Smedley in his *History of the Underground Railroad in . . . Pennsylvania* says that slave catchers coming north in pursuit of escapees always lost the scent at Columbia, Pennsylvania. "There must be an underground railroad somewhere," they concluded. But similar stories can be traced to other localities. They could all be true, for at a time when railroads were a novelty the terminology was on everyone's tongue.

Head and shoulders above all other Railroad agents were Thomas Garrett and the even more famous Levi Coffin, both Quakers, both born in 1789, both capable businessmen who voluntarily devoted their time and their money to the struggle against human enslavement. Garrett was born in the North, but moved south to Delaware where pro-slavery feeling was strong. Coffin was born in North Carolina but moved north to Indiana. Both Garrett and Coffin began helping slaves in boyhood, stimulated to action by the brutality and injustice they had seen.

When Thomas Garrett was eighteen, a Negro woman employed by his father was kidnaped. This kidnaping of free Negroes in order to sell them into slavery was in fact one of the chief stimuli to the formation of the Railroad. Garrett went after the woman and succeeded in bringing her back. Thereafter he helped Negroes to freedom whenever he could.

In 1822 he moved to Wilmington. For forty years he continued his work in spite of the hostility of the surrounding community, and in spite of frequent threats of murder. In 1848 he was finally brought to trial for helping two child slaves to escape.

Convicted, he was fined $8,000. Everything he owned was sold to meet the fine. When the sale was over, the auctioneer turned to him and said, "Thomas, I hope you'll never be caught at this again."

"Friend, I haven't a dollar in the world," Garrett answered, "but if thee knows a fugitive who needs a breakfast, send him to me."

Nearly sixty, Garrett started all over. Friends loaned him capital and in time he grew prosperous again. He continued helping slaves until the Civil War.

"The war came a little too soon for my business," he said near the end of his life. "I wanted to help off three thousand slaves. I had only got up to twenty-seven hundred!"

Levi Coffin, raised as a Quaker in the innocent belief that the Christian message meant what it said, was also shocked by the brutal beatings, the callous separation of mother and children which went with slavery. His first overt act, as in Garrett's case, was to prevent the attempted kidnaping of a free Negro. Then he helped one who had been set free in his master's will but was re-enslaved by a prejudiced court. Next he aided a slave who had been outrageously beaten. By these gradual steps he came to helping any escaped slave who came to him.

Leaving North Carolina in 1826, when he could no longer endure the daily scenes of brutality, he moved with his wife and infant son to Newport (Fountain City), Indiana, where several lines of the Underground Railroad converged. There he found free Negroes trying to aid the fugitives who came through. It was clear that they needed his help.

"I thought it was always safe to do right," he decided. "The Bible, in bidding us to feed the hungry and clothe the naked, said nothing about color, and I should try to follow out the teachings of that good book." And so the big, raw-boned, gentle Quaker went about the Lord's work as his conscience laid it out for him, though at the risk of his business, his reputation, his safety.

When friends in the neighborhood observed the fearless

manner in which Levi Coffin and his wife took in the refugees, they began to help with gifts of clothing or with transportation.

As a leading agent, Coffin soon became known along the Ohio River where fugitives usually made their break for freedom, and along the routes leading to Canada. "Depots were established on the different lines of the Underground Railroad, south and north of Newport," Coffin explains, "and a perfect understanding was maintained between those who kept them."

Three principal lines from the south converged at his house. A gentle rap at the door announced the arrival of a "train." Springing from bed, Levi Coffin would open his door to whatever group of fugitives might be climbing out of the usual two-horse wagon. After a whispered conference they were led inside. Then Levi would lock the door, cover the windows, strike a light and build up the fire. After Mrs. Coffin had fed them, the fugitives were placed on pallets before the fire. Sometimes as many as seventeen arrived in a single night. Eliza Harris, immortalized by Harriet Beecher Stowe in *Uncle Tom's Cabin* as the mother who crossed the ice-filled river with her child in her arms, was one of those who found her way to the Coffin's. Levi, who says that she and her baby stayed with him for several days, authenticates the story of the river.

When slave catchers were around, it was often necessary to resort to one trick or another. Often Mrs. Coffin would hide a young woman between the straw mattress and the feather bed, and then smooth the blankets so that nothing showed. Often the girls who came through had fair complexions and could, with a veil over their faces, easily be passed off as white.

When Coffin became widely known as an agent, it was essential that he avoid any action which might lead to his being prosecuted. If a wagon was to be hired, he gave the money to a second person to hand to the driver. Negroes who owned no property were usually employed as drivers.

The need for money went beyond anything Coffin could himself supply. When money was needed he called on some of the "stockholders" to furnish it. On one of these occasions he called at the pork-house of Henry Lewis. In addition to Lewis, his brother and the bookkeeper, there were three strangers sitting in the office—all slaveholders from Kentucky.

"Henry, I want to raise a little money for a family of poor people," Levi Coffin said. "They are in need, and I am called on for help."

Henry, knowing well enough what was afoot, said, "Are they very poor?"

"Yes, among the poorest of the poor, and must suffer if they are not helped; thee knows I am often called on in such cases."

Before leaving the office, Coffin collected six dollars for his fugitives, including donations from the slave owners.

Though the Underground Railroad itself was too dangerous an activity to be openly organized in most places, there were other kinds of voluntary group activity which could help the cause along. In 1838 Levi Coffin and some of his friends got together to see how they could spread the sentiment for emancipation. They decided to establish an anti-slavery library which could give or loan books, tracts and periodicals about slavery. Twenty-five dollars was subscribed and invested. Thereafter Levi Coffin kept up the supply with his own money. Interest in abolition increased. Meetings were often held—"library meetings," they were called, in order to prevent their being broken in upon by mobs.

At about the same time the local societies joined together to form the Anti-Slavery Society of Indiana. Anti-slavery lecturers canvassed the state, always stopping with the Coffins when they reached Newport.

But as the movement gained strength in the forties the opposition also grew stronger. Mobs began to interrupt anti-slavery meetings. When the Negro speaker Frederick Douglass made his first tour through Indiana he was pelted with rotten eggs, stones and brickbats. But gradually public opinion shifted again, growing so strongly anti-slavery that Coffin began to keep fugitives in his house openly.

Another source of help was the Anti-Slavery Sewing Society.

Learning that the fugitives often arrived in rags, the ladies of Cincinnati where Levi Coffin was living after 1847 formed a group to provide badly needed clothing.

The cause which had led the Coffins to Cincinnati was Free Labor. A two-day convention had been held the year before at Salem, Indiana, the outcome of which was a resolution to raise $3,000 and loan it to a suitable merchant who would develop a wholesale business dealing only in goods produced by free labor. The idea was to discourage slavery and promote emancipation by economic pressure. Coffin was urged to take on the job and to move to Cincinnati where the facilities for such a business were available.

Coffin was happily established at Newport where he had now lived for fourteen years. He had recently built himself a new house. His business was flourishing. He was no longer young. But the committee kept pressing him, knowing perhaps that his Quaker conscience would force him to accept, as it did.

He sold his business at Newport, rented his house, and leased a store and dwelling house in Cincinnati. Then he went East to buy his stock. Orders came in faster than he could fill them. It was soon apparent that there were not enough free cotton goods available to meet the demand. Soon he was organizing the supply of free cotton in the South and arranging to have it ginned by free labor.

As the most active of all Underground Railroad people, Levi Coffin deserved the title of President which was popularly bestowed upon him. But it was an honorary title. The Underground Railroad never had a president, never had officers. It is unique among voluntary associations for the efficient way it functioned without formal organization. It may have carried as many as 75,000 slaves to freedom. It engaged the active services of hundreds of "agents," "conductors" and "engineers," including the author of *Uncle Tom's Cabin* who also operated in Cincinnati and who in the characters of Simeon and Rachel Halliday portrayed such a Quaker couple as Levi and Catharine Coffin.

Wilbur Siebert, leading authority on the Underground, catalogued over 3,200 people who served the Railroad. In its organization, Siebert points out, small and scattered localities and even individual families were important. "These little communities were in general the elements out of which the Underground system built itself up." Through them, the Railroad had grown into a widespread institution before 1840, with a network of routes stretching from the South to Canada. Lines converged and branched in so many places that it was almost impossible for slave hunters to trace runaways through a single county without getting off the track. Where anti-slavery sentiment was strong, the whole countryside threw a protective blanket over the escaping slaves, and in addition to the few thousand who did the active work there were many thousands who aided with money or clothing, or who directed the fugitives to the right place or slave catchers to the wrong one. The Underground Railroad seized the imaginations even of those who played no active part in it, and the tradition of it carries on even today. In many a town the houses where slaves were hidden are still pointed out, and the back windows through which they escaped if the pursuit got too hot.

Since the work of the Railroad was contrary to the law of the land, formal organization would only have increased the danger. Officers formally elected could have been too easily seized and convicted. One of the strengths of the organization was its ability to operate without any elaborate apparatus. It was moral force—a strong sense of the rightness of the cause and of individual responsibility to it—which held the Railroad together.

Another binding force was its terminology. Special signals, passwords, messages guarded by figurative language provided what was known as the Railroad's grapevine telegraph. Fugitives were referred to as "U.G. baggage" or "bales of black cotton." Contributors were "stockholders," houses where slaves hid were "stations." The special language provided a valuable symbol of unity for the thousands of agents who never saw each other and who were held together by no constitution or set of bylaws.

In the larger cities, however, some organization was necessary. In Philadelphia in 1838 the Vigilance Committee of the Pennsylvania Anti-Slavery Society put through a formal plan of organization. Robert Purvis, the president, had a room so constructed in his cellar that it could only be entered by a trap door from the room above. Active agents in Baltimore and to the south directed runaways to Purvis, who hid them in his underground room when the chase was hot. The records of the Committee, kept by the Negro secretary, William Still, and hidden in the loft of Lebanon Seminary, contained an account of every fugitive it aided.

In some centers regular conductors or agents were employed to handle transportation problems, while the volunteer stationkeepers received and cared for the arrivals until they could be sent northward. In Philadelphia the Dorcas Societies, made up of colored members, provided clothing while the Philadelphia Association for the Moral and Mental Improvement of the People of Color raised money and supplied food, clothing and employment. In this way the Railroad was supported by a great many other voluntary associations whose activities did not have to be as secret as the actual moving and hiding of fugitives.

*　*　*

David Putnam, Junior, was Railroad agent at Point Harmar, Ohio. One day in August, 1843, he received the following note:

Belpre Friday Morning

David Putnam

Business is aranged for Saturday night be on the lookout and if practicable let a cariage come and meet the carawan

JS

Putnam used the back of this note for the following penciled memorandum:

Aug.	13/43	Sunday Morn.	2	o'clock arrived
		Sunday Eve.	8½	" departed for B.
	16	Wednesday Morn	2	" arrived
	20	Sunday eve.	10	" departed for N.
Wife & children	21	Monday morn.	2	" arrived from B.
		" eve.	10	" left for Mr. H.
	22	Tuesday "	11	" left for W.
A. L. & S. J.	28	Monday morn.	1	" arrived left 2 o'clock

Clearly, an agent of the Railroad had to be willing to lose sleep over his avocation. In this sixteen-day period Putnam was up four times in the middle of the night, when he and his wife must have lost several hours sleep feeding and settling their guests. If he accompanied the fugitives who left his home, he was out all night on five other occasions, and would have needed most of the next day to get back home.

Frequently disguise was the means of getting away from a hot pursuit. A pretty mulatto girl eighteen or twenty years old had managed to get as far as Crawfordsville, Indiana, without help. Here, just as her owner was catching up with her, she was taken into the home of John Speed. Losing her trail, the owner went through town until he was sure he would have overtaken her. Then he returned to Crawfordsville, learned about Speed's Underground activities, and had a watch kept on his house. Meanwhile the Railroad made plans for her escape. When they had been completed, she was led out at night through the gardens to the home of a free Negro family named Patterson. There she was dressed in a fine silk dress and supplied with a white baby and one of the Patterson girls to act as her attendant. Thus disguised, she was put aboard a northbound train.

As the train pulled out, she discovered that her master was in the same car with her! He was apparently going to the end of the line to catch her whenever she came along.

Somehow she managed to hold herself together until she reached Detroit. There she went aboard the ferry which would carry her to Canada and freedom. When her borrowed nurse and baby went ashore and the gangplank was raised, she saw her owner standing on the dock. As the boat pulled away from shore she lifted her veil and waved him a pert good-by.

There were hundreds of other cases when former servant girls were tricked out as fine ladies, or as plainly dressed Quaker women. Light-colored men, in truth as well as in *Uncle Tom's Cabin,* were passed off as white gentlemen while the dark-skinned acted as their servants.

In the back country and in the early days, most of the transporting had to be done by wagon. The Reverend Calvin Fairbank once abducted a whole family—father, mother and six children—from Covington, Kentucky in a load of straw. But when railroads became common, the whole process was immensely speeded up. Henry Box Brown was hidden in a box, delivered to Adams Express, and carried from Richmond to Philadelphia in twenty-four hours. Such an exploit obviously called for some form of organized co-ordination.

Even more co-ordination was needed to whisk off five slaves from the tobacco plantation of a Colonel Hardy near Washington. The slaves disappeared on a Sunday night. Colonel Hardy called in an accomplished slave catcher as soon as he discovered his loss. But almost before the slave catcher could get started, there arrived in the mail a copy of *The Liberty Press,* a paper printed in Albany, with a marked article which read:

"Arrived this morning by our fast line three men and two women. They were claimed as slaves by Colonel Hardy of the District of Columbia, but became dissatisfied with the Colonel's ways and left the old fellow's premises last Sunday evening, arriving at our station by the quickest passage on record." The article concluded by advising the Colonel not to trouble himself about his slaves any further, as they would be under the protection of the British Lion before the paper could reach him.

The article also mentioned incidents which only the Colonel's servants could have known. "Nobody but Kate would have told that story!" said the Colonel, and called off the search.

What the Colonel did not know was that at that minute his slaves were no farther away than Baltimore. The Underground had arranged for the notice in the Albany paper so that Hardy's people could go north without fear of being pursued.

It had all begun when Jo Norton, one of Hardy's slaves, had been approached by a stranger one Sunday night on a dark road. The stranger offered to carry him to freedom. Two weeks later they met again, when it was agreed that three weeks hence Jo was to come to a clump of bushes by an old cemetery. He came, waited for the signal, and was amazed to find that when he stood up, four other forms also arose out of the dark. All four were friends of his from the Hardy plantation.

Following the directions that had been given them, they started to walk down the road at the sound of a second signal until they met their "conductor." He told them to walk to the railroad, and then to follow the tracks thirty miles until they saw a man waiting for them. If he said his name was Ben, they were to go with him.

It was dawn when they found Ben. He led them to a hiding place in a corn rick. Ben, a free Negro, had stacked his corn close to the tracks on the theory that no one would think of looking for runaways in such an exposed place.

The next night another agent appeared and led the two women of the party away. The three men were kept a few days longer. After the Colonel had received the newspaper and called off the search, they were sent on to Baltimore. They were given money to buy peanuts and fruit, and were told to walk openly through the more crowded streets, keeping in sight a sharp-faced Negro boy who would guide them to the outskirts. Here, again at night, they met the two girls. From the man who had led the girls there they received directions for the next lap of their journey.

In Philadelphia they were hidden in Quaker homes, then sent

on a fishing boat to Bordentown. From there to New York they traveled by train, the men hidden among crates and bales, the girls veiled and dressed as ladies. At Albany they separated, some of them going on to Canada.

Planning as elaborate as this proves the existence of a pretty efficient organization.

That members of the Underground Railroad were quick to make use of any opportunity that came their way is clear from the case of the letter which was dropped by mistake into the slot in the *Philadelphia Ledger* office instead of into the U.S. Mail. The letter was from a Maryland lady who had come to Philadelphia to seek a runaway slave. It was written to a noted slave catcher named Alberti, asking him to call on her.

A clerk at the *Ledger* office opened the letter, passing it on to the Vigilance Committee. Cyrus Whitman, a member of the committee, fitted himself out in an imposing set of whiskers and called on the lady, introducing himself as Alberti's assistant. Whitman took down the name and description of the slave and departed.

In a few hours a poster was printed and stuck up throughout the city, warning everyone of the lady's intentions. The fugitive meanwhile was located and sent north to safety.

* * *

The abolition movement and the Underground Railroad kept on in spite of hostility not only in the South but in the North, where it was so strong that men like Wendell Phillips and Thomas Wentworth Higginson felt that their stand against slavery had lost them their comfortable prestige in the New England literary world. Harriet Martineau attended an anti-slavery meeting in Boston only to find that she had forfeited the good opinion of Boston society. Theodore Parker could find no ministers to exchange pulpits with him. The colleges of the East were full of pro-slavery feeling, and when Charles Sumner spoke to the Harvard students in 1848 he was booed and hissed because he was an abolitionist—even though a Harvard man.

Three years later Emerson was similarly treated when he spoke in Cambridge on the fugitive slave law.

Northern ministers felt no Christian challenge in slavery. The most prominent of them defended it, including the president of Dartmouth and the Episcopal Bishop of Vermont. The Methodist General Conference of 1836 censured two of its members who had favored abolition.

When Miss Prudence Crandall tried to educate Negro girls in her school at Canterbury, Connecticut, the legislature passed a special act so that she could be prosecuted. In Canaan, New Hampshire, a similar school was pulled away by a hundred yoke of oxen and dumped into a near-by swamp. In New York City the home of Lewis Tappan, champion of abolition, was sacked. Mobs also destroyed other homes and churches known to be tainted with the belief that all men are created equal. The murder of Lovejoy in 1837 was only one instance of the pro-slavery feeling in the North.

Against such displays of mob violence, the abolitionists had one principal weapon—voluntary group activity. Not only the anti-slavery societies, but hundreds of sewing circles, reading clubs, libraries, newspapers were formed to support the cause. Plain people, taking the Declaration of Independence seriously, in time made their weight felt. Gradually the societies were displaced by the anti-slavery political party, or became adjuncts of it. Not Garrison's, of course—he never was willing to enter politics.

But whenever a new sort of job was to be done, a new association was formed. So Eli Thayer of Worcester organized the Emigrant Aid Company which was to colonize Kansas for freedom. The first party arrived in 1854 and settled Lawrence. Hostile invaders later set up a slave government there, but the free residents refused to recognize it. By voluntary association they set up a government of their own, called a convention, and adopted a constitution which was sent to the United States Senate in 1856.

When war came, the energies of abolitionists were channeled into Freedmen's Aid Associations. Help to escaped slaves continued throughout the war, only now it was not necessary to send them on to Canada.

Finally in 1870 the Fifteenth Amendment became law and the work of the anti-slavery societies was over. Levi Coffin was invited to speak at a large meeting held by the colored people of Cincinnati.

Explaining how he had received the title of President from slave hunters who could not find their slaves once they reached his hands, he said:

"I accepted the office thus conferred upon me, and . . . endeavored to perform my duty faithfully. Government has now taken the work out of our hands. The stock of the Underground Railroad has gone down in the market, the business is spoiled, the road is now of no further use." He then resigned an office he had never held in any formal sense. But someone had to be the symbolic leader of the vast voluntary movement which had grown up out of thousands of private convictions and against great odds. Not all the hostility in the North and South could stop it—not laws, or economic pressure, or social ostracism. Not even the power of government could stop the Underground Railroad, illegal as its operations were.

Whether war would have come without the anti-slavery movement is an open question. Whether an easier solution to the slave problem might have been found if the Railroad and the anti-slavery societies had never sprung up is also a question without an answer. But these questions are really beside the point. A great surge of voluntary activity was the characteristic response of Americans when confronted with their greatest domestic issue. Hundreds of groups formed. All shades of opinion were represented. New needs brought forth new groups to perform special functions. And through all this ferment of activity, through the free and voluntary marshaling of conflicting programs and ideas, a road to the future was finally built. Against tremendous odds—against all kinds of social and economic and legal pressure—the voluntary associations won out.*

We hope we shall never again have to face so divisive an issue, nor do we wish to see one decided at such a cost in blood. But we ought to take pride in the fact that for almost a hundred years, without material gain of any kind for themselves, thousands of Americans gave incredibly of their time, their money, their reputation, their health, even their lives because they believed in freedom for all men. Such an outpouring of disinterested service had hardly been seen anywhere in the world before. Characteristically, it was poured out through the habitual channel of voluntary association.

Today many organizations carry on the tradition of the Sons of Liberty and the abolitionists, standing guard over the liberties guaranteed us in the Constitution. They too are voluntary, depending on the responsibility of the citizens for membership and support.

Such associations are essential to freedom, since even the most benevolent government tends to resent criticism, to encroach upon the rights of men, to enlarge its sphere of operations, to take over responsibilities that could as well be left to local or voluntary groups.

As long as Americans are free to organize and free to join any kind of organization—except, of course, those bent upon violent overthrow of the government or those dominated by foreign powers—they will be able to maintain a dynamic, responsive culture superior to any totalitarian power. Any attempt to prevent freedom of association is a threat to the American way of life at its deepest core.

---

* A voluntary association of a very different nature was the Ku Klux Klan, organized in 1865 to intimidate the freed Negro and to maintain white control.

VIII

Paradise, Inc.

"We are all a little wild here with numberless projects of social reform," Emerson wrote to Carlyle in 1840. "Not a reading man but has a draft of a new community in his waistcoat pocket."

One of these communities had got far enough out of a waistcoat pocket to be excitedly discussed in Transcendentalist circles during the winter of 1840. The pocket belonged to George Ripley, a Unitarian minister who after fourteen years had grown tired of preaching, and who had determined to form an association for those who wished to combine "plain living and high thinking" in a practical way. The result was Brook Farm.

Ripley was a cheerful-hearted, hard-working man who cared nothing for worldly possessions and not much more for fame. Philosophy was his love, and to found a community in which philosophy would have the importance it deserved was all he asked. Every ship from Europe was bringing Owenites, Christian socialists or Fourierists to found their communities under the invigorating influence of the American air. Ripley, aroused by this atmosphere of "association," had ideas of his own.

So in the spring of 1841 he and his wife, Sophia Dana, settled in West Roxbury on a farm of 192 acres which had been purchased by the sale of twenty-four shares of stock at $500 each. The old farmhouse in the shade of an ancient sycamore was christened "The Hive." Buildings began to go up—the Eyrie, the Nest, the Cottage, the Pilgrim House. Then came the members to fill them, until at the peak six years later there were 140. Hawthorne, beginning to be known as a writer of stories, arrived. He hoped to find at the farm a way to earn a living which would also permit him to marry Sophia Peabody and to have time free for writing. But after playing "chamber maid to a group of cows," milking "the transcendental heifer" (only a poet could milk a heifer, surely) and forking dung out of "the gold mine," he regretfully gave up, finding it impossible to write there. Charles Dana came fresh from Harvard; he was later to gain fame as editor of the *New York Sun*. Two of the early members went on to follow Brook Farm ideals in other places—Isaac Hecker, who later founded the Paulist Fathers, and George P. Bradford, who moved to Plymouth where he taught Greek and hawked the vegetables he raised with his own hands.

Brook Farm had about twenty members at the start. Some were farmers and workingmen. Some were artists or Boston Brahmins. There was an English baronet's son, a Spaniard, two Filipinos, the son of a Louisiana planter. There were Transcendentalist girls with beautiful eyes and high purposes, their hair flowing to their shoulders instead of being caught up in a prim New England bun.

High purposes were in fact the hallmark of Brook Farm, which aimed at nothing less than "1. To indoctrinate the whole people of the United States with the principles of associative unity. 2. To prepare for the time when the nation, like one man, shall reorganize its townships on the basis of perfect justice." In short, the Farmers were perfectionists.

All were to share in the work—not only in order to become self-sufficient, but "to insure a more natural union between intellectual and manual labour than now exists." If everyone worked, no one need slave and there would be plenty of time for uplifting relaxation and elevating conversation. That, in any case, was the theory. But Ripley found that he had to be up before dawn if all the tasks were to get done. Dressed in a blue tunic and cowhide boots, he milked, cleaned out the stalls, carted vegetables to market, and directed the activities of his associates. His wife worked just as hard—washing, scrubbing floors, working in the kitchen. Her family thought it all foolishness, but she seemed to enjoy it.

As important as the farming was the school, which supplied a good part of the income, and sometimes the only cash. Ripley taught philosophy and mathematics, Mrs. Ripley history and Dante—the latter in Italian. Charles A. Dana taught Greek and German. It was a remarkable school, and it turned out some remarkable students, among them the man who later played a leading part in breaking up the Tweed ring, Francis C. Barlow.

But the chief end of Brook Farm was to enhance the intellectual and spiritual development of its members. Brook Farm was full of conversation, of sitting around in groups on stairs and floors. John Sullivan Dwight held classes in botany and geology in the near-by woods. Ripley gathered the members around him in the snow of a winter's evening in order to tell them about the stars. Sometimes they would walk or drive the ten miles into Boston to a concert, a lecture by Emerson or an anti-slavery meeting.

There was gaiety as well as culture—dances, picnics, boating parties, plays, games. And there were plenty of visitors. At first only the Transcendentalist inner circle came—Emerson and Margaret Fuller and Bronson Alcott and Theodore Parker. But as the Farm's fame spread, visitors poured in by the hundreds.

"A perpetual picnic, a French Revolution in small," Emerson called it, refusing an invitation to become a member himself. In its idyllic setting near the Charles River, with its pine woods and green meadows and its framework of rolling hills, with its groups of young men and maidens wandering across the landscape, Brook Farm did have something of the look of a picnic. It was fresh, new, spontaneous. There was the constant novelty of living in one household with a hundred people, gathered together voluntarily and sharing similar ideals. There was the sharing of playtime and of labor, the brilliant conversations, the little jokes and phrases—even the bad puns—which drew them together. "I have just gotten a reseat in full for these pantaloons," said Lemuel Capen after getting his trousers back from the Mending Group. The blue tunics, the brown hunters' frocks, the muslin dresses with flowers and ribbons were not so uniform as to be dull, yet managed to suggest their groupishness.

Yet, it must be admitted, there was a somewhat naïve innocence about the place. Though the members were intelligent and high-minded, they had failed to come to grips with the world as it was. While the industrial world was beginning to boil and seethe around them, they tried to retreat to an economy of hand labor. They would labor eight hours a day in winter, ten in summer. But what if the hay had not all been got in after ten hours? And what if their inexpert hands could not compete with skilled labor?

In near-by Lawrence and Lowell the machines were already turning. Hand labor was no match for what the machines could do. The men and women of literary bent who were attracted to Brook Farm simply did not make the best workers. The products they tried to produce for sale failed to make money. Instead of being self-sufficient as they had planned, the Farmers found that they were eating into their capital.

For four years the associates enjoyed their "age of reason in a patty-pan." But financial erosion proved that they must somehow do better. Tall, harsh-voiced Albert Brisbane and famous Horace Greeley came to visit and aroused their interest in the doctrines of Charles Fourier, the French socialist. They voted to reorganize on Fourier principles. Fourier, more than a little mad, had felt himself to be the only human being who understood the harmonious plan which God had made for the world. He had set it all down, in amazing detail, in half-a-dozen books. Part of his fantastic plan involved the division of all mankind into mathematically exact Groups, Series and Phalanxes. Fourier decreed that each Phalanx should contain 1,620 people. There were to be exactly 2,985,984 of them in the world when his plan was fully realized!

Brook Farm, in electing to be one, seemed at first to renew itself. New members poured in, bringing new capital and new enthusiasms. But something important had been lost. Fourier's obsession with numbers rather than human considerations gradually killed off its spirit. "Fourier has skipped no fact but one—namely life," said Emerson. The plays and picnics ceased. Emerson, Thoreau and the others stopped coming. The spontaneity was gone. Burdensome detail and needless complexity of organization replaced the warm family feeling. New members brought new discontents.

The community threw all its effort into the building of the "Phalanstery" specified by Fourier as the necessary center of each phalanx. True, Brook Farm was unable to come up to Fourier's dream of a building twenty-two hundred feet long, with wings 500 feet long and parallel rows of out-buildings with the whole gracefully landscaped. All Brook Farm could produce was a plain, three-story frame building 175 feet long. Its attic was full of rooms for single members, its second and third floors divided into apartments for families. The first floor housed a big dining room, kitchen, parlors and a spacious hall and lecture room.

On a Tuesday evening, March 3, 1846, the members were enjoying a dance in the Hive, celebrating the resumption of work on the Phalanstery after the winter's halt. The structure was nearly completed; most of the community's liquid funds were in it.

A member noticed a light in an upper window. A moment later the dance was broken up by the cry: "The Phalanstery is on fire!"

The building burned to the ground. There was not a penny of insurance. Brook Farm died the next year, in 1847, but not before leaving a permanent mark upon American education and social organization.

It is easy now to smile at the idealism of those good people as, in their blue tunics, they mixed literary conversation with the shoveling of cow manure. Yet all of them, when they came years later to look back on the experience, remembered it as the springtime of their lives, the high point of faith and intellectual flowering. John Thomas Codman, who went to live at Brook Farm at the age of seventeen, has best rendered the atmosphere of the place.

"The summer came on with joy and beauty," he wrote years later in his *Brook Farm*. "I recall the long waves of nodding grass, that swayed in the June wind and were chasing each other, fugue-like on the broad meadows. How beautiful it was, tipped with its various hues of green, yellow, red and purple, bending and rising as each breath of wind passed over it! The crops looked well, and the table was supplied with varieties of garden produce. . . . There never was a more gentle, kind, amiable, trusting, self-respecting, loving set of young folks anywhere assembled. . . . This I know, that the sympathy and friendship which sprung up in those days has lasted all these years, and will remain as long as life. . . . They were seeking something which, had they found the realization of, would have carried peace to troubled hearts, contentment and joy to all conditions and classes. They were builders, not destroyers. They proposed to begin again the social structure with new foundations."

Even Hawthorne who had left returned wistfully to say to the saintly George Ripley:

"Even though I went away, the clay of which my body is molded is nearer akin to these crumbling furrows here than to any other portion of the earth's dust."

* * *

During the nineteenth century the United States was host to over a hundred groups who associated themselves for the purpose of trying to achieve a richer and better life than society at large was providing. Over a hundred thousand people were involved. Many of these groups were attempting to establish the principles of the Sermon on the Mount and the community of the Apostles described in Acts iv 32, 34–35:

And the multitude of them that believed were of one heart and of one soul: neither said any of them that ought of the things which he possessed was his own; but they had all things common. . . .

Neither was there any among them that lacked: for as many as were possessors of lands or houses sold them, and brought the prices of the things that were sold,

And laid them down at the apostles' feet: and distribution was made unto every man according as he had need.

Many of these communities were formed by Europeans who came to America in order to start fresh in a new land, where there was space in which they could be alone and where they would be free of the customs and economies which had bound them at home. The Shakers, the Owenites, the Fourierists, the various groups from Germany were of this sort. It is significant that America attracted them, and that their experiments thus became part of our history. But they did not grow out of American soil.

There was, however, an American tradition of associating to form voluntary communities such as we have seen at Plymouth, along the Connecticut, and in the westward settlement. There was a tradition of holding all things in common, too, though not with the conviction that this was the way things should be. The Pilgrims and the first settlers at Jamestown had experimented with communism because the merchant adventurers who staked them demanded it. The Jamestown settlers, who apparently agreed to make the voyage in return for their keep—and perhaps the hope of finding some gold on their own—finally had to share the work and the food in order to keep alive. But they hadn't pretended to like it.

The groups who came to set up communities in the nineteenth century were seeking a way out of the squalor and poverty brought on by the industrial revolution. They were in revolt against the homelessness and helpless dependence of the worker upon his employer. But the most spectacular and the most successful of all these experiments (with the possible exception of Amana which will be described later) was a home-grown product which sprouted in the rocky soil of Vermont.

John Humphrey Noyes was born in Brattleboro in 1811, studied at Dartmouth, and had begun the study of law when at the age of thirty he was converted and decided to become a minister. He went to Andover Seminary, thought it deficient in earnestness and moved to Yale. There he made his great discovery—that Christ promised and demanded perfection here on earth. "Be ye therefore perfect, even as your Father which is in heaven is perfect," he read in Matthew v, 48. Clearly, then, current religious teachings were all wrong.

Noyes began to preach his doctrine right under the noses of his Congregationalist professors with their Calvinist beliefs. He was nearly expelled from the seminary. When his license to preach was revoked he said:

"I took away their license to sin and they go on sinning; they have taken away my license to preach but I shall go on preaching."

And he did. For fifteen years he traveled about the country preaching Perfectionism and convincing so many people that the orthodox clergy considered him a serious menace.

In 1839 with a group of relatives and neighbors he organized the Putney Bible Class at Putney, Vermont. By 1846 it had become the Putney Community—thirty or forty people living together like the members of the primitive church and practicing Complex Marriage which was Noyes' own invention. The citizens of Putney objected so strenuously to this novel arrangement that they broke up the community and drove Noyes out of town.

But Noyes was convinced that he was right. He believed that the Second Coming had occurred centuries ago, that sinners had then been divided from those who were saved, and that he was among the saved. It was therefore proper for him and his Perfectionists to follow the laws of heaven rather than of earth, and in heaven, as everyone knew, "they neither marry nor are given in marriage." Noyes believed that sexual love was a sacrament—that it should be integrated with the religious life, and that it should be shared by the whole community of believers. Private ownership of women was no more to be endured than private ownership of property in a community which would bring heaven to earth.

Moving his group in 1848 to a broad, fertile valley in western

New York, Noyes established the famous Oneida Community which was born, so to speak, out of wedlock, saved by a steel trap, and preserved in memory by the Community Plate which descendants of the community still make today.

The first years were hard. But everyone—men, women and children—labored to build the community. Gradually the colony grew in numbers and in wealth. By 1851 there were more than two hundred members. Providentially, one of these was an Oneida neighbor named Sewell Newhouse, who before joining the community had manufactured steel traps on a small scale in his blacksmith shop. When the community decided, in 1852, that it needed a profitable manufacturing business, Newhouse was persuaded to teach the community how to make traps. One of the community's agents took a trunkful to Chicago, where they sold immediately. By 1860 this trap had become the standard throughout the United States and Canada. Professional trappers would use nothing else. For seventy years all the traps used by the Hudson's Bay Company were made at Oneida. Noyes himself worked at a forge, and in the early days women and children all joined in the work whenever a large order came in. By 1864 they were making six kinds of traps, hiring forty outsiders to help, and realizing a handsome profit. Oneida traps went as far as Australia, Russia and Uruguay.

This commercial success supported a unique social system, the most remarkable aspect of which was its sexual relations. In a holy community, Noyes taught, there was no reason why sexual relations should be restrained any more than eating and drinking. Among Perfectionists, sex was not a matter for shame or for exclusiveness, but an expression of universal love. Any man in the community might cohabit with any woman if she wished to accept him. To avoid embarrassment, the invitation was given through a third party. The only thing insisted upon was that these relationships should not become fixed. "Special love" —showing a preference for one person above others—was the one sin which could not be tolerated. For it indicated a selfish, exclusive frame of mind. At Oneida, all were members of one family, and all—in theory, at least—were equally to be loved.

One other thing was insisted on too. Along with Complex Marriage went Male Continence—which meant that the male was to control himself so as to prevent any chance of conception. Young men were encouraged to pair with older women until they had become perfect in this art. For propagation—which Noyes regarded as a function quite separate from "amativeness" —twenty women and twenty-four men were selected. In addition, every man might if he wished be the father of one child. Long before the word eugenics was known, Noyes had carried out a eugenic experiment.

Sexual love was thus looked upon as the fullest expression of unselfish feeling, and not as an evil. It was the final intimacy which bound the whole group together in love and mutual regard. Noyes insisted that this unique social relationship, with the restraint it placed upon the male, was freer of licentiousness than were worldly marriages. There were no signs at Oneida of the passions and quarrels which would certainly have resulted if the system had been purely libidinous. For more than thirty years three hundred men and women lived happily under the arrangement. Pierrepont Noyes, one of the children born in the Community, testifies that "the opportunity for romantic friendships also played a part in rendering life more colorful than elsewhere. Even elderly people, whose physical passions had burned low, preserved the fine essence of earlier associations; child as I was, I sensed a spirit of high romance surrounding them, a vivid, youthful interest in life that looked from their eyes and spoke in their voices and manners."

The system of Complex Marriage was, as later events proved, a necessary part of the economic system. When it was abandoned because of pressure from outside, the community flew apart. Because so long as the children were regarded as belonging to the whole community, as long as the men and women shared their love among one another, no division of property was possible or necessary.

Living together as one family, eating together, worshiping

and playing together, the Oneida folk had no need of private property. All that they needed was supplied to them—even to the common wardrobe from which clothes for travel were drawn. They were industrious and they prospered. In 1860 they built the huge brick house which still stands. They proved to be good businessmen and women, full of inventiveness and good management. They made their own machinery for making traps and working silk. Women as well as men were allowed to follow their own bent and as at Brook Farm attained an equality which placed them far above their sisters in the world outside.

With all necessities provided for, there was no need to strive for individual wealth. Luxuries and vanities were no temptation because simplicity of dress was the rule and there were no Joneses to keep up with. Jobs were rotated as far as ability permitted, yet those who proved capable of only humble tasks were praised and valued as much as factory superintendents.

Living together like a family, the Perfectionists were able to govern themselves without government. Twenty-one standing committees and forty-eight departments carried on the affairs of the community, from manufacturing to hair-cutting, waterworks and photography. The children were well taught. There was entertainment of all kinds—music, dances, plays, chess, cards, picnics, pantomimes. Every evening the whole community gathered together for worship, discussion of community affairs and relaxation. Exclusiveness was frowned upon. Members were encouraged to "keep in the circulation." Comfortable sitting rooms were scattered through the big building to stimulate association. Bedrooms, though comfortable enough as sleeping quarters, were built small to discourage exclusiveness.

From the beginning, the New England custom of doing things in "bees" was followed. When strawberries were ripe the whole community including the children went off to pick them. When a carload of peaches arrived at the canning factory, everyone pitched in to prepare them. In the Oneida Community everyone worked and all kinds of work were considered equally honorable.

Most remarkable of all the voluntary acts in this voluntary association—as remarkable anyway as the voluntary restraint exercised by the males—was the institution of mutual criticism. This was Oneida's substitute for law, police, punishment, or force of any kind. It was the device which made Oneida a truly voluntary community.

The criticism was conducted by a committee which, in the presence of the subject, opened up to him his shortcomings and his accomplishments. Frankness and friendliness prevailed, but no one held back the truth, even if it hurt.

Charles Nordhoff, a writer who was allowed to be present at the criticism of a young man, reported that about fifteen people were present, including Noyes himself. Charles, the young man, sat in the middle of the group. He began by saying that he had been assailed by doubts and a weakening of faith, but that he had been trying to combat this evil tendency.

His first critic remarked that he had been hardened by too much success and had therefore come to think too well of himself. Others, concurring, gave him examples of his own conduct. A young woman said that he was haughty and supercilious. Another young woman said that he was guilty of "special love," calling certain people by pet names and showing his preference for them. So it went on, while the young man grew paler. Drops of sweat broke out on his forehead.

After half an hour, Noyes summed up by saying that though the young man had some serious faults, he was earnestly trying to improve himself. As an example of his earnestness, Noyes remarked that Charles was one of those chosen to become a father. "Under these circumstances, he has fallen under the too common temptation of selfish love, and a desire to wait upon and cultivate an exclusive intimacy with the woman who was to bear a child through him." Noyes told how the young man had come to him in this difficulty, and had decided to isolate himself from the woman and let another man take his place at her side, and had done so "with a most praiseworthy spirit of self-sacrifice."

As a result of the institution of criticism, life at Oneida was unusually free of backbiting and scandalmongering. Since every member of the community would sooner or later be subjected to criticism, those who spoke up at one were careful in what they said. If any spitefulness appeared, this was corrected by other members. The whole procedure was democratic.

Far in advance of their time, the people of Oneida used criticism as a means of curing psychosomatic disorders. "If you are sick," said the Oneida *Circular*, "seek for someone to tell you your faults . . . let them put their finger on the very sore that you would best like to keep hid. Depend upon it, there is the avenue through which disease gets access to you." At Oneida, many years in advance of Freud, remarkable cures of apparently chronic ailments were achieved through criticism—achieved more rapidly and effectively than is commonly the case through psychiatry, perhaps because they took place in a more favorable setting. At Oneida everyone took criticism. It was the normal thing to do. The person criticized felt himself to be a part of the community which did the criticizing. He was, in a sense, both critic and subject of his own criticism. He felt himself part of a community which cared for his well-being. Recent experiments in group therapy have returned in effect to what Oneida practiced a hundred years ago.

So for more than thirty years the three hundred people of Oneida lived together like one great family. They prospered, raised children, developed industries, and enjoyed a life the cultural level of which was far above that in the world around them. No compulsion held them together. They were a voluntary community, free to leave if they wished, though few did. They were secure in the knowledge that they would be cared for in old age—not by charity, but as members in a community to which they had contributed their labors. The children, after a good schooling at Oneida, could go on to college if their talents permitted. They could come back to take their place in the community.

The towns in the neighborhood of Oneida, after an initial

hostility and suspicion, came to think well of the Perfectionists. They never got into trouble, were never drunk or lawless, and always kept their word and paid their debts. So much could not be said of the non-Perfectionist communities. So in spite of their radical principles and their novel social practices, the Perfectionists were let alone for twenty-five years. They made no secret of their belief and practice—in fact they discussed them freely in the weekly paper which they issued (the recipient to pay whatever he felt able to contribute) with the hope of converting the world to their way.

Then in 1872 young Anthony Comstock, a fanatic whose name was to become a synonym for narrow-mindedness, organized the New York Society for the Suppression of Vice and in 1873 persuaded Congress to enact a bill which made all information on birth control lewd and obscene. The Oneidans could no longer print or write anything about their unique method.

Professor John W. Mears of near-by Hamilton College now decided that the Perfectionists were an offense and must conform or be destroyed. He wrote to newspapers, preached sermons, called for a holy crusade. At last he won the backing of several church bodies in central New York and called a conference which met at Syracuse in 1879. The conference strongly denounced the Perfectionists—which certainly came as no surprise—but failed to resolve that the community be exterminated as Mears demanded. The press ridiculed Mears, defended Oneida for its high reputation. Legal authorities showed no disposition to act.

But unknown to Mears, internal dissatisfaction had already begun in 1876 when Noyes tried to transfer his leadership to his eldest son who had little talent for leading, and when a trouble-making newcomer with a will to power had begun to agitate the community. Those loyal to Noyes realized that if a complaint were lodged against him with the District Attorney, and if the dissidents in the community should then give testimony against their leader, serious results might follow. In the summer of 1879, therefore, Noyes secretly left during the night and crossed into Canada. Then, after having defended his system against the world for thirty years, he wrote back to propose that Complex Marriage be abandoned—"not as renouncing belief in the principles and prospective finality of that institution, but in deference to public sentiment." In deference also, maybe, to the fact that he was now sixty-eight years old.

The proposal was accepted with only one dissenting vote, and on August 28, Complex Marriage came to an end. Thereafter many couples were married. No one had foreseen it, but orthodox marriage dealt the deathblow to the community. For now that separate families were formed, economic individualism appeared. As Pierrepont Noyes remarks, "Monogamy is the main support of economic individualism. For the sake of the family, millions endure the chaos and misery of our competitive regime." The community staggered on for a while, but in 1880 Oneida went over to the system of private property.

* * *

The Hopedale Community, founded by Adin Ballou near Milford, Massachusetts, began in 1841 without theological dogmas but on a base of Christian socialism. It was opposed to slavery. It stood for women's rights, non-resistance, the relief of human suffering. It guaranteed employment to its members, and the opportunity to each individual to raise himself to the highest point his abilities permitted. Fellowship, religion and the opportunity for cultured living were promised.

By 1854, 235 members were enjoying the benefits of a democratic society in which all had an equal voice. They practiced mutual criticism and, with the exception of the patent rights on their manufactures, held the means of production in common. But this one exception led to the death of the community. Ebenezer Draper, who owned the patents, and his brother George gradually got control of three-quarters of the joint stock. Nothing in the constitution prevented them from doing this. So after fifteen years, the community dissolved.

* * *

In 1874 Charles Nordhoff visited all the communities then operating in the United States, from the Shakers in New England to the German colony of Aurora in Oregon. He concluded that life as lived within the communities was invariably on a higher level than life lived in the neighborhood around them. He found them clean, well-ordered, relaxed, giving a decency and dignity to humble life which it too often lacked outside. The members did not have to toil as hard as their neighbors, and lived much better. They were honest, with a reputation for fair trading and for making goods of high quality. Convenience and comfort were conspicuous. Food was abundant and well cooked, health good. Nordhoff believed that they lived longer than the rest of the population as a result of regular habits, temperance, and being relieved of the care and worry which beset the rest of the world. He could not discover the lazy men who according to outsiders would be sure to hamper or destroy any plan of living which assured every member the needs of life. On the contrary he found that when they entered these communities, men enjoyed working together and did their best without urging. And of course the position of women in the communities was far above that on the outside.

Even while they were struggling to build their communities, says Nordhoff, "the Communists enjoyed a greater amount of comfort, and vastly greater security against want and demoralization, than were attained by their neighbors or the surrounding population, with better schools and opportunities of training for their children, and far less exposure for the women, and the aged and infirm."

Nordhoff called these societies "communist," as of course they were. But their form of communism was so totally different from what we mean by communism today, that it would be better if they could be designated by some other word. They lacked all the attributes which characterize modern communism—the authoritarian one-party control, the savage disregard of human life, the stamping out of individual thought and speech, the slave-state. These communities were voluntary. No one had to belong to them. They were mostly democratic rather than authoritarian, and they earnestly sought to place life on a higher level of culture, religion and brotherliness. Though sooner or later and for various reasons they came to an end, they lasted long enough—some for over a hundred years—to show that their system could work, and work well.

Longest-lived of any was the Amana Society which continued its communal form from 1842 until 1932, when it transformed itself into a joint-stock co-operative which continues successfully to this day. The founders of Amana were members of a religious sect who came from Germany to settle near Buffalo in 1842. There they bought five thousand acres of the old Seneca reservation. Within a few years over a thousand had come from Europe to make up the community. They transformed the land into a garden and set up a woolen factory for those accustomed to millwork rather than farming.

Though they had not practiced communal living in Europe and had no idea of doing so here, they soon found that they must pool their resources in order to clear the land and establish industry. By 1855 they had prospered so greatly that they needed more land and moved on to Iowa, where they established seven villages on an extensive plain. The members dined together in large groups, supplied their simple needs through stores at which each member had an annual credit allowed him, worked regularly at their allotted tasks though without haste or overexertion, and spent much of their time at religious meetings.

Religion was the core of Amana's life. It was based upon a belief in the divine inspiration of the community leader, and upon a congregational sharing of the service, either by reading or singing. The Amana folk had written and printed two huge collections of hymns from which they sang at some length and —according to a spectator—with no spectacular musical success. Women were regarded as inferior creatures, and Rule XVIII of the twenty-one "Rules for Daily Life" advised the brethren to "Fly from the society of womenkind as much as

possible, as a very highly dangerous magnet and magical fire."
Marriage was permitted but not greeted with joy. Amana wed-
dings were as somber as funerals.

All that is changed now, and Amana women have equal rights
with men. Good schools, free medical service and other marks
of progressiveness now characterize the communities, and the
church no longer controls everything.

* * *

All these communities enriched our history with experiments
in voluntary group activity which embraced every aspect of
life—which offered to their members a complete and integrated
existence, with religion an essential part. In new ways they
achieved that beloved community, that mothering warmth
which Bradford had dreamed of. They proved that men can
live happily as voluntary members of a society whose aims are
not the acquisition of wealth and power, but living creatively
—loving their work, loving each other, working, playing, thinking and worshiping together in brotherly affection. Without
despising comfort or culture, they overcame the temptation to
worship possessions for their own sake. They lived fuller,
better lives than they could have lived otherwise. They realized
the ideal of living not only for and in themselves but for and in
each other.

Best of all, perhaps, they proved that men have within themselves the power to conceive and to create social forms in which
all controls are voluntary and whose members can feel that
service to each other is perfect freedom. Nowhere else in the
world did voluntary community ever put forth so many flowers
of achievement. It is an achievement which gives faith and
strength to all our voluntary activity. Man, if he wishes, can
make a better world. That dual faith—in the power of human
capacities and the power of voluntarism—is the cornerstone of
the American point of view, and of the several movements we
shall look at next.

IX

Women, Temperance and Culture

In 1826 Josiah Holbrook (1788–1854), graduate of Yale and son of a well-to-do Connecticut farmer, became possessed by an idea. He sat down and wrote to the editor of the *American Journal of Education* about it.

"It seems to me that if associations for mutual instruction in the sciences and other branches of useful knowledge could be started in our villages . . . they would increase with great rapidity, and do more for the diffusion of general knowledge, and for raising the moral and intellectual taste of our countrymen, than any other expedient which can possibly be devised."

Then, instead of resting in the righteous satisfaction of having written to the editor, Josiah Holbrook went out and followed his own advice. At Millbury, a village near Worcester, Massachusetts, he gathered a group together and explained his plan. In November the "Millbury Branch, Number 1, of the American Lyceum" was formed. The name, of course, came from the place in Athens where Aristotle had taught.

Holbrook had visions of a nation in which every town, every village would have its lyceum. County and state lyceums would draw the separate associations together, and a national lyceum would crown the whole structure.

Josiah Holbrook was not only a letter writer and a visionary. He was also an organizer. He therefore threw himself into establishing the program he had put before the nation.

Twelve or fifteen towns around Millbury soon had their

lyceums. Holbrook united them in the Worcester County Lyceum. Next he dipped down into Connecticut and with help from the Reverend J. S. May encouraged a number of towns there to form associations and to unite themselves in the Windham County Lyceum. Not only a visionary, a letter writer and an organizer, Holbrook was also a lecturer. He now went around to the lyceums to help fill the need for speakers, talking on geology and natural history. Everywhere he went he explained the purposes of the movement he had started, handing out circulars and still writing letters to editors. He encouraged the local lyceums to make their own collections of geological specimens, and many a New England attic still contains a box full of dusty rocks whose labels have fallen off or grown illegible. He set up a factory to turn out "philosophical apparatus"— that is, equipment for scientific experiments. He published a sample plan of organization and articles of association which towns could use in forming their own lyceums.

Article 2 committed the members to "procure a cabinet, consisting of books, apparatus for illustrating the sciences, and a collection of minerals." Regular meetings were to be held for discussion, scientific demonstrations, lectures. The usual membership fee was two dollars a year.

By 1828, according to the *Boston Advertiser,* more than fifty societies had been formed. Daniel Webster chaired the meeting held in Boston to consider forming the national body. By the following year branches had been formed in nearly every state in the union. Massachusetts alone now had seventy-eight, with three county lyceums. State conventions were being held. Still the movement grew—from nine hundred town lyceums in 1831 to three thousand in 1835. Massachusetts alone had 137 in 1839, with 32,698 members. Salem with 1,200 boasted the largest membership. Nine or ten of the Massachusetts lyceums had built their own halls.

Sir Charles Lyell and Louis Agassiz the zoologist were amazed, when they reached Boston in the forties, to discover how universal was the interest in education. Philip Hone, the

American diarist, wrote that the New York theaters were deserted for the lyceums meeting nightly in the Tabernacle and in Clinton Hall. "It is a matter of wonderment," he wrote, "to witness the youthful workman, the over-tired artisan, the worn-out factory girl . . . rushing . . . after the toil of the day is over, into the hot atmosphere of the crowded lecture room."

What they got at the lyceums was no frivolous entertainment or watered down scholarship. The finest scholars and thinkers of the age came to the lyceum platforms. Emerson's reputation with the public came far more from his appearances at lyceums throughout the country than from his writings. "My pulpit is the lyceum platform," he said, and went on to praise the lack of stiff conventions prescribing any particular style or method. "Now here everything is admissible," he added, "and philosophy, ethics, divinity, criticisms, poetry, humor, fun, mimicry, anecdotes, jokes, ventriloquism are the breadth and versatility of the most liberal conversation."

Thoreau found the lyceums his only dependable source of income. Wendell Phillips, it was said, gave his lecture on "The Lost Arts" to two thousand lyceum audiences. Henry Ward Beecher, William Lloyd Garrison, Charles Sumner and Robert G. Ingersoll toured the lyceum circuit. So did Oliver Wendell Holmes, Susan B. Anthony, Julia Ward Howe, Josh Billings, Bill Nye, James Whitcomb Riley and Mark Twain.

The lyceums usually met once a week through the winter. Their program was not restricted to hearing distinguished lecturers. As voluntary associations, the lyceums relied upon their own resources. Members might bring in samples of minerals or plants they had been collecting, and would then help each other to classify and arrange them. They contributed books to the library, borrowed from it, or discussed what they had read.

"From the manner in which they associate," wrote a contemporary, "each may become, by turns, a learner and a teacher." Discussion and informal debate were frequent.

Holbrook's dream of a national lyceum was realized in 1831 when delegates from three state and several county lyceums in other states came together in New York on May 4. Annual meetings continued to be held through 1839. But they were not particularly well attended. The strength of the lyceum was in the small local group where the members could actively take part.

Though the lyceums developed out of the vision and practical good sense of one man, it was the membership which made them. Holbrook sensed a need which was universal. It does not matter much that this thirst for knowledge came partly—perhaps largely—from a conviction that it provided the stairway to wealth and advancement. But it does matter greatly that the need was expressed and answered through voluntary association.

One of the things Holbrook hoped to accomplish through the lyceums was to raise the wretched standards of the common schools. He realized that if the taxpayers, the citizens got excited about education for themselves, they would soon take an interest in what their children were learning at school. And he was certain that the lyceums would in effect provide teacher training, since the town schoolmaster would be certain to attend the lyceum in his community.

Holbrook was right about this too. Teaching, which had often been the resort of those who could do nothing else, began to be respected as a profession. Teachers began to look for better methods. While the lyceum was increasing the knowledge of the teachers who attended, it also encouraged them to organize.

The twelve counties of Vermont and two counties in New Hampshire held conventions on education in 1831 which were attended by the indefatigable Holbrook. Teachers were encouraged to meet weekly, and in semiannual county conventions, to improve their profession. Meanwhile lyceum members were active in improving their schools. From the start, Holbrook had wanted two things of the lyceums. He wanted them to raise individual standards of knowledge, and he wanted them to raise school standards. The first appealed to self-interest, the second to community pride and the healthy urge to work together for some useful end. This is a combination any association needs if it is to succeed.

From their support of teachers and schools the lyceums went on to champion the novel idea of state control and supervision. It was the interest in education fostered by the lyceums which led directly to legislation in this field. As early as 1828 the lyceums were advocating county and state boards of education, and to some extent the state lyceums acted like boards of education. Massachusetts, where the lyceums were most active, was in 1837 the first to have a state board. Edward Everett, a vice president of the national lyceum from the beginning, was Governor when the board was created. It was Everett who, under the prompting of Josiah Holbrook and with the help of Daniel Webster and some other leading citizens of Boston, had founded the Boston Society for the Diffusion of Useful Knowledge in 1828. This was the lyceum idea adapted to Boston's size and intellectual pretensions. But one such association was not enough for Boston. There soon followed the Natural History Society, the Mercantile Library Association, the Mechanics' Apprentices' Association. Impressed with the value of the movement Holbrook had started, John Lowell established the public lectures which bear his name. Boys invited their girls to go to the lectures, walking home afterwards to end the evening with an oyster supper.

The lyceum movement pioneered many of the institutions and services we now take for granted. "The United States Weather Bureau, library extension, the museum of natural history, the scientific laboratory, free textbooks, the village improvement society—all are there foreshadowed." The National Education Association, government-backed geological and mineralogical surveys, the writing of town histories and making of maps—all trace back to the lyceums.

Because they were voluntary associations, the lyceums performed in the new states of the West a function Holbrook had not foreseen, but which he was quick to note when he visited there.

"Coming, as do the inhabitants in all the new States, from different sections of the country, they bring their habits, notions, and prejudices with them. . . . Yet in every instance where the lyceum has been proposed, every party, so far as I know, has united in it without the least jealousy." And Holbrook concluded that if people with such varying backgrounds could find any common ground, they would soon become assimilated. By providing a way for people to get together, therefore, the lyceum was filling a vital need.

As valuable as anything the lyceum movement did was to show the need for services important to society, filling the need until government could take over, and creating the public opinion which would lead to government action. If the lyceum had done nothing except to bring about state boards of education in this way, it would have fulfilled its function.

No more vigorous system of adult education has ever existed than that of the lyceum. It was vigorous because it met a deeply felt need, and because the people who felt the need *were* the lyceum. Once again the instrument of voluntary association was responsible for a major advance in American life.

To supply the lyceums with lecturers, James Redpath established the Boston Lyceum Bureau about 1868, and thereafter he furnished many of the outstanding speakers and performers to local organizations or to the Lyceum Committees which took the place of the older lyceums. In 1913 about twelve thousand towns were supplied in this way.

The lyceums never entirely died, for in the Chautauqua idea they were reborn.

They had another curious rebirth too.

One of Josiah Holbrook's unrealized plans was to build at Berea, near Cleveland, a Lyceum Village which would be the headquarters of the whole movement. Holbrook persuaded another Yankee, John Baldwin, to put up most of the money. When the plan failed, Baldwin was left with the mortgages. Seeing no way out, he opened his problem in prayer, promising that if the Lord would get him out of this difficulty he would devote any fortune he made to whatever cause God should direct. The Lord's answer was to send Baldwin to a huge ledge of grind-

stone rock right on his own farm. Baldwin made a fortune on it.
He also kept his promise, pouring his wealth into schools and
colleges.

As for Josiah Holbrook, his end was unfortunate but appropriate. He was drowned at the age of sixty-six while collecting mineral specimens near Lynchburg, Virginia.

*   *   *

Chautauqua, begun as a summer institute for Sunday School
teachers, filled a void left by the decline of the camp meeting
and ended by becoming an instrument of "culture" for the
masses.

The Reverend John Heyl Vincent had no such end in view
when in 1874 he opened the first of these "assemblies" on a
former camp meeting ground at beautiful Lake Chautauqua in
western New York. He wanted to raise the standards of Sunday
School teaching, and in that he succeeded. But the "assembly"
idea proved to have a wider appeal than he had intended. Singing and innocent entertainment had been a part of the first
assembly. In the following years lectures, music and readings
were added to furnish "pure, wholesome entertainment" for
the Sunday School teachers who had come to improve their
knowledge of the Bible.

To bring the Bible to life, Vincent built a scaled model of
Palestine, complete with its lakes and mountains. Students
could walk around it, visualizing the places where Jesus and
the disciples had walked.

From such educative devices as this the Chautauqua program
rapidly broadened to include lectures in literature, the arts and
sciences. By 1879 a regular group of schools with graded courses
of study was established, with an eight-week session which grew
until two hundred courses were being offered—all this in addition to hundreds of lectures, readings and musical events.

Combining the spirit of the revival meeting with that of the
county fair, Chautauqua naturalized culture in America. It also
made summer education a part of the American landscape, for

it is the mother of all the summer schools, summer theaters, summer camps for painting and dancing and music which erupt from Maine to California and flourish with the same burst of energy which our climate bestows on Indian corn.

Chautauqua combined religion with entertainment. It combined culture with a lakeside holiday. The whole family came along. There was swimming and boating and sports. Each year more activities were added, more land was bought up and more buildings were built, until thousands came to crowd the auditorium, the amphitheater, the lecture rooms. Though the secular program came to outweigh the religious, a strong spiritual tone continued to control and direct the whole.

Here was the kind of "package deal" dear to the American heart—uplift, culture, the out-of-doors, physical exercise, gregariousness, high spirits, group activity, a family outing, the practical wedded to the ideal, a sense of doing something worth while and of having a good time. Chautauqua both expressed and suited the American character.

Meanwhile, as the fame of Chautauqua spread, similar institutions sprang up throughout the country—at Bay View, Michigan, at De Funiak Springs, Florida, at Monterey, California, at Sandusky, Ohio, and Winona Lake, Indiana. Something about combining culture with fresh air made an irresistible appeal.

In 1904 the idea was taken up by traveling companies. Tent Chautauquas popped up like mushrooms all over America. Though they had no connection whatever with the original Chautauqua, they used the name. Those who were growing up in the twenties will remember the tent that arose overnight on an empty lot or ball field. We were taken there to be filled with culture, though all we may remember now is the tent itself, and some of the best citizens wearing big badges like the ones they awarded to prize cattle at the county fair. These were the members of the local committee who had agreed to serve as sponsors and sellers of season tickets. The "season" was five or six days, which was about all the culture most towns were capable of absorbing.

At the height, ten thousand Chautauquas gathered in as many as forty million Americans during a single season.

Though attendance at Chautauqua was a matter of choice, those who came had little to say about the program. They could take it or leave it. But they did not make it. So Chautauqua hardly qualifies as a voluntary association. But out of Chautauqua grew another program of group activity—the Chautauqua Literary and Scientific Circle.

This was another brainchild of the indefatigable Vincent who in 1878 announced a course of reading which would bring to those who like himself had missed a college education all the usual college subjects except mathematics and the abstruse sciences.

Vincent, who had a gift for stagecraft and spectacle, had the stage dressed with a telescope, a microscope, a globe, and a table piled with books and scientific apparatus when he announced the new program to the Chautauqua audience on the afternoon of August tenth.

Vincent asked all those who wanted to join the new group to write their names and addresses on slips of paper. He had forgotten to provide paper, or to draw up any description of the course, its regulations and fees. Seven hundred people managed to find scraps of paper to write on, and before the session had ended, most of the regular Chautauquans had signed up.

One thing Vincent had made definite: the first reading would be Green's *Short History of the English People*. There was a rush to the bookstore, where the half dozen copies in stock were seized. An order for fifty more was telegraphed to Harper Brothers in New York. Telegrams soon had to be dispatched for another fifty, then for a hundred and then for several hundred. Puzzled, Harpers asked why an unknown place in the wilderness of western New York was trying to corner the supply of Green's *History*.

When the vacationers went home from Chautauqua and spread word about the Circle among their friends, eight thousand four hundred members signed up. By 1891 there were over a hundred thousand. In addition to the four-year course leading to a diploma, special courses—nearly a hundred—ultimately had to be worked out to meet the demand.

Membership in the Circle sometimes had unexpected results. A man and wife who had found it impossible to continue living together set up separate quarters. Once every two weeks the husband called to see his children, and on one of these occasions he mentioned that he had joined the C.L.S.C. and started on the readings. His wife asked what the letters meant. When he explained the plan, she also joined the Circle.

The next time he called, he stayed to discuss the books they had both been reading. Soon he was coming weekly, and then nightly. The common interest in the books, the excitement of sharing ideas together, healed the breach.

Members of the Circle were spread around the world. One woman, the wife of an army officer, wrote that she was stationed among the Indians, a hundred and twenty-five miles away from any other non-Indian woman. When she got her bundle of books, she wept for joy. Reading them, she felt, brought her into fellowship with the thousands who were reading the same books and thinking the same thoughts.

One young woman sailed for South Africa shortly after signing up. There she taught in a girls' boarding school. When June came around, she appeared at school one day in her best dress.

"Is this your birthday?" the girls asked.

"No," she answered. "It's Commencement Day at Chautauqua in America, and everybody dresses up on that day."

Like these two women, about half of the Circle members read by themselves. But the other half organized themselves into local Circles—sometimes all the women in a community who were interested, sometimes the members of a church. They came together to discuss what they had read, to read reports. Often they took turns in the chair. After they had completed the prescribed course, members of the Circles were unwilling to relapse into unrelieved domesticity. They took up civics or politics or literature. In one way or another, they kept going.

*　*　*

Of course the women's organizations have a still deeper root —the movement for women's rights which began early in the nineteenth century.

As a child of ten, Elizabeth Cady had learned what it meant to be a woman. She was standing in the room that served as her father's law office in Johnstown, New York, one day when he came in with Flora Campbell. It was Flora who brought the eggs and chickens and other farm products to the Cady household. But this time Flora had come with a problem so burdensome that tears ran down her cheeks when she explained to Judge Cady that her husband without her consent had mortgaged the farm her father had left her. Now his creditors were taking it over. She wanted his help.

Judge Cady took one of the many books from his shelves. He read her the law. "The law plainly states that on marriage a woman's property becomes her husband's," he explained. Mrs. Campbell would get no help from the law.

As she left the office, Elizabeth ran after her. It was not the first time she had seen a woman leave her father's office in despair after he had quoted the law to her. Each time he had taken down a book, she had noted the page and put the book back upside down on the shelf.

"Don't cry another tear," she said to Flora. "I have all those wicked laws marked and I will cut every one out of the books tonight."

Agitated as she was, Mrs. Campbell managed to let Judge Cady know of his daughter's plan. Without letting her know that he had learned it, he told her how laws were made and how many law books there were in the world.

"When you are grown up," he told her, "you must go to Albany and talk to the Legislature; tell them all you have seen in this office . . . and if you can persuade them to pass new laws, the old ones will be a dead letter."

In 1825, when Elizabeth Cady was ten years old, the status of women was not a great deal better than it had been in medieval days when the lord of the manor had the right by law to take to his bed every girl who was married in his domain. A married woman was under the absolute control of her husband. Everything she had or might earn was his. He could pick her companions for her, separate her from her relatives, choose her religion. For a woman to speak in public was regarded as a disgrace. Oberlin was the only college in the United States which admitted women. Not one doctor, lawyer or ordained minister was a woman. Very few jobs were open to a woman, and if she did get into a field where men were employed, her pay was but a fraction of what the man received. As if to maintain the helplessness which was supposed to be feminine, women were encumbered with heavy and voluminous skirts which dragged in the mud or made their household tasks burdensome. They were forced to lace themselves into corsets which destroyed their natural shapes and made it impossible to draw a full breath.

Twenty-three years after she had learned about the inequality of women, Elizabeth Cady, now Mrs. Stanton, was a happily married mother of three boys living in Seneca Falls, New York. Happily married, yet not altogether happy. The inequality of women was still on her mind. She had seen it again in 1840 when, just after her marriage to Henry Stanton, she had gone to London with him to attend the World Anti-Slavery Convention to which he was a delegate. There the women delegates from America were denied their places at the convention. Slavery, it appeared, was bad for Negroes, but quite all right for women.

In London she met Lucretia Mott, the sturdy Quaker advocate of emancipation. Lucretia was one of the delegates denied her seat. The two women struck up a friendship which was renewed when Lucretia made a visit to Waterloo, near Seneca Falls, in 1848. Here Elizabeth Stanton visited her and here she met three young mothers, Quakers, who like herself were interested in the place of women.

Why not hold a convention, Elizabeth asked—a convention on women's rights? Lucretia Mott and the three younger women heartily approved the idea. Together they drafted a call for a convention to be held a week later in Seneca Falls and then sent it off to the *Seneca County Courier*.

The convention was to last two days, July 19 and 20. The first day was to be for women only, but men were invited to attend the next day's session, when Lucretia Mott was to speak.

Meanwhile Elizabeth Stanton and her friends started to prepare a declaration of principles and a set of resolutions. Reading the Declaration of Independence for inspiration, Elizabeth hit upon the happy idea of rephrasing it to dramatize the bondage in which women were held. Eighteen legal grievances were easily found to match the eighteen in the original Declaration.

Carriage loads of men and women drove up to the Wesleyan chapel on the morning of July 19. The interest was so great that the original plan of admitting only women had to be abandoned. On the second day the declaration was passed by a unanimous vote. Then the resolutions were taken up one by one. Finally Elizabeth Stanton rose to resolve that women must "secure to themselves their sacred right to the elective franchise."

The resolution seemed so radical that the debate was long and sometimes heated. Elizabeth Stanton's friends had advised against it. Even her husband had left town and boycotted the meetings because of her insistence on this point. Finally the resolution passed by a small margin—the first formal demand in the United States for woman suffrage.

Newspapers picked up the story and either ridiculed or viewed with alarm. Some of those who had signed the declaration asked to have their names removed. But those who believed in the movement went on with it. Another convention was held at Rochester. The declaration and the resolutions were again proposed and passed. It was more than a movement that Elizabeth Stanton and her four Quaker friends had started around that mahogany table in the home of Mary McClintock at Waterloo—it was a revolution.

❋   ❋   ❋

When Susan B. Anthony returned to her home in Rochester from teaching at Canajoharie, she found her Quaker family full of talk about the convention. Her mother, father and sister had all signed the declaration and resolutions while her cousin had served as secretary of the convention. They all talked so much about the beautiful and accomplished Mrs. Stanton that Susan wanted to meet her. The opportunity did not come until 1851 when she went to Seneca Falls in May to visit Amelia Bloomer —the lady who did *not* invent bloomers though a quirk of fate gave her the credit for them. When Amelia Bloomer introduced her to Elizabeth Stanton, they immediately felt attracted to each other. From that time on, they were drawn closely together in the interlinked movements for temperance, emancipation and rights for women.

When Susan was invited to a meeting of the Sons of Temperance in Rochester the following year, she rose to speak but was instructed by the chairman that "the sisters were not invited there to speak but to listen and learn." This was all that was needed to arouse Susan B. Anthony. She made arrangements for the first Woman's State Temperance Convention, to be held in her home town of Rochester. She persuaded Elizabeth Stanton to preside. When the convention voted to establish the Woman's State Temperance Society, Elizabeth Stanton was elected president and Susan one of the secretaries.

From then on Susan B. Anthony (whose parents came from the same Quaker meeting in Adams, Massachusetts, from which the Farmington settlers had gone out) spent her life organizing conventions, meetings, societies, lectures. Where Elizabeth Stanton —five years her senior—charmed audiences with her vitality and dignity, Susan did the spade work which brought out the audiences. At the state convention held in Albany in 1854 Mrs. Stanton gave the speech which she delivered a few days later to the legislature, thus fulfilling the mission that had rested on her since childhood.

"The wife who inherits no property," she told them, "holds about the same legal position that does the slave on the Southern plantation. . . . She can get no redress for wrongs in her own name in any court of justice." She went on to list the many abuses a woman had to submit to by law. "We are moral, virtuous, intelligent," she said, "yet by your laws we are classed with idiots, lunatics and Negroes."

The legislators praised her. But they did nothing to change the situation.

Then came the Civil War. There was little time for conventions now, but women were getting a chance to show that they could be useful in a crisis. Susan B. Anthony and Elizabeth Stanton organized the Women's Loyal League to help win the war and free the Negroes. But when the war was over, they went back to the main task—woman's suffrage.

The first Woman Suffrage Convention to be held in Washington opened on January 19, 1869. It was a large convention, with twenty states represented. The Fifteenth Amendment, for the enfranchisement of the Negro, had already passed Congress and was about to be submitted to the states. Mrs. Stanton pleaded with the convention to support a Sixteenth Amendment to enfranchise women. Together with Susan Anthony she persuaded George W. Julian of Indiana to introduce it in the House. Then Susan and Elizabeth together toured the western states to push the amendment. Everywhere they went they were well received, and everywhere new suffrage organizations sprang up to carry on the campaign.

But when the Equal Rights Association met in May at Steinway Hall in New York it refused to follow these ladies in their belief that all women must be enfranchised along with Negro men. So Elizabeth and Susan organized a meeting and formed the National Woman Suffrage Association, starting off with a hundred women from eighteen states who had come to the Equal Rights convention. Those who believed that the vote for women should be set aside until the Fifteenth Amendment had been ratified promptly assembled at Cleveland and formed a rival organization—the American Woman Suffrage Association. Susan B. Anthony, as a leader of the other group, was not invited. But she went anyway. Suffrage was her concern, no matter who called the meeting. Elizabeth Stanton was on an extended lecture tour for the New York Lyceum Bureau in order to put her children through college, but she was proud of her friend's pluck—though certainly not surprised.

Susan was recognized in the audience. Judge Bradwell of Chicago moved that she be invited to the platform. Thomas Wentworth Higginson, who was presiding, tried to turn the suggestion aside, but Bradwell persisted and Susan took her seat to a solid round of applause. None the less, the suffrage movement was split down the middle. The National Association under Elizabeth Stanton and Susan Anthony was for militant methods and was willing to discuss any subject relating to woman's emancipation, no matter how controversial. The American Association took a more conservative position. It avoided controversial subjects like birth control, sensible clothing and divorce, concentrating on the vote alone, and that mostly at the state level. Each group did useful work, but for twenty years they worked apart.

Finally in 1887 the American Association suggested that Lucy Stone and Susan Anthony look into the possibility of reuniting the two groups. Union was finally brought about in 1890, and Mrs. Stanton became president of the National American Woman Suffrage Association.

It was to take another thirty years before the country would finally give the vote to women. But the Association kept pushing. Every Congress was urged to adopt the amendment, though when it finally got around to it, it had become the nineteenth instead of the sixteenth.

By the time Elizabeth Cady Stanton died in 1902 the revolution for which she had fought was not complete, but it had begun. Women could get a college education, enter the professions, approach economic independence. No longer were they accused of trying to destroy the foundations of society, of "French infidelity and communism," of setting divine law at defiance and establishing legalized adultery. All these things and more had been said of Elizabeth Stanton and Susan Anthony. Nor had the battle stopped with words. They had been hissed, whistled at, jeered, mobbed, pelted with rotten eggs, threatened with knives and pistols. Stubbornly they had kept on.

"Lifting woman into her proper place," Elizabeth Stanton had said, "is the mightiest revolution the world has yet known."

The mantle passed from her to Susan Anthony, and from her to Carrie Chapman Catt who in 1900 became president of the Association. When victory was finally in sight in 1919, Mrs. Catt proposed a League of Women Voters to take the place of the old Association. The league would have three main purposes— educating new voters, supporting needed legislation and arousing all citizens to take part in the governing process.

Optimistically, the League assumed that practically all the women in the country would join the Association in order to learn their duties as voters. Optimistically, it thought that its work would be done in five years so that it could disband.

But twenty million women did not run eagerly to the polls, nor did they join the League by thousands. So the League had to find ways of getting to them. This it did by information booths for voters, meetings at which political candidates told where they stood on leading issues. Small discussion groups were sponsored. Whenever an important public issue arose, the League sought for ways to dramatize it, to get the facts on it, and to get the facts to its members and to the public.

From the beginning the League has relied on its members to choose the things they want to do. Six months before every biennial convention the local Leagues begin to discuss the issues they want to put in the national program. These recommendations go to headquarters where they are organized into a proposed program. This goes out to the leagues for a second discussion, and the program is finally settled by a vote of representatives at the convention.

One of the most vigorous and remarkable voluntary associations on the national scene, the League is non-partisan. It stands for full recognition of the constitutional rights of all citizens and the removal of legal discriminations against women and minority groups, equal opportunity in education, efficiency in government, conservation of natural resources, co-operation of government with farm, labor and industry in maintaining a sound economy, and a co-operative approach to international problems. It uses every method it knows to make people look at facts and be guided by them rather than by the visceral response so often cultivated by the rabble-rousing type of political figure.

There is no parallel organization for men, which raises the interesting question why women appear to have taken their duties as voters more seriously and more sensibly. It is no answer to say that men are active in the political parties, for women are there now too. The League encourages its members to take an active part in party politics as individuals. It hopes to make them better able to take part through its program of education.

As its president, Mrs. John G. Lee, has pointed out, our system of voluntary association involves women in many services which in other countries would be performed by government. "Invariably foreigners who visit the United States and are interested in government," she says, "ask why there aren't more women in public office. . . . Our unique system of voluntary association takes out of the hands of government many enterprises of a public character. For example, hospitals, churches, charitable institutions, independent schools and colleges . . . our political parties, labor unions and most of our major reforms, political and social and moral, have been instituted by voluntary associations . . . I used to think we greatly overdid this sort of thing in the United States—that all our communities were badly overorganized. I see it differently now and I believe this multitude of voluntary associations constitutes a tremendously important safeguard in American life. . . . They do, however, in a very real sense keep out of politics many worthy people. . . . Volunteer work for the benefit of our communities is an accepted part of the American pattern. But it is far more than that. It is really the basis of our society. It has prevented the necessity of turning to government to do that multitude of things we want to have done. We choose rather to do them ourselves voluntarily, even competitively."

The League itself is one of those associations, and one of the most useful.

*   *   *

If the General Federation of Women's Clubs had a patron saint, he would have to be Charles Dickens. For the great novelist was in a way responsible for the mountains of dainty sandwiches, the Alpine heaps of cookies and cupcakes which sustain the many millions of members who belong to the women's clubs throughout the country.

In 1868, the year before the two Woman Suffrage Associations were formed, Dickens was making his last reading tour in America. When he reached New York, the Press Club had a dinner in his honor—a Lucullan banquet of three dozen elaborate dishes. Dickens was so exhausted from his reading tour and so wasted with illness that he almost failed to get there. There were some others who did fail to get there—the women of the New York press who had been refused admittance. Responding to this slight in the characteristic American way, they formed a group of their own which they called Sorosis. Its initial interest in women's grievances led it to investigate the conditions under which women worked and then the causes of infant mortality. It petitioned to have women admitted to universities.

Finally, in the same year (1890) when the two suffrage associations united, Sorosis called a convention in New York. Sixty-one clubs, answering the call, formed the General Federation of Women's Clubs. There are now fifteen thousand clubs and eleven million women in the Federation, which seems to prove that if hell hath no fury like a woman scorned, voluntary association is the best way of harnessing her energy.

As many as 80 per cent of the public libraries in the country were first established and supported by these clubs, and through the years women's groups took the lead in demanding juvenile courts, prison reform, conservation of resources, public health measures, adult education, and other cultural and civic advances.

Often the clubs had their roots in the temperance crusade. Americans seem to have made more effort than any people in the world to stay sober. The history of temperance societies goes back at least as far as 1808 when a society was formed in upstate New York. Backsliding was apparently a frequent occurrence, since it became the custom, whenever a drunk staggered down the street, to remark: "There goes another member of the temperance society." But that was before the women took charge.

Within twenty years there were over a thousand local societies. In 1852 Susan Anthony organized the first women's group on a statewide basis. In 1873 a group of women in Hillsboro, Ohio, started a crusade that really got results. Their strategy was to go right to the saloons and pray them out of business.

In Washington, Ohio, about forty women and a few men gathered in church and began to pray. Then the men continued praying and the church bell kept tolling while the women marched out into the streets. They visited the eleven saloons and three drugstores where liquor was sold. They talked to the proprietors. They stood praying in the street outside. The men who went into the saloons looked mighty sheepish. Before long they drifted away. One saloon keeper poured his whole stock into the gutter while bells rang, women prayed and men shouted. The crusade swept to twenty-three states in fifty days. In 1874 the Women's Christian Temperance Union was formed. In its first year of activity it got twenty thousand men to quit drinking —or to say they would. In ten years—thanks largely to the energy of Frances Willard—it had circled the globe. (Back in Washington, Ohio there were more saloons than ever before by 1884.)

Temperance, emancipation and rights for women were logically and inextricably mingled. Much of the evil women suffered came from drunken husbands, while the slavery from which the Negro suffered had its counterpart in the subjection of women. Sometimes the same leaders were active in all three movements. Sometimes interests clashed. Associations were formed to tackle one or all of the evils. But in the very process of trying to free themselves, women found that their strength was in association, in working voluntarily together. And finding this, they found that their subjection grew less. For if they could associate, if they could unite their strengths, they were no longer weak.

Their emancipation was a long time coming. But it came—thanks to the power of voluntary association.

X

Knights of Labor—and Some Ladies

In 1877 the country was deep in the longest depression in its history. The panic had begun in 1873 with Jay Cooke's failure. In the winter of that year the unemployed had tried to demonstrate in New York and had been ruthlessly routed by the police. The wages of those who still managed to hold jobs were cut. Pinkerton men were active in Pennsylvania, helping railroad officials to break up the unions.

On July 19 the Pennsylvania Railroad, then highly unpopular with the public, followed up its wage reductions by doubling the length of its freight trains. Trouble flared immediately at Pittsburgh. The railroad men struck, trains were held up and mobs gathered in the streets. Local regiments of the National Guard were called out, but their sympathies lay with the strikers, so six hundred troops were sent in from Philadelphia. The day they arrived, July 21, they killed twenty-six people. Then they took refuge in the roundhouse and machine shops. By this time the citizens of Pittsburgh were in open revolt against the troops. They set fire to the shops and cars and laid siege to the roundhouse. The troops were disbanded and left to get out of town as best they could.

For a whole day the city was torn with looting and rioting. When it was over, five million dollars' worth of property had been destroyed. The whole community had joined in the revolt against the railroad.

Riots burst out in other cities, all the way to California. For the first time a revolution of working people seemed possible in the United States. The rioting had exposed a deep cancer of despair and discontent. At the same time it had demonstrated their terrible power.

Fear led the courts to clamp down all the harder. And the wage earner, grown desperate, began to look for a way to save himself. In the bitterness of his disappointment, he was tempted to take up the European theory of class warfare. There were plenty of immigrants from Europe on hand to lead American labor into socialism and Marxism. And they had plenty of material to work on. The press was largely subservient to the employers, the corporations. Workingmen who had the bravery to demand considerate treatment or who joined unions in order to get it were fired. Labor organizations were attacked from the pulpit. Yet men who suffered hideous deaths in the mines and steel mills had to leave their families destitute while the wealth piled up by their labor went to build fantastic fortunes.

In spite of all this, the American labor movement did not go Marxist. And one important reason why it did not was the deeply engrained habit of voluntarism—of organizing not to create a revolution or a government which labor would control, but to get directly from the employer (rather than through government intervention or regulation) a fair share of the product labor had created.

The labor movement in 1877 was far from new. The Constitution had hardly been drawn up when craft unions had come into existence. They were local affairs, for markets at that time were mostly local. But by the 1820s all the crafts in cities like New York and Philadelphia were setting up trades-councils, similar to the city centrals of a later time. And by the sixties there were also at least thirty-two national unions which made some attempt to unite all the workers of a single craft.

Efforts logically followed to draw the various trades together into one big workingman's organization. But because such organizations were built from the top down, they did not amount to much.

The men who had gone into revolt at Pittsburgh and else-where were the victims of a changing economy. Industrialism had left them at the mercy of the employer. The old way of life, hard but self-sustaining and based upon the soil, had disappeared for many millions of people who had found no other form of security to supplant it. They were scared. They were desperate. Then suddenly, when their discontent might easily have left them open to alien ideologies, they discovered a home-grown cure.

In 1869 a man named Uriah Stephens was chiefly responsible for turning a dying local of garment cutters into a secret society which he called the Noble and Holy Order of the Knights of Labor. Stephens, born in 1821 of Quaker ancestry, had studied at a Baptist seminary but had been forced by lack of funds to leave it and learn a trade. After years of travel mixed with political and union activity, he envisioned an organization which would lift all those who toiled out of their poverty and despair. A Mason, an Odd Fellow and a Knight of Pythias, he introduced Masonic elements from these orders into the ritual of the new organization. Early in 1870 Stephens was named Master Workman of the fraternity.

At first even the name of the society was kept secret. The secrecy was so deep as to inhibit growth, so gradually it was relaxed and the body grew larger. But the Knights grew very slowly. At first the local—or "Assembly," as the Knights called it—was composed of members from one trade. Then "sojourn-ers" were admitted—members of other trades who would later form assemblies of their own co-workers. Much later mixed assemblies were formed. In their district assemblies, however, the Knights brought together men of various trades. Their method of organization therefore had a double appeal—it allowed the various trades to carry on their own affairs, but united them in a common front with men of all trades. Skilled and unskilled were welcome, and in the early years anyone who sympathized with labor—just so long as he was not a professional gambler, a liquor seller, or a lawyer.

Members took the following oath:

"I do truly and solemnly promise that I will to the best of my ability, defend the life, interest, reputation and family of all true members of this Order, help and assist all employed and unemployed, unfortunate or distressed Brothers to procure employment, secure just remuneration, relieve their distress and counsel others to aid them, so that they and theirs may receive and enjoy the just fruits of their labor and exercise of their art."

In 1877, the year of riots, Uriah Stephens' vision of a united laboring man's society suddenly blossomed. The old personal relationship between employer and journeyman was fast disappearing. The workingman might never see his employer, and unless he could form a labor group as big and inclusive as the vast corporation he worked for, he was helpless. It was this need which the Knights of Labor met.

In 1878 a general assembly—that is, a national organization —was formed. Between 1879 and 1885 membership rose from about 10,000 to 110,000. But in the following year it leaped to over 700,000. During that year more assemblies were formed than in the previous sixteen. In February alone 515 assemblies were organized. Newspapers predicted that the Knights would pick the next President. Branches sprang up in England and Belgium. The ritual was translated into half a dozen languages for the benefit of immigrant members.

Leader of the Knights during most of its national existence was a self-taught, humorous young Irishman named Terence V. Powderly who had come up through the ranks, learned the machinist's trade, and been black-listed for union activity so that he could never keep a job for long. At the age of twenty-nine he was elected Mayor of Scranton and was twice re-elected. He had become corresponding secretary of the Knights of Labor when a district assembly was established at Scranton in the riot year of 1877. From 1879 until 1893 he was Grand Master Workman of the national body.

Slender, with mild blue eyes behind gold-rimmed glasses, Powderly looked like a poet or a philosopher among the big, heavy-set men who acknowledged him as their leader. In his double-breasted black broadcloth coat and stand-up collar, he looked like a man of breeding rather than a laboring man and the son of a laborer. The walrus-like moustache which dipped to his chin and covered his mouth gave him a misleadingly somber appearance.

Powderly was anything but somber. Estimates of his ability vary, but he had a large following and he had the interests of labor at heart. When outstanding leadership was needed, however, as in the railroad strikes of the eighties, Powderly lacked the necessary skill in negotiation.

At first these strikes were spectacularly successful. For the first time in history American labor was sufficiently united to compel big corporations to bargain on terms of equality. In 1885 Jay Gould himself had to meet the representatives of the Knights. Gould controlled the Missouri Pacific, the Wabash railroads and several others—in all about ten thousand miles of lines. When these lines tried to reduce wages, strikes broke out. After a good deal of jockeying, the executive board of the Knights went to Gould's office in New York. Ultimately they got an agreement that no railroad officials would discriminate against any employees who were Knights or question their right to belong to the order. All old employees were to be reinstated before any new ones were hired. No future strikes would be called until a conference had been held with railroad officials. When this agreement was reached, the strike was called off.

The public saw a great victory for the Knights of Labor and exulted in the way Jay Gould had been brought to terms. Gould himself—who had recently broken the telegraphers and was about to break the railroads—announced with a straight face that he approved of labor unions and wanted to see all his employees unionized. The Knights of Labor were now at the peak of their prestige. New members poured in.

Industrialization had changed the face of America. The old ties of neighborhood were disappearing. Immigrants from most of the countries of Europe were flooding the land. Differences in religion, language, custom threatened a complete breakdown in the social structure. Old animosities were brought from Europe. New misunderstandings grew where strangers had to live close together. Into this chaotic scene the Knights of Labor stepped with a uniting ritual, a formula for emotional harmony and brotherhood among all who toiled. The creation of a community of feeling tends to be neglected in historical writing. It is harder to pin down than economic or political pressures and activities. Yet it underlies all. At a time when unemployment and low wages had led to desperation and broken out into widespread rioting, the Knights of Labor offered an alternative. It offered order instead of chaos, by means of voluntary association. And it offered unity. Workers both skilled and unskilled were welcome, both craftsmen and industrial laborers.

But as every life has in it the seeds of its own death, the Knights of Labor had several fatal flaws. One of these was that the members hardly knew what to do with themselves at weekly meetings once they had gone through the ritual. There was no great amount of business to do. The national leaders recommended study, but apparently failed to provide any definite program or guidance. The organization grew too fast to be properly consolidated. Strikes were called at the local level and the national leaders—who were opposed to strikes on principle—were run ragged trying to settle or prevent them.

Then, on May 4, 1886, there was a demonstration in Haymarket Square, Chicago, led by a small group of anarchists. When policemen tried to break it up, a bomb exploded. Seven policemen and four people in the crowd were killed. Over a hundred were injured. Opponents of organized labor used the incident—quite unjustly—as a club to beat the Knights with. And from this point on the Knights kept running into bad luck.

Public opinion, which had been behind the Knights, turned abruptly against them. The very success of the order now proved to be its worst enemy. With that fear of bigness which has always characterized American opinion, the public now regarded the Knights as a danger.

This fear of bigness is worth examining, since it plays an important part both in the formation and structure of voluntary associations in America.

It is rather ironic that in other countries bigness is regarded as the dominant feature of American life—big land, tall buildings, big motor cars, big business. We are feared for our bigness. Yet few foreigners know that the fear of bigness has run like pedal point throughout our history, and that since early colonial days we have fought bigness and monopoly wherever we have found it. Little Plymouth faced the problem with the growth of Massachusetts Bay. It resisted and lost. The small states were reluctant to come into a union with the big ones until equality in the Senate reassured them. Once the Union was formed, every effort was made to keep the federal government from gaining power at the expense of the states. Strong local control has remained an ideal, if not always an actuality, in every phase of American life.

The instinctive response of Americans has been to preserve their heritage of local, voluntary activity against the encroachments of big government, big business, big labor. Loyal Americans stoutly resist and loudly grumble against what they regard as too much government in Washington. Little businessmen are suspicious of big business, and big businessmen talk as if their huge corporations were family groups. They talk that way because they feel that way—because they too feel that the neighborly group is the true American ideal. Industries which are on their toes therefore encourage voluntary group activity among their employees.

Voluntarism, from the beginning, has been the American way of combating bigness and keeping control at the local level. "We can tend our own affairs." That is the characteristic attitude. Only when voluntary associations grow big and top-heavy, do they too come under suspicion.

It was this fear of bigness which toppled the Knights. The fear was present not only outside the ranks, but within, among the crafts which feared that they were being snowed under by the all-labor organization. The Knights of Labor was organizing trade union members and swallowing up whole locals of already established unions. Some at least of its leaders believed that the trade unions were a thing of the past, to be superseded by the Knights as a unified body speaking for all labor.

This, according to the American faith in the strong local group, was heresy. So in 1886 a group of trade union leaders called a meeting "to protect our respective organizations from the malicious work of an element who openly boast that 'trades unions must be destroyed.' " Thus in the year when the Knights were at their peak, the process of dissolution was started. Before the end of the year a federation had been formed which was to supersede the Knights, and Sam Gompers stepped forward as its leader.

From 1887 to 1894 the American Federation of Labor and the Knights of Labor used up a good part of their energy fighting each other. The federation was, as its name implied, to be controlled by the trade unions which composed it. Trade autonomy was therefore its basic principle.

Sam Gompers, formerly a socialist, now came forward with the idea of "business unions." Unions were not to mix in politics, but to gain for workingmen their fair share of the national income through collective bargaining.

"So long as we have held fast to voluntary principles," said Gompers, "and have been actuated and inspired by the spirit of service, we have sustained our forward progress. . . . I want to say to you, men and women of the American labor movement, do not reject the cornerstone upon which labor's structure has been builded—but base your all upon voluntary principles."

One reason why the Federation insisted upon voluntarism was its fear that government was not to be trusted—was too much under the influence of business. Laws favorable to labor could be passed only after exhausting struggles, and then might be so interpreted by the courts as to do more harm than good. Labor could still remember how federal troops, court injunctions, and all the forces of government had been used against them. The

Sherman Anti-Trust Law had first been applied against labor rather than business, while the Lever Act, intended to curb racketeering, was used by the courts to break a strike.

The federal system of government also made difficulties, since it was hard to make laws of national scope which would be satisfactory. Then there was the peculiar nature of political parties in America. Neither party could attract the votes of all workingmen. Each party tried to appeal to all the major economic groups in the country, and could not afford to adopt a platform conspicuously favorable to any one.

Gompers and his followers had also learned by experience that labor laws could never keep up with rapidly changing economic conditions, that any laws made to establish minimum rates tended to become maximums, that reliance on legislation tended to make workers too dependent on government rather than on their own resources.

Through collective bargaining, on the other hand, labor could keep abreast of the times and fit its demands to varying local conditions. It would have to keep on its toes and rely on its own resources. This way it was more likely to get its share of the profits earned by the product it turned out. Voluntary association, in other words, was a more sensitive and effective instrument than the legislative process. And the labor union would be strong as long as it remained true to its principles as a voluntary association.

With the rise of a new industrial labor organization in 1905—the Industrial Workers of the World—Gompers had to face a new threat. The I.W.W. organized all kinds of unskilled workers —lumbermen, migrant laborers, miners. It was huge, potentially dangerous to the A.F.L., but loosely organized. Its left-wing philosophy kept it from becoming acceptable to the majority of Americans, however, and it finally dissolved in 1925.

The next attempt at industrial organization, that of the Congress of Industrial Organizations, was more effective. During the thirties it successfully organized such major industries as steel and automobiles which the A.F.L. with its craft union point of view had hardly touched.

The depression, which marked the growing power of the C.I.O., also dealt a hard blow to the A.F.L. belief that labor unions should keep out of politics. The Federation was forced to support legislation dealing with unemployment and labor relations. But as organized labor turned more and more to political action to achieve its goals, it tended to divide its members and disrupt its organization. Then it had to appeal to government to force workers into unions or prevent members from resigning.

The C.I.O., meanwhile, thoroughly approved the entrance of unions into politics and the reliance upon legislation. But in the popular reaction against unions exerting too much political power, wise leaders would see a familiar storm warning. Public opinion has always gone against any indication of overbalancing power in the hands of any economic group. It has always favored the organization which could stand on its own feet instead of leaning on government. That is one reason why collective bargaining rather than the formation of a labor party has dominated the labor movement in America. When workers appear to be losing local control, when the decisions of distant officials seem to take initiative out of their hands, the public loses confidence in their organization. The same resentment is felt against industries which are remotely controlled, or against government which from a distance interferes in what citizens feel to be local matters. We are emotionally much closer to town meeting, the wagon train or the husking bee than our industrialized, urbanized life may indicate. For our human-ness is deeper rooted than our industrialization, our urbanization.

In the labor movement, four forms of activity stand out through the years—fraternalism, collective bargaining, co-operation and politics. Most of the early unions provided fraternal benefits for their members, but this once important service has become of little importance in comparison with the national social security legislation. Many unions tried co-operation as a way out of the slavery imposed by low wages, but this phase is now of little importance. Labor's importance as a pressure group influencing legislation is of course very great. But throughout the years, labor's greatest success has come through collective bargaining—a process which however painful is essentially voluntary rather than compulsory, democratic rather than dictatorial.

* * *

What the unions did for labor, the trade associations did for employers. These groups grew up during the Civil War, were widely established by the end of the century, and were greatly increased by government sponsorship during the first World War. Suddenly involved in broad economic planning for which it was unprepared, the government encouraged the formation of trade associations to make its task easier. In 1913 there were only 240 regional and national associations; by 1919 there were about two thousand, by 1930 four thousand. President Hoover encouraged them when he came to the White House, and thereafter the N.R.A. and the second World War stimulated their growth, until at present there are twelve thousand, counting state and local groups and including a trade association of managers of trade associations!

As they grew, the trade associations went through a remarkable change. Instead of watching each other in mutual jealousy, the members began helping each other out. American businessmen today are pooling know-how and sharing trade secrets to a degree little realized by the public. For this they have a vast number of associations. The Society of Automotive Engineers and the Automotive Safety Council, for example, bring about a cross-fertilization of ideas which would be ruled out by any theory of cut-throat competition. A member of the American Warehouseman's Association can call on the know-how of any member in the country to help him in handling a special problem. Through the trade associations members can get information about administration, stock handling, supplies, labor problems, packaging. This interchange of information has immeasurably increased production, quality, efficiency. Trade secrets have almost become a thing of the past. Voluntary association has been industry's way of escaping both monopoly and cutthroat competition.

Recently a good many efforts have been made to pool the information possessed by universities, industry, labor and government. Thus by cross-fertilizing, new potentialities are opened up in every area of American life. A series of conferences sponsored by the Advertising Council took up the subject of "A Free Dynamic Society." Members of the conference included such notables as Chester Barnard, president of the Rockefeller Foundation; Erwin Canham, editor of the *Christian Science Monitor;* Russell Davenport, Peter Drucker, Lewis Galantiere, Harry Gideonse and Walter Wheeler, president of Pitney-Bowes. Paul Hoffman was moderator. These men exchanged ideas about what gives the dynamic push to American society. The many answers they came up with pointed in one direction: not toward individualism or private enterprise (America has no monopoly on these), but to a kind of free and mutual collectivism—a constant exchange of ideas among men of many professions and trades, the underlying motive of which is the improving and enriching of American life. The instrument through which this has been accomplished is voluntary association.

The Advertising Council is itself an excellent example. An organization of businessmen aware of the vast changes in our way of life, it has undertaken to explore and interpret these changes, and to advertise to the nation the existence of public dangers which cannot be overcome without the voluntary cooperation of millions of citizens. The Council spreads its warnings against inflation, accidents, inadequate educational facilities. It is nonpartisan, and it counts on the existence of alert voluntary groups throughout the country to respond to its warnings with appropriate action. This is one of the most remarkable things about its way of operation—that it needs no organization of its own to act on the advice it gives. For it knows that the country is full of associations able to respond locally to local needs.

The activities of the business or labor leader are not limited to the associations directly affecting his business, however. A good share of his time goes into meetings of local church, hospital, Y.M.C.A., Community Chest, school or library boards. Sooner or later he will be called on to take a state or national board membership. A typical entry in *Who's Who* shows one industrialist involved in the Eye Bank for Sight Restoration, organizations devoted to international friendship or relief, Travelers Aid, National Safety Council, Regional Plan Association, United Negro College Fund, museum and university trusteeships and assorted cultural activities.

"The central characteristic of corporate enterprise," Lewis Galantiere points out, "is a diffusion of ownership so wide that it has become as anonymous as ownership under nationalization. This has placed upon management responsibilities of a 'trustee' nature, not only towards the owners but towards society as a whole." Or as Paul Hoffman puts it, the new socially conscious capitalism in America is "a system based on widespread ownership, diffusion of initiative, decision and enterprise and an ever-widening distribution of its benefits."

Such a diffusion of ownership, management and benefits relies, not upon government guidance and control, but upon the activities of hundreds of associations, from the trade and labor groups to the welfare organizations whose activities constantly raise standards of health, culture and education.

The number and complexity of these national associations is indicated—though no doubt incompletely—in the twenty pages of the *World Almanac* which attempts to list them. When the Department of Commerce tried to make a count of national associations in 1949, it listed 4,000. Of these, 1,800 were business, 500 professional, 200 labor, 100 women, 55 for farmers. Including local branches and chapters there were 16,000 organizations for businessmen, 70,000 for labor, 15,000 civic and professional groups—and 100,000 for women, who seem to be the greatest organizers of all. Trade and professional groups are most prominent. They include influential groups like the National Association of Manufacturers, the U.S. Chamber of Commerce (significantly a voluntary association while similar bodies abroad are semiofficial), the American Medical Association. They include the many professional bodies which meet to exchange information and raise standards—or, occasionally, to prevent competition.

But then there are the religious, fraternal, patriotic, service and youth organizations—all of them with programs more or less dedicated to raising standards in one way or another. There are associations devoted to health problems, ethnic problems, public affairs. Those who would simplify spelling, lower the birthrate, wipe out profanity, reform the calendar or honor an ancestor or a general always seem to form associations. Women, veterans and sports fans are active joiners. Anyone with a hobby is sure to find kindred spirits through such associations as the Society for the Preservation and Encouragement of Barber Shop Quartet Singing in America (28,000 members), The Blizzard Men of 1888 (750), the Society for the Perpetuation of Circus Street Parades, The Guild of Former Pipe Organ Pumpers (3,500), or the First Avenue Boys—whose official address is on Third Avenue. The National Grandmothers Clubs apparently lumped their slogan and president into one; her name was Bea Good.

It is easy to smile at ourselves for rushing around to one meeting after another—easy to smile at the bulging wallet full of membership cards, the home-town paper with its columns full of announcements, at the list of President Truman's affiliations —Shriner, Elk, Moose, Lion, Eagle, and member of the Society for the Preservation and Encouragement of Barber Shop Singing in America. But this is the sort of people we are. We may waste a lot of energy, but we have succeeded by associating together in raising the highest standards of health, education and general welfare yet achieved by man.

*   *   *

A clothing factory in Holyoke, Massachusetts, had been organized by the Amalgamated Clothing Workers. During a slump, its lack of capital became so serious that there seemed to be no choice but bankruptcy or a wage cut. At this point an arbitrator was called in. He knew from a look at the books that the company was really on the rocks, and he told the employees so.

Most of the employees were girls, and they had a few things to say about the way men were running things. "Why don't you make a more efficient shop instead of cutting wages?" they wanted to know. Then they pointed out that layout and routing were inefficient, that some workers were on piece rates and others on weekly rates, with no co-ordination between them.

The arbitrator encouraged them to submit a plan. He advised the owner to give them every encouragement, to welcome every suggestion, and to be sure the girls got credit for originating the plan. Result: the company stayed in business.

In the 1920s a big strike usually resulted in picket lines, "goons" hired by the company to beat up the pickets, police attacks with clubs or worse, and men sent to the hospital. In 1949 during the steel strike the company served hot coffee to the workers on the picket lines while union members were patrolling company property to protect it from damage. When a reporter asked one of the strikers if there was likely to be any fighting, he said, "Nah, the union has grown up—and so has the company I guess."

The two thousand workers of a steel mill near Pittsburgh had joined a new union in the midst of the depression, but were uneasy about their jobs and the future. Wild-cat strikes kept breaking out. The owner was uneasy too; he had all his money invested in the plant and times were bad. The head of the union, Joseph Scanlon, had been an accountant. He explained to the union members that the company was close to insolvency. After an all-night meeting the men voted to take a wage cut of 25 per cent for three months, and to see what they could do further to help management save the mill—and far from incidentally—their jobs and homes.

Union and management working together drew up an efficiency program. Workers contributed their suggestions. Soon costs began to drop, the mill began to show a profit, and the full wage was restored.

Workers, like people everywhere and in all the relationships of life, want to feel wanted. The job is a big thing in every man's life. He has got to feel about it one way or the other. He will feel loyal to it, interested, involved—or sour, uninvolved, hostile. But he would rather feel loyal, if given the chance.

There is no such thing as economic man. Man is a much more complicated organism. His emotions get into everything he does. And if his emotions are positively involved and channeled, they will release unsuspected energy, skill, devotion. Hundreds of studies have proven that employees who feel that their opinions are wanted work better than those who are merely ordered about and never consulted. Even pay cuts do not lower the production of employees who are made to feel recognized and important.

When changes are to be made in a plant—if jobs are to be shifted, new machinery moved in or methods of working changed—workers are immediately suspicious if the plant is run autocratically. But if they are told what's going on and asked to help with the planning, the change becomes a part of them. It is "ours" instead of "theirs." Everyone needs this sense of identification in order to do good work. The impulse must come from inside, not from a barked command, an order from outside. And this impulse from inside is the basis of voluntary activity.

It has also been proved that men work best in small groups where they can know each other well and build up a sound structure of emotional relations. And it has been proved that groups work best when they are allowed to share in the plans and decisions. Autocratic or anarchistic groups flop badly by comparison—a matter which is of international significance these days.

Social scientists are rediscovering what Americans have known instinctively all along—that voluntary shared activity for creative ends is the most rewarding and the most productive form of human behavior. For a time, the impact of big business and big cities obscured the importance of the small voluntary group. But now new ways of putting it to use have opened up in industry, though there is much still to be done. There is still a long way to go in the big cities where millions have failed to find any meaningful group as an outlet for their creative and gregarious instincts. The settlement house was one attempt to solve this problem, and there have been others. Wartime emergencies always draw people together, for danger is a great stimulus to solidarity. But the sense of neighborhood, of shared dangers and responsibilities, fades away as the danger passes, and city areas which have momentarily felt the bonds of brotherhood relax into anonymity again.

We have not yet found that moral equivalent of war for which William James was searching. But the instrument for it is always at hand, always being retested and reused in a thousand ways, always being rediscovered and readapted to emergent needs. A growing awareness of the power of voluntary association is evident nowadays on many fronts, and ways of harnessing the powers of individuals through group functioning are constantly being developed. Perhaps we may even achieve, in time, that moral equivalent for war. If we do, the instrument is sure to be voluntary association.

XI

The Good Seed

Oliver Hudson Kelley had been around. Born in Boston in 1826 to a family that boasted kinship with the Holmeses and Sewalls, he had gone west at the age of twenty-one, clerked in a drugstore and reported for the *Tribune* in Chicago, and become a telegrapher at Peoria. There he is supposed to have pioneered the reading of messages by sound instead of from tape. By 1849 he had gone to Iowa, where he married. But he and his bride soon moved on to Minnesota where Kelley took up farming and trading with the Indians. He put up the first frame barn and ran the first reaping machine in Minnesota, having arrived there the year it became a Territory. It was also in Minnesota that Kelley became a Mason—an act which twenty years later was to affect history.

After two years of marriage, Kelley's young wife died at the age of nineteen, leaving him with an infant daughter. A year later he married again. Temperance, his second wife, gave him four more daughters. Meanwhile Kelley was becoming a leader among the farmers of Minnesota. He was secretary of the county agricultural society. He began to write for farm papers, urging farmers to study, experiment, and improve their crops and income. His articles were noticed by the Department of Agriculture, then in its infancy. In 1864, when crops were bad, he went to Washington and joined the Department as a clerk.

Two years later President Johnson asked the Commissioner of Agriculture to have a survey made of Southern farming as a basis for reconstruction measures. Kelley was chosen for the job, and after an interview with the President set out on an extended tour.

Now forty years old, Kelley was an impressive-looking man— tall, with firm mouth, dark, active eyes and a chin whose forward thrust showed through the full beard which had already begun to turn white. A Yankee, Kelley was greeted with suspicion in the South until he made use of the Masonic membership. The value of this fraternal bond was a thing he did not forget. What he saw during that tour, combined with what he had seen of farming in the West, convinced him that farmers needed an association of their own to help them out of the situation they were in.

Back in Washington, he began to talk with half a dozen friends about such an organization. In 1867 a preamble to a constitution was drawn up and a ritual prepared. The organization was named Patrons of Husbandry, but each unit was to be called a Grange. Toward the end of the year the first Grange meeting was held.

But so far the organization which above all others needed grass roots had none at all. The Washington Grange was made up of government clerks. How were they to persuade the farmers of the nation that they should join a secret organization they had never heard of?

Kelley decided to go on an organizing tour. After he and his friends had pooled their resources and invested in a railroad ticket to Harrisburg, he had $2.50 in cash to start him on the road! His only other asset—besides good health, faith and a sense of humor rare in zealots—was a letter empowering him to establish Granges and collect fees.

At Harrisburg Kelley did actually manage to collect $15 for a charter, but no Grange was organized. He had no experience at organizing. He was a poor speaker. He made the mistake of trying to get farmers to come into town instead of meeting them out in the country. And when he asked them to put up hard cash for membership, any enthusiasm he had managed to convey rapidly evaporated. The only Grange he succeeded in establishing was at Fredonia, New York. It has been continuously active ever since.

By the time he reached Madison, Wisconsin, Kelley was penniless. From the master of the local Masonic lodge he borrowed enough to buy a rail ticket to his home in Minnesota which he reached on May 1, 1868. Tired and discouraged, he was ready to give up. But his wife was not. She had just received a legacy of $500. She no doubt had thought of twenty good ways of spending it around the home, or even of saving it for a rainy day or for the education or trousseaux of her daughters. Instead, she handed it to her husband and told him to go out and try again. Without Temperance Kelley's $500, the Grange would have died. If the Patrons of Husbandry have a patron saint, Temperance Kelley should occupy the niche.

Just as Kelley was starting out again, good news came from Iowa. A Grange had been formed there in response to some publicity sent out from Washington. Another stroke of good fortune was the arrival from Boston of Mrs. Kelley's niece, Caroline Hall, a level-headed girl who became an invaluable secretary and assistant. Thanks to her, women were invited to membership and to positions of importance.

Now things began to hum. Nearly a dozen Granges sprang up in Minnesota within a few months, and early in 1869 the first State Grange was formed there. Once the movement was under way, it grew like corn in July. Granges popped up throughout the Midwest, then spilled over into Vermont, South Carolina and Canada. By the end of 1872 there were 1,105 Granges throughout the country and Kelley was living in Washington where he could devote his full time to the organization. In 1873 the first regular delegate session of the National Grange was held at Georgetown, D. C., with representatives from eleven State Granges. From this time on, the Grange was in the hands of the farmers. The organization grew so rapidly that by the following year there were twelve thousand Granges in thirty-two states and two territories. All over the country Grange Halls began to appear—plain, barn-like buildings usually, to which farm families flocked twice a month for meetings which combined secret ritual with business, culture, fun and food.

Now the difficulty was to keep people out instead of enticing them in. Lawyers, salesmen, speculators, politicians and agents discovered that they were "interested in agricultural pursuits" as the regulations required, "but only as the hawk is interested in the sparrow" as Worthy Master Adams wryly remarked.

Like the Knights of Labor, the Grange was fertilized by a period of general discontent and watered by despair. The years from 1870 to 1873, usually regarded as prosperous, had been hard on farmers. The westward advance of the railroads, the homestead law, immigration and demobilization had greatly extended production and consequently had lowered prices. Then came the panic of 1873. Farm prices tumbled further. Mortgages were foreclosed. The labor of years was wiped out in foreclosure sales. Floods and plagues of locusts added to farm misery.

Its treasury comfortably filled, the Grange could afford to help bring relief to areas of special need. Supplies and money were sent to flood victims in Louisiana, to farms eaten up by grasshoppers in Nebraska, and to distressed farmers in Minnesota, Iowa, Dakota, Kansas and Alabama. The benefits of rural brotherhood were already beginning to show.

It was this fraternal aspect of the Grange which had been uppermost in the minds of Oliver Kelley and the other founders. They wanted to give the farmer and his family something like a rural Masonic Order. They wanted to supply a social outlet for the loneliness of farm life, and they hoped in time to raise the cultural and educational level of rural America.

But a voluntary association—responsive to the times and to the interests of its members—rarely follows any preconceived pattern. Its strength is its responsiveness. And when the farmers decided that legislative action and co-operative enterprise were what they wanted, the Grange program had to meet their needs. It had already brought them together, putting an end to the isolation which had prevented any strong farmer action in the past and giving them an organization through which they could work. It soon found itself in the midst of a fight.

Western farmers were bitter against the railroads, which had been given whole principalities of land, had persuaded towns to buy stock in order to get on the line and had then watered the stock, charged outlandish rates to carry farm products while giving special privileges to other shippers, and corrupted state legislatures by means of passes and other gifts. To fight the railroads was what the Western farmers wanted to do more than anything else. The railroads had money, but the farmers had votes. So the Granges sent their members into the state legislatures. Although Granges were supposed to be nonpolitical, they got around the prohibition by formally adjourning Grange meeting and then immediately taking up political affairs. They held State Grange meetings in the state capitals while the legislatures were sitting. They sent out questionnaires to candidates for office, and only those who answered satisfactorily got farm backing.

When the Granges began to get results the railroads denied the right of the states to regulate their rates. They refused to obey the new laws and used every method of obstruction they could think of. When they refused to lower passenger rates in Illinois, some farmers climbed aboard anyway, paid the legal fare to the conductor and gave him the choice of accepting it or trying to throw them off. By altering its schedules to inconvenience passengers, the roads were often able to force repeal of legislation they disliked. In every state but Illinois the laws regulating the railroads were repealed before they had had a fair trial.

In addition to fighting the railroads, the other major Grange activity was setting up co-operatives. Irritated by the high prices they had to pay for machinery, for crop storage, for all the things they had to buy and the commissions they had to pay for the sale of their crops, the farmers decided to set up their own stores, factories, commission merchants. Grain elevators were purchased, shipping associations were organized, fire insurance companies were established.

But in their enthusiasm the Grangers overextended themselves. The National Grange, well supplied with funds, decided to break the monopoly on farm machinery. The officers bought up patents of all sorts and planned to set up a number of factories. Their action nearly wrecked the Grange. The harvester factory set up in Iowa failed in 1875, bankrupting the State Grange. Other failures followed, patent suits were brought, and Granges began folding up for fear they would have to pay up for the losses.

Yet the era of business activity had its benefits. For one thing, the Grangers learned that middlemen and manufacturers had their uses, and that the distribution of crops was something more than a parasitic function. When the co-operatives were finally established on Rochdale principles (sales at market prices, with savings paid back to members in the form of dividends), they proved successful and are still operated by many Granges today. Insurance against farm hazards also proved a successful venture and is still carried on. Co-operative creameries, packing plants and supply houses are still important Grange activities. More than a quarter of the products of its members are marketed co-operatively.

Though manufacturing and co-operative failures chipped away at membership throughout the eighties until there were hardly 100,000 members left, the vitality of the Grange idea was proven when membership began to pick up again. By 1915 it had risen to half a million. Today it is over 800,000. Other farm organizations have come and gone; the Grange seems to be here to stay.

There is no doubt that one reason for its lasting success is in its ritual, and in the emotional bond which that ritual creates. The role of secret societies in American life has been too often ridiculed and too rarely understood. In a society as mobile as ours, men and women often find themselves among strangers. Or they may be separated from their neighbors by their religious beliefs or by mere physical distance. The secret society provides the same sort of emotional warmth which the primitive tribe or the small village naturally possessed. It provides a set of acceptable symbols which (like the primitive totem animal) unifies the members, giving them a sense of their own dignity and importance, giving them a recognized place in a group, idealizing their daily activities and elevating to universal significance the lives they live and the things they do.

Certainly the Grange did all this for the farm family. That it took in women and children from the beginning was a source of strength. Today there are 1,800 Juvenile Granges whose members may transfer to the adult group at fourteen. It was one of the earliest national organizations to give prominent positions to women—and well it might, since it would have been still-born but for Temperance Kelley. The lot of the farm wife in 1870 was even harder than that of the farmer. Life on the farm was a hard life, with little chance for rest or recreation and none for education. The Grange helped to change this. In addition to ritual and business, its meetings included discussions of contemporary affairs as well as entertainment. Special programs in home economics were developed, with good effects on the comfort and health of farm life. But even more important, the opportunity of doing things together helped to strengthen the bonds between men and women, helped to raise the quality of family life. In many isolated areas the Grange came as a unique social opportunity. And getting together socially brought about an improvement in dress and manners.

"Crabbed men came out of their shells and grew genial," Solon Buck reported. "Disheartened women became cheerful; repressed children delighted in the chance to play with other boys and girls of their own age."

The Grange also brought back the old-time virtue of neighborly aid. The ritual emphasized charity, and members responded by harvesting crops for a sick brother or helping to rebuild a house destroyed by fire or tornado. When the National Grange sent aid to stricken areas, the deed strengthened the feeling of unity within the Grange and helped draw the country together in a feeling of mutuality.

The Grange gave scope to men whose talents extended beyond farm tasks. Those with business sense could help organize the co-ops, the insurance companies. The meetings were training grounds for public speaking and parliamentary procedure— arts which were of value especially to Grangers who were elected by their brothers to public office. Then, thanks to the Grange, there was a spurt in the publication of farm journals. "If the Granger movement had created nothing else than this desire to read," wrote Solon Buck, "it would have been worth while. For after the farmer began to read, he was no longer like deadwood floating in the backwaters of the current."

In addition to what the Grange offered the farmer locally, it sponsored national legislation which improved farm conditions everywhere. Because the National Grange could speak authentically for close to a million farmers, it always had the respectful attention of Congress. And it could speak authentically because it was a true voluntary association made up of strong local units. Resolutions adopted by the local or Subordinate Granges were passed up through the Pomona (or district) to the State Granges, and then to the National Grange composed of delegates from the states.

It was in this way that rural free delivery came about. During a discussion in a western Grange a woman asked why farm mail wasn't delivered, the same as city mail. The local Grange passed a resolution and sent it on up to the Pomona Grange. Taken up by the National Grange, it was pushed for more than ten years before Congress agreed in 1893 to try it out. Despite the predictions of Congressional leaders that it would destroy rural life with its dangerous socialistic tendency, it proved a great success.

The first major legislative effort of the Grange was to get the Department of Agriculture raised to cabinet status. The notion that farmers deserved a cabinet officer was greeted with ridicule,

but the Grange kept pegging away until finally in 1889 they succeeded.

Other Grange objectives included the graduated income tax,
agricultural experiment stations, parcel post and postal savings.
The Grange advocated state police systems, better highways,
rural electrification, an agricultural extension service of advice
on farm problems and home economics, control of utility and
freight rates, and a good many other things which were of benefit not only to the farmer but to the general public.

Locally, the Grange is a real asset to the community. It is active in all kinds of improvement projects, from draining mos-
quito swamps and sponsoring village clean-up days to establishing town forests and putting up welcome signs. Granges help
the schools with support to hot lunch programs, prizes, and advice on school gardens. They help the churches by staging benefit entertainments and contributing needed equipment.

*   *   *

During the years of the Grange's decline, other voluntary
groups tackled the farm problem. Greenback Clubs, formed
mostly in rural areas, were for easier money. In 1878 about a million votes were cast for Greenback candidates. Though the West
was the stronghold of Greenback sentiment, it was Solon Chase
of Maine who put forward the argument that appealed to
farmers. "Inflate the currency, and you raise the price of my
steers and at the same time pay the public debt," he said. "Them
steers" gave Chase wide popularity. But inflation did not appeal
to enough voters as the solution of their needs, and the Greenback movement died.

But not the problem. In 1893 an English visitor found American farmers full of the same discontent that was seething in
Europe. His comment on the way Americans were tackling it
was illuminating.

"In England," he wrote, "they are hoping for aid from councils
of all kinds; in France they have put on protective duties which

have been increased in vain twice over; in Germany they put on and relaxed similar duties and are screaming for them again; in Scandinavia—Denmark more particularly—they limit the aggregation of land; and in the United States they create organizations like the Grangers, the Farmers' Leagues, and the Populists."

There it is in a nutshell: "In the United States they create organizations." The practice is so common that every schoolchild in America knows more about rules of order and parliamentary procedure than many a university graduate in Europe.

After the Grange had declined and the Greenback Clubs had died, the National Farmers' Alliance tried to do something about low prices, high interest on mortgages, high freight rates and inequitable taxes. The Alliance got under way in 1880 when the Grange had begun its decline. It jumped into politics and got control of the state legislatures in Tennessee, Arkansas, Mississippi, Georgia and the Carolinas. It was able to elect several governors. Similar farm organizations were soon sprouting in various parts of the country, and although by 1890 most of these were declining, they helped provide the platform of the new People's Party.

The Populist Party, as it is usually called, came out for cheap money, a graduated income tax, government ownership of railroads, the eight-hour day and direct election of Senators. Its presidential candidate polled over a million votes in 1892, and two years later nearly half again as many Populist votes were cast. But then in 1896 Bryan carried the free silver platform into the Democratic platform and the bubble burst. Rising farm prices completed the job.

But while other farm organizations disappeared, the Grange, having got its second breath, went steadily forward. Although it has fought for laws that would benefit the farmer, its stated aim is to advance legislation of benefit to all the people. Its attitude toward the free seed program is illuminating, and the story has symbolic as well as practical significance.

Any farm organization would of course support a program of

free seeds supplied by the government—wouldn't it? Not the Grange.

Those whose memories can reach back to the twenties and who had anything to do with gardening will remember the manila envelopes with pink labels franked by a Congressman which, in response to a simple request, brought packets of flower and vegetable seeds into any American home by way of the postman. The arrival of the envelope was one of the signs of spring which always brought joy to a youngster's heart, together with a tangible realization of the wealth and magnanimity of a government which could give away things you usually had to pay good money for at the store. Why our Congressman could not also supply pencils, marbles, jackknives and the other essentials of living we never bothered to inquire. But we had the impression that he could have done all this too if it had occurred to him.

According to the Grange point of view, however, this largess was far from the innocent and charming friendliness on the part of a kindly government which it had seemed to the young.

For half a century the government spent about a quarter of a million dollars yearly on the seed program. Congressmen were enthusiastic; they optimistically figured that each packet meant a vote (they must have forgotten that we hadn't reached voting age), and even when the Grange began to protest, they went right on appropriating the necessary funds.

But the seeds were something less than perfect. If they sprouted, they often turned out to be anything except what the package said they would be.

Wrote one irate Granger: "Our Congressman is sending to this post office large packages of seed regularly to a half-dozen names of people who have long been dead, some for more than ten years. In a way I suspect it is better to send the seed to dead people, for I do not know of any live people who want the trash. Can't the Grange take up this matter and stop it?"

The Grange did take up the matter. It protested that the

mailing of more than 60,000,000 seed packets was a waste of government funds. It managed to convince the Secretary of Agriculture, but not Congress. Year after year, though by diminishing majorities, Congress voted the seed money. Year after year the Grange fought it. It disappeared at last in 1923.

The Grange's objection to free seeds was not only a matter of money. It was a matter of principle. Good farmers hated to see poor seed propagated. Good seed was the basis of all farming, and seeds were symbolic of the farm, the field, the country life. They were outraged at the thought of seed being used as a cheap way of buying votes. And when they fought it, they were fighting for the dignity of their way of life.

*　*　*

Two other farm organizations continue to play an important part in the national picture. They are the Farmers' Educational and Co-operative Union, founded in Texas in 1902, and the American Farm Bureau Federation. The Union began among farmers of low income. Spreading across the Great Plains, it reached into three-quarters of the states and now numbers nearly half a million families. It has advocated co-operative buying and selling, along with legislation which guarantees the farmer's cost of production.

The Farm Bureau Federation, numbering one and a quarter million families, is an interesting example of the way Americans prefer voluntary group action to government control. For here is an organization which grew out of a government program, and is such a mixture of government and voluntary group activity that the two cannot be unscrambled.

In 1903 the Department of Agriculture decided to show Texas farmers how to grow cotton in spite of the boll weevil. Out of this program grew the demonstrators or county agents who went onto the farms and showed farmers how to improve their crops and their working methods. Under President Wilson's New Freedom program the state agricultural colleges were given funds to carry on extension programs for farmers, and the county agent system spread rapidly.

In any other country the program would have developed as a pure government project, with a head bureau in the nation's capital, instructions sent out to the regions, reports meticulously returned to headquarters, and farmers obediently following the instructions of the government agents.

In the United States it turned out differently. From the beginning there was a strong voluntary twist to the program. In the early phases local groups had got together to raise money for the work and to help the agents make contact with the farmers. The Smith-Lever Act of 1914 recognized these voluntary groups as a source of the funds that would be necessary to match the federal grants. When the state legislatures passed laws to take advantage of the federal offer, they usually required that any county wanting to take part should set up an association of farmers—a farm bureau.

So here was a program which, beginning as a federal demonstration, had stimulated voluntary groups to extend and carry it on, and had blossomed into a federal-and-state-supported service which required the organization of voluntary supporting groups at the local level! Cumbrous? Inefficient? A visitor from abroad might be excused for thinking so. Yet it works. And one reason why it works well is that local people have a stake in it. It is their organization. They are not being bossed by outsiders.

During the first World War the Farm Bureaus were encouraged by government as a channel for increasing food production. With help from the Department of Agriculture the American Farm Bureau Federation was launched in 1919. More than three-fourths of the states now have Farm Bureaus, but the heaviest membership is in the Corn Belt, as the Federation's point of view often indicates.

Members of the Grange and the Farmers' Union have been known to resent the fact that county agents are closer to Farm Bureau farmers than to the rest of the farming population. They don't like the idea of county agents promoting membership in the Bureau when their pay comes partly from federal funds.

A Congressional investigating committee in 1942 found evidence that the Farm Bureau was using the Extension Service to build its organization, and the following year the Grange and the Union joined forces to prevent federal funds from going to states where county agents worked for the Farm Bureau. The move was not successful.

In addition to the educational activities of the county agents, the Federation is busy promoting legislation favorable to farmers. Since few people are quite sure to what extent the Bureau is a government body, it enjoys an informal semiofficial status. But when the members get together in the community house down the road to eat strawberry shortcake and prepare for the membership drive, they are obviously a voluntary association.

It is all very confusing. But it works.

* * *

The conflict of interests among farm groups illustrates the fact that in the United States there is no such thing as division along class lines. The same conclusion comes from even a casual consideration of the differing viewpoints of labor and business organizations. The American scene is too richly complex and too dynamically mobile to be divided up into clearly marked classes. To what class does the industrial worker belong who lives in the country where he grows his own vegetables, keeps chickens, and invests his savings in the stock market?

This complexity of interests results not only in conflict between associations, but within them. "Organized interest groups," as David Truman points out, "are never solid and monolithic." Some members of the Farm Bureau, for example, are buyers of feed while others sell it. Some farmers produce milk for butter, others raise soy beans for oleomargarine. The National Association of Manufacturers has both protectionists and low tariff members. The American Medical Association embraces specialists, medical professors and general practitioners. Some doctors are quite happy with the *status quo* while others believe in compulsory health insurance. The members of the American Legion are even more diverse. Among them are union members and anti-union employers, real estate men and advocates of public housing, professional men and unskilled workers. Whether or not they are able to reconcile their varying viewpoints, their common membership tends to unite them emotionally and to create a climate for understanding.

Still further, a man may join half a dozen groups, and when these groups take a stand on national issues, a multiple-member may find the national leaders lining him up on both sides of the fence. If you are a merchant who likes to live in the country, and if you are also a veteran whose favorite hobby is hunting, you might belong to your trade association, the local Chamber of Commerce, the American Legion, the Rod and Gun Club and the Grange. The trade association and the Chamber of Commerce may be fighting imports while the Grange favors them. The Rod and Gun Club may be trying to preserve wild life cover which your Grange friends want to cut and sell. And at the Legion you will meet men whose labor, professional or trade associations pull them in various directions, or are pulled by them.

Does all this sound hopelessly confused? It is, of course, much more complicated than the totalitarian way. But the complexity is itself the best guarantee that we shall not be victimized by a dictator. There is always the danger that federal control of welfare programs, economic stability and defense measures will weaken local initiative and tempt the citizen to leave his affairs in the hands of government.

Voluntary association—voluntarism—is a constant bulwark against this threat. As members of even one national association, we are represented in the web of influence which determines the decisions of government. As members in several associations we further complicate the pattern. But as active members of local unions, Granges, Chambers of Commerce, voters' leagues, welfare associations, churches, parent-teacher groups and goodness knows what else we are constantly weaving the tapestry of the national life and adding our own bit of color or line to the pattern.

No one forces us to belong to anything. But the tradition is behind us and around us. To carry a conviction into action by associating with other like-minded citizens—that is an old American habit. To be sure, there are plenty of associations which seek privileges for their members instead of seeking the general welfare. But even these have their place. They are part of the pattern but they cannot dominate it. The pattern is a complex one; to some it appears ugly or meaningless. But to those who help with the weaving and who know what human materials go to make it, the finished product—or rather, the ever-unfinished product—is worthy of praise. It lacks the geometric precision of the totalitarian state, but it has the irregular charm of life itself. So long as you can exterminate the bad seed and plant the good, life has hope.

XII

A Nation of Joiners

In Bennington, Vermont, a remarkable thing happens once every two months.

At midmorning a station wagon and a truck arrive at the Elks Barn from Burlington, bringing six nurses and two drivers. The men carry beds and equipment into the Barn—a recreation center for the local chapter of the Benevolent Order of Elks (a voluntary association). Meanwhile the volunteer services of the local Red Cross chapter have been busy. As chairman of the blood program Esther Parmelee has been busy for several weeks past, making contact with people in the community. She has checked with Betty Clark to make sure that volunteer clerical aides will be on hand. She or Mrs. Gardner at the Red Cross office has lined up some volunteer nurses and doctors. The canteen volunteers have been alerted to prepare a noon meal for the workers and serve light refreshments during the afternoon. Nurses Aides, trained by the Red Cross, and Gray Ladies similarly trained, arrive at the proper time. The volunteer transport service is ready to go. General R. W. Buzzell, recruitment chairman, has been busy with his committee. Newspaper publicity, prepared by a volunteer, has been appearing.

When the doors open at eleven-thirty the Elks Barn is ready to operate as a blood center. They are all there, those volunteers —six more nurses, three doctors, a technician, seven Staff Aides, six canteen workers, four from the motor corps, six Nurses Aides, two Gray Ladies—a wonderful demonstration of the efficiency

of voluntary effort and devoted hard work. But they are use-
less until another group shows up—the citizens who will take a
half hour or so out of their busy day, get over to the Elks Barn,
and donate a pint of blood.

Will they come? Esther Parmelee is always a bit nervous at
this point. Suppose nobody shows up? It's a possibility, for there
is nothing which assures attendance.

Yet they do come. And they have always come—always in
numbers sufficient to fill the quota of 135 pints. They give their
blood to someone they will never know, someone in another city,
or perhaps in Korea or at an army base in some other distant
part of the world. A good many of them come regularly and in
the past five years have given a gallon, or two, or three. If all
this happened only in Bennington, and only once in ten years,
it would seem a miracle. But because it happens several times
a year, and happens all over the country, we take it for granted.

Behind the local volunteers stand the resources of the American Red Cross, a voluntary association which makes the Bloodmobile a possibility and which co-ordinates the program in Bennington with Vermont and the whole nation.

The American Red Cross traces its origins back to the Sanitary
Commission, a voluntary association organized in 1861 to look
after the health and comfort of the Union Army. The commission, privately financed, provided cooks, nurses, hospitals,
medicines, bandages, clothing and food for federal troops. Meanwhile Clara Barton, a Patent Office worker, was visiting the
hospitals in Washington. After Bull Run she began working
under fire at the battle fronts, with time out to raise money for
needed supplies.

Worn out by her self-imposed war work, Clara Barton went to
Europe to recover. There she heard of the Red Cross, founded a
few years before by Henri Dunant, a young Swiss businessman
who had been horrified at the lack of medical care for soldiers
when he had happened to come on the scene of the bloody
battle of Solferino. Dunant wrote a book proposing the formation of voluntary national societies to care for war wounded

without distinction of nationality. When sixteen governments
sent representatives to Geneva in 1864 to discuss a treaty, the
experiences of the Sanitary Commission were of great value in
proving that belligerents could work together as Dunant proposed. The idea of an international organization appealed to
Clara Barton. She took part in its work during the war of 1870
and returned to the United States determined to get her own
country to sign the Geneva Treaty. In 1881 the American Association of the Red Cross was established with Clara Barton as
president, and the next year the United States ratified the
Geneva Convention.

Impressive as the Red Cross is at the national and international level, its real strength lies in the local chapters and in
the volunteers who give their time to its various programs. The
Gray Ladies and Nurses Aides who help at the Bloodmobile also
give their time to the local hospital. The Staff Aides also do
clerical work at the chapter offices. Then there are the First Aid
courses given to the police force, industrial groups, ski slope
operators and high school students. There is the water safety
program which teaches children to swim, the course in home
nursing given at the local high school. The Home Service, with a
paid secretary, takes care of family problems arising out of
military service. Disaster Service is ready to go into action if
an emergency arises—to warn and evacuate the victims, provide medical aid, shelter and food, to register those involved
and help locate the missing, to answer queries and supply public
information, and to provide necessary supplies of all kinds.

* * *

Before the Civil War, New England towns like Bennington
got along very well without the Red Cross. Not so very different
from Plymouth two hundred years before, Bennington still
found that church and town meeting could satisfy most of its
needs—care for the poor, educate the children, keep the roads
and bridges in repair, preserve the peace, and keep people
reasonably contented. To be sure, there were signs that these

basic institutions no longer met every need. The lyceum movement arrived to satisfy the thirst for learning among an eager-minded people whose formal education had stopped at grammar school or at the most with the local academy. William Lloyd Garrison, during his brief residence, had proposed an association to combat slavery. Even in 1880 the only organizations listed, beside some professional and fraternal groups, were the Grand Army of the Republic, the Grange, a temperance group, a young men's group, the Young Ladies' Shakespeare Club and the Ladies' Dickens Club. The web of associations now so familiar to us had not been woven. But the threads were being spun.

In 1844 a young London dry goods merchant, George Williams, after holding meetings for prayer and Bible reading with workers in his trade, formed the Young Men's Christian Association. The idea caught on, spread throughout Great Britain, and in 1851 was imported to the United States where the first group was organized in Boston. Within three years enough cities had followed suit so that a convention (including groups in Canada) was held in Buffalo. The program soon expanded to include housing, reading rooms, clubs and study groups, and a vigorous physical training department. In 1869 at Salem, Massachusetts, a boys' program was started which was quickly copied in a good many other places. Now there is hardly a community of any size in the United States which does not have its Y.M.C.A. Its building is one of the principal landmarks of the smaller city, the shouts from its gymnasium one of the familiar American sounds, the lights from its windows a friendly beacon for the young. Of all voluntary associations, it gives the firmest impression of stability and permanence. Its feminine counterpart, organized somewhat later, has similar programs and objectives.

During the Civil War, the Y.M.C.A. worked in camps and hospitals. It has provided important social services during wartime ever since.

A direct outgrowth of the Christian belief in social action, the Y.M.C.A. came just in time (1890 in Bennington) to fill a growing need as society changed from its predominantly rural, small-town, family base to an urban pattern with young people living away from home. Its service to youth was important to a society which no longer used the time and energies of its children in farm or family tasks. When youngsters began going to high school in significant numbers, when factories replaced the farm or the family business in which they were needed, teen-agers were left with time and energy on their hands. The Y.M.C.A. could help to channel energies which might otherwise have exploded in strange forms and unwanted places.

In 1910 another association with the accent on youth was imported from England—the Boy Scouts. When it got here, it found two similar native organizations already at work, or at play—Ernest Thompson Seton's Woodcraft Indians and Dan Beard's Sons of Daniel Boone. Dan Beard became the patron saint of the Scouts, which grew with amazing rapidity on a program of teaching boys all the crafts of the outdoors which their ancestors had learned as a matter of course. Moral and intellectual training were also an important part of the program, but no boy joins an organization to improve his mind or soul.

In addition to having fun and learning new skills, the Scouts also made themselves useful in any number of ways—preventing forest fires, helping in clean-up and safety campaigns, turning out in emergency or disaster, and salvaging waste or distributing posters during the war years. The Scout idea, non-military but disciplined, and based on a boy's need for gang life, was and is a great success—partly because it helped bring the frontier into the city boy's life, but also because it recaptured the principle of boy-training which all primitive or village societies understand.

*   *   *

The community which began to need such associations to care for its young people also began to need other services. The town "poor farm" was no longer an adequate way of caring for those who could not care for themselves. The small budget for poor relief no longer met the needs of an industrial age with its sudden and frightening epidemics of unemployment. In small towns the church still served as a social center, but in the cities where even neighbors were strangers, something else was needed.

In 1886 the Neighborhood Guild—later called University Settlement—was founded in New York City by Stanton Coit who had studied settlement work in England. His hope was to organize poor neighborhoods into groups of about five hundred people, and to lead them to carry out on their own initiative and through their united strength the reforms that were needed for their own betterment. These Guilds could then band together to undertake tasks too big for each one alone. Coit's idea was to provide a minimum of assistance from outside. He expected the Guild members to form a self-directing organization which would raise the moral and material standards of the neighborhood.

Eleven years after the first settlement was established there were 74 of them throughout the United States. By 1900 there were 103, and by 1911 the number had grown to 413.

The settlement answered a need of low-income groups. But they were not the only ones whose social roots had been disturbed by urban industrial life. To meet the wider need came the school center. Since the public school was found everywhere, and since it was nonsectarian and publicly owned, it seemed ready-made for a community center. In 1907 Rochester, New York, began a program (initiated by a joint committee of voluntary associations) of using the schools for social and recreational purposes. Labor unions, women's clubs, and social services combined to launch the program. When the president of the Board of Education spoke at the opening of the first school for this purpose, he stressed the idea that the school center was an institute through which the members of the community could serve themselves. The school board supplied the facilities, but it was up to the people to decide what use to make of them. Edward J. Ward was put in charge of the school center program. He envisioned the school as a place where community problems could be discussed. In addition to recreational and cultural activities, he wanted voters' leagues to unite the people for civic improvement. He thought the school should also serve as a polling place. When the ward bosses caught on to the fact that people might learn the political facts of life at these centers, they killed them. Ward went on to organize school centers throughout Wisconsin.

The idea of a community center was meanwhile being developed, with local variations, all over the country. In Brooklyn the People's Institute helped neighborhoods to set up their own organizations. Public School 63 in New York City seemed to have discovered a formula by which all the city's schools could become centers of community life. After exploring their own needs, the members of such a center would set up a program to meet them. As Clinton S. Childs saw it, "There must be a unifying social bond of feeling, tradition, experience, belief, and knowledge, a common meeting ground, spiritually and concretely speaking. But there must also be a community expression through activity, self-government, and self-support."

Mary Follett in *The New State* saw these neighborhood groups as political units in which men would learn not merely to influence politics but to be politics.

As the movement gained speed, New York City found itself with five major types of community organization at the neighborhood level—settlements, neighborhood associations, community centers operated by the Board of Education, independent community center associations and community councils. Other cities experimented with various forms of the community center, no longer limiting the experiment to low-income neighborhoods.

Then came the depression, bringing the block-aid plan as a means of relieving unemployment by voluntary means. In the state of Washington the state government encouraged the formation of local community councils as a means of preventing the relief program from becoming merely a state handout. It wanted voluntary associations to help communities assimilate the new public welfare program. It wanted to encourage the habit of local responsibility.

War brought a further development in neighborhood organization—the defense council. Over eleven thousand of them were established throughout the country. Though their primary purpose was to protect the civilian population in case of attack and to encourage civilian contributions to the war effort, some of them were concerned with the dislocations caused by war—a heavy influx of workers into war industries, the resulting burden on housing, health and recreation facilities. In some cities block plans were set up to encourage neighborly feeling and foster the sense of mutual trust which would be essential if an emergency arose.

Some cities held on to the machinery set up by Civilian Defense, turning it to peacetime uses. Ninety communities in Tennessee converted their Citizens' Service Corps to permanent community councils.

* * *

The Community Council idea was already well established in many American cities. It was a natural result of the proliferation of voluntary agencies which had been going on since the latter part of the nineteenth century. So many services, if they were to keep from stepping on each other's toes, needed to march in some sort of order. So in 1909 the social agencies in Milwaukee and Pittsburgh set up Councils. Now four hundred cities have them.

"A Council," according to Community Chests and Councils of America, Inc., "is fundamentally a citizens' movement—a voluntary coming together of the citizens of a community for their mutual benefit."

Behind this concept lies the idea that while the individual citizen is primarily responsible for his own health, support and behavior, society does things to some individuals which prevent them—perhaps only temporarily—from caring completely for themselves. Or the whole community is confronted, as in the case of a polio epidemic, with a problem which cannot be solved individually. Or there are recreational needs which must be planned with the whole community in mind.

Agencies to meet these problems grew up haphazardly in America. They grew so luxuriantly that in the larger cities they nearly created chaos. Hence the Council, bringing together all the health, welfare and recreation services. Since service clubs, women's clubs and other civic groups contribute valuable services to the community, they are represented too. Also the Parent-Teacher Association, churches, veterans, nationality groups. The idea is to make the Council a true cross-section of the community. But above all, it must be based on the desire of a group of people to do something themselves to improve conditions in their neighborhood.

It was this desire that aroused the people in the Hough area of Cleveland. Their neighborhood was sliding rapidly downhill when a Catholic bishop, a Presbyterian minister and a social worker suggested the formation of a Neighborhood Council. A public meeting was held, and those who came filled a large hall.

"You can live in a better neighborhood without moving away," they were told. With that promise as their slogan, they formed the Council, set up committees and went to work. They organized a drive to rehabilitate the old houses which had given the area its shabby look, persuading owners to clean up their property and clubbing together to clean up vacant lots or rake up litter and rubbish. They turned the tide against encroaching slum conditions, and their example encouraged other areas to do the same.

The Tremont area had a similar problem. Twenty years ago it was so notorious as a breeder of criminals that people from the area when looking for jobs were afraid to tell where they lived. Dilapidated property, overcrowding, poor sanitation and the poverty of the residents had created an area of blight in which crime, delinquency and sickness festered.

That was before the Tremont Area Civic Association was formed—the first Area Council in Cleveland. They too cleaned up their housing. And as the housing improved, the delinquency rate dropped. Then they persuaded the city to build them a large playground and a swimming pool. Ultimately the Family Service Association decided to close its office there because the need for it had dropped off.

The twenty-five Neighborhood Councils of Cleveland have put on health exhibits, sponsored talent contests, organized youth councils, sponsored chest X-ray campaigns, rat control campaigns, fly campaigns, clean-up campaigns, safety campaigns. They have worked for better family relations and race relations. They have organized youth councils through which teen-agers have been given a stake in the community by helping in door-to-door campaigns. There is no standard pattern. The activities depend on the needs of the neighborhood. They are assisted and advised by Cleveland's central council—the Welfare Federation.

In Troy, New York, the Council of Community Services was faced with the problem of what to do about the railroad yard slums known to everyone who ever passed through Troy on a train. First, students of Russell Sage College called at every shack in the area. They uncovered shocking conditions—so shocking that the conservative local newspaper came out for a Public Housing Authority and the voters approved it, over the protests of some real estate interests.

The Council shifted its investigation to other areas. As quickly as it gathered the facts, the newspaper published them. Interests opposed to doing anything despite the facts threatened to destroy the Community Chest, but the Chest refused to call the Council off.

Today, Troy has its first housing project with more on the way. The railroad slums will soon be cleared, making available space which is badly needed for business use. The new construction will benefit as much as anyone the very real estate interests which fought the clean-up.

In Greenville, South Carolina, the Community Council faced up to the community's biggest problem—the needs of the Negro. The Council had the wisdom to assert that the problem was everybody's business, involving the attitudes and behavior of all the citizens. So it set up a committee of white and Negro leaders, about equally divided as to race and representing the professions, business, trades, social workers and church leaders.

Their first business, the committee decided, was to get the facts. Fact-finding committees were established for twelve fields of service—everything from population and sanitation to housing, employment and community participation. Co-chairmen, white and Negro, headed each committee. They found more than two hundred people who would help make the survey. Ministers rode buses to see what happened on public conveyances. Housewives called on their neighbors. Doctors looked over health facilities. Other professionals studied the facts in their fields. Once the reports were written, discussed and revised, they were sent out to those concerned. One result was that the transportation company made the suggested improvements before the report got into print.

As a result of the facts which had been dug out, things began to happen in Greenville. Housing and slum clearance projects got under way. The Women's Auxiliary of the County Medical Society started a clinic for prenatal care. Negro doctors were invited for the first time to Medical Society meetings. Blinker lights were installed near Negro schools. A state park for Negroes was promised.

Perhaps more important in the long run than all these things was the fact that by working together on committees, white and Negro leaders came to know each other for the first time.

"The survey got people together," said one member. "Meeting and working together—not as people of two races, but as citizens with a common purpose—has been a release and a relief."

In Shreveport, Louisiana, where another careful survey of the Negro community was undertaken by a thousand volunteers working through the Council, publication of the facts brought these results: formation of a permanent committee to improve conditions; a $1,000,000 demonstration in financing low-cost housing with 684 units—privately financed and F.H.A.-approved —under construction and more on the way; extension of the sewage system to areas previously not served; a $20,000,000 bond issue for new schools, over half of which will go into Negro schools; a comprehensive slum clearance program and building code; Negro doctors for the first time admitted to practice and operate in private hospitals, and private rooms made available to Negroes.

The Greenville and Shreveport programs dramatize the importance of digging out the facts about a community—a major function of Councils. Other major functions are: co-ordinating the member agencies, joint action, improving service and efficiency, providing common services such as information, volunteer bureau and community calendar, and keeping the public informed on community problems.

Many Councils set up a volunteer bureau in order to recruit citizens who are willing to work, and to assign them to places where they are needed. Several years ago when the Detroit Volunteer Bureau held its annual presentation of awards at City Hall, 14,810 volunteers had given 986,519 hours of service in health and welfare agencies. One club alone had 450 members who had given a hundred hours each.

Outstanding among Councils is the Welfare Federation of Cleveland which has 168 member organizations, each voluntarily modifying its program of action according to plans worked out jointly by all the members. Together, these organizations spend over $50,000,000 a year. This is big business, and the Federation is organized to cope with it. Five allied councils co-ordinate work for health, children, case work, group work and hospitals. More than thirty central committees cut across functional lines to undertake such various activities as guiding international visitors, studying alcoholism, promoting proper nutrition, investing Federation funds, stimulating action on sex delinquency, and studying the needs of the chronically ill.

Planning, obviously, is an important part of the job. Twelve hundred citizens in Sacramento considered it important enough to give their services during 1952 to the committees of their Community Welfare Council. Through the leadership of a voluntary board of directors, they worked on study committees dealing with adoption, family service, day care, summer camps and civil defense—to name only a few. Their study of the aging led to the formation of the Golden Autumn Club at the City Library for those who wanted to talk about books, and to the Silver Thread Dance Club for folk dancing. When a public controversy arose over the Oak Park Well Baby Clinic, a citizen's committee sifted the facts and came up with twenty very specific suggestions.

Summing up the work of these volunteers, the *Sacramento Union* said: "Here is an instance at the grass roots of democracy in action. Here is proof that citizen participation, on a voluntary basis, in community welfare is inestimably the best way to handle such problems."

The importance of such planning is illustrated by what happened in a small city in upstate New York. The executive officer of its Council chanced to overhear at his service club lunch the remark that the Downtown Shelter was going to open an eye clinic for low-income people. The speaker knew what he was talking about, because he was a member of the Shelter's advisory board, the moving spirit behind the idea—and an optometrist. After lunch the executive had a chat with the chairman of the Shelter's advisory board who was also a member of the Council. He readily agreed that the eye clinic idea should be cleared through the Council.

Next came some fact finding, which disclosed that the Department of Public Welfare already took care of people on relief who needed eye care, that the eye clinic in a local hospital was far from overworked, that the schools screened out children in need of attention and followed up to see that glasses were provided, that service clubs and P.T.A.'s paid for these glasses when parents could not afford them, and that all these services were already well co-ordinated.

The Shelter gladly abandoned its plan.

In Norfolk, Virginia, the Community Chest requested the formation of a Council in order to review the work of the agencies it was supporting. The findings hurt some feelings. They showed that one agency should be discontinued, three others merged under one executive, professional standards raised throughout, buildings renewed or replaced. To check the report, the Chest and the city government asked two outside consultants to investigate. Their findings confirmed what the voluntary committees had said. The Chest then launched a special building fund campaign for $1,250,000, professional standards were raised, and the other changes recommended were made. One result was that while individuals on relief began to receive more, the total disbursements for relief grew less.

Community Councils reflect the growing complexity of our society. They also reflect the healthy tone of voluntarism, which is able not only to organize in order to meet community needs but also to join these separate associations together in a super-association.

"A Community Council," says the Cleveland Federation, "is a group of people in a geographical area who have decided to plan and work together to make their homes, factories, streets, schools, playgrounds and places of business better places in which to live, work, play and grow up. More than that, it is a way in which the men and women who participate become better neighbors, better citizens, and better Americans."

This De Tocqueville would have understood. So would William Bradford, the Vermontville settlers, or the people in the wagon trains. The idea of making a better community has fascinated Americans from the very beginning. They have always known that the way to do it is through voluntary association, which can change as the needs change, merge and dissolve, ebb and flow with the rhythm of life itself. Yet they never quite achieve what they are after, because they keep setting their sights higher and because ornery human nature is always back-sliding.

Still they keep on trying; they keep on volunteering. They do not say it, but they know that the volunteering is itself a way of living and that a community full of volunteers must be on the right track. For is this not what life is for—this exchange of mutual services?

*   *   *

Many nineteenth-century "charities" were built around the idea that the deserving poor, if they were properly grateful, might reasonably expect to be kept from starving by strategically timed handouts. The beautiful word charity thus took on a sanctified odor which, though noticed first by the recipients, eventually became offensive to bystanders and even to well-meaning donors.

Meanwhile the concept of service began to replace the idea of "charity." In 1851 the Boston Y.M.C.A. began its program and became the first group work agency. Two years later came the first foster home service for children, in New York. In 1854 the first day nursery opened, again in New York, following the crèche idea imported from Paris. It was 1877 before New York began the first visiting nurse association, and in the same year Buffalo opened the first family service society. Buffalo proposed to do away with the "charity" approach, the indiscriminate alms-giving which chiefly benefited the shameless, encouraged syco-phancy, and failed to help those who were too proud to beg. Buffalo's Family Service Society was deliberately planned to "organize the charitable impulses and resources of the com-munity in behalf of families in need according to their need." This was a great step forward.

This co-ordination of previously haphazard services moved across the country. Meanwhile the need for another form of co-ordination was becoming apparent—in the field of fund-raising for community services. So in 1887 Denver brought all these services together under the Associated Charities, making one united, community-wide appeal. The ten agencies which had united in this experiment found that they raised more money than they had ever collected through ten separate campaigns, and at less cost.

In 1913 Cleveland added the ideas of budgeting and social planning to the united appeal. Then in 1917 the war emphasized the need for fund raising to support voluntary programs for soldiers both overseas and at home. Three hundred cities organized War Chests for this purpose, and when the war was over, they continued the joint idea which Rochester, New York, christened the Community Chest—a name now widely used. In 1928 the New Orleans Chest hit upon the red feather as a symbol, as by coincidence did Duluth. Meanwhile the various Chests and Councils had formed a national association of their own in 1918. In 1945 Community Chest became the official name and the Red Feather the approved symbol for all the members of this association. By 1953 there were more than 1,700 Chests and other "united funds," more than 400 Councils. More than two million men and women worked in the 1953 campaigns to raise $280,000,000. Many of them went on working throughout the year on the various committees of the Councils.

Of that $280,000,000, it is interesting to note that nearly half went to youth—to the Y.M.C.A., Y.W.C.A., Boy and Girl Scouts, foster care, day nurseries and the rest. Health and family services took almost another quarter, leaving the rest for hospital care, welfare planning and Councils, USO, administration and miscellaneous services. Through the Councils, the work of the private agencies was co-ordinated with public agencies which of course spend a vastly greater sum—around fifteen billions.

To a foreign observer the picture must look hopelessly confusing. Why not turn the whole business over to government? Taxes would then supply the money needed and everyone would be saved the nuisance of fund raising.

Eduard Lindeman, the famous authority on social work, put it this way: "It is difficult to imagine what American life minus its volunteers would be like. . . . Public agencies would take on more and more of the coloration of bureaucracies. Private agencies would, I believe, wither and die. And when private institutions no longer exist, Democracy will have committed suicide."

Community Chests, Councils and agencies, like all the other voluntary associations, are an organic part of American life. They grew because they were needed; they were not organized from the top down. The socialist or the communist or the fascist would persuade or force government to do these things. But if government does them all, dictatorship is inevitable. A people who are content to leave it up to government will soon be the pawns rather than the determiners of government. But a people who are willing to take part, voluntarily, in serving the community will find themselves not only doing a service but living a life. Their service not only cuts the cost of government but raises their own level of experience, sharpens their responses, enlarges their compassion and humanity, broadens their horizons, gives them goals and purposefulness, makes them bigger people.

The Community Chest slogan compresses it all into four words: "Everybody benefits—everybody gives."

* * *

The Bennington Evening Banner is a small-town paper which has the good sense to put some of its local news on the front page. On one front page, picked at random, the following events are recorded:

1. Bennington County Forums is holding its final meeting of the season with speakers from the United Nations and United World Federalists. The public is invited.

2. The Bennington Merchants' Association has just had a dinner meeting at which one state Senator and two town representatives discussed bills before the legislature.

3. A variety show is being put on by volunteers in order to raise money for a family which has been burned out and lost all its belongings. Proceeds will pay for purchasing and moving a small structure to the old foundation.

4. The Community Chest members have met and voted to change their annual meeting from September to January.

5. Blood donors are needed for the Bloodmobile which comes to town tomorrow.

6. The Taxpayers Association will meet at the Y.M.C.A. tomorrow at 7:30.

7. B.P.O. Elks is holding its regular meeting at 7:45.

8. The Knights of Columbus announce a social for tomorrow night.

9. A representative of the Vermont Heart Association will speak at the Bennington White Chapel P.T.A. tomorrow evening.

10. Transportation to the polls and free baby sitters are offered by the Citizens' Committee.

A typical picture of the sort of thing that goes on in Bennington or any other small town. This catches only the more important events, of course. There are more on the inside pages.

Important changes have taken place in the first half of the twentieth century. Bennington's needs are no longer met by a dozen organizations. Today there are more than a hundred. They include the fraternal orders, the service clubs, three associations of businessmen, a handful of professional organizations, unions, the Grange and Farm Bureau, church groups, two veterans' societies, half a dozen women's organizations including those described in other chapters, a Dale Carnegie alumni group, a wonderfully fine community chorus, and a Family Service Center which is largely supported by another useful volunteer organization—the Thrift Shop.

This network of associations is bound together by no formal plan, for Bennington has no Community Council. Yet it is a web strong enough to support the unfortunate and the distressed as well as to maintain a constant onward drive the object of which, in that homely American phrase, is to make Bennington "a better place in which to live."

No doubt there are services Bennington lacks. No doubt there is poor co-ordination and overlapping. But informal as the system is, it works because there is informal agreement about fundamentals—that the town is a good one which can always be made better, and that voluntary service is the way to do it. These are postulates every American takes for granted. The system works, too, because people know each other, know what is going on and can pretty well supplement each other without toe-treading. Active citizens belong to all the general civic associations because a contribution gives them membership. They attend the annual meetings of perhaps half a dozen organizations, go to a weekly or bi-weekly service club or to several women's groups, serve on several committees and act as chairman or president of at least one activity. They see each other, work together, know what is going on, and by informal contact keep the thing in balance. The chief fault in their performance is not their fault at all; it is that not enough people get into the act. One of the major advantages of all these associations is that they bring together people of differing occupations, neighborhoods, religions and incomes. They therefore help to make Bennington a true community by preventing it from falling apart into cells and cliques.

Most of these associations have state and national affiliations. Officers who go to conventions thus get a sense of belonging to something a good deal bigger than the home chapter. They carry this feeling back with them to the chapter. Usually there is a national publication which reinforces the feeling of solidarity. Sometimes the scope is truly international. Actually, therefore, a member of Rotary who helps dig post holes for a fence at the new deer park, attends the Vermont–New Hampshire district meeting, visits other clubs while traveling, listens to a talk from his district governor who has been to an international convention, and reads constantly in his magazine of what clubs in other communities are doing—this citizen feels his kinship with other citizens on several levels. He may also be having similar experiences in several other organizations.

As our cities have grown bigger and our civilization more complicated, membership in voluntary associations has provided a substitute for the tightly integrated village life. It has provided a way for people to belong to several communities, great and small. And as improved transportation and communication have made states, then the whole country and then the world interdependent, membership in voluntary associations has provided the emotional culture which ties individuals into these wider groupings. So the network of membership in local associations is only a small part of the picture. American society is held together by an intricate and voluminous weaving of voluntary relationships which give stability and strength to the whole structure. This is one of the unrecognized benefits of voluntarism.

* * *

What makes people volunteer?

The Vassar Summer Institute of Family and Community Living tried to get the answer to this several years ago, in a three-day symposium headed by outstanding leaders in the field of social work.

Leading reasons given were the desire to do something useful and the need of an interest outside the home.

"Because you meet interesting people," was high on the list. Also "because friends are working at volunteer jobs," "because it gives you a feeling of prestige and importance" and "because you are prodded by a need felt for self or family."

"I have so much energy," said one young mother, "I just have to do something."

Another said, "I felt I wasn't making enough of a contribution by keeping house and bringing up children."

Said a maturer woman: "I am scared by the wave of reaction in this country, so I feel it important to do something about it."

"Why don't we say something about the fun of working with others?" asked an experienced volunteer.

"Especially when it's something you really believe in," another woman added.

"Sure, there are tough spots, but it's like family life—your ultimate goal carries you over the bumps. And the net effect is fun."

"You can't put volunteer work into a pigeonhole," added a thoughtful woman, "because it's not apart from living."

"You do volunteer work because you are what you are," still another woman agreed. "It comes naturally, like breathing."

"It's not apart from living—it comes naturally, like breathing." These statements express, off-hand and unself-consciously, what this book has been trying to say. Their very off-handedness proves the point.

It only remains to try to state somewhat more systematically the underlying philosophy of this nation of joiners.

XIII

A *Dangerous Freedom*

How do voluntary associations affect life in the United States? As soon as it is phrased, the question seems absurd. We cannot imagine life in America without these associations, for they are not only a part of that life; they provide the pattern on which it is formed, the mold in which it is cast. They make possible the continuous dynamic balance among economic groups which prevents any one group from getting control over the economy. They find the sore spots in our social order and attempt to heal them. They promote the discussion of public affairs, guard our civil liberties, deepen the cultural life, elevate standards of health and community living. To their members they give a purpose, a sense of moving toward a goal.

Some form of group life is essential to all normal people. We must belong to something bigger than ourselves, bigger than the family. But when it gets too big, it gets too vague. Membership in the human race is rarely capable, alas, of stirring up such an intense feeling of brotherhood as one has in his Masonic Lodge, Kiwanis Club or Grange. Membership in such groups as these rewards the member with the warm sense of being part of something, of being accepted, recognized, appreciated. Sociologists call it status.

We like to make fun of ourselves for joining things. One reason we make fun is that we have been brought up to believe that individualism is the highest human achievement. It is therefore weak of us to want to congregate and we must there-

fore laugh off this weakness. In fact, however, it is our individualism we ought to laugh about. There is no need to be shamefaced
about being joiners, for that persistent habit of getting together
"to do something about it" is responsible for most of what is best
in American life.

"Multiply your associations and be free," said Proudhon.
Americans have been doing just that for several hundred years.
If you are a young student of sociology who makes a study of life
in Harlem you may, like Mary Ovington, spark the formation of
a group to do something about the conditions uncovered. This
was the origin of the National Association for the Advancement
of Colored People. If you are alarmed by political bosses who try
to stifle free speech, or by states which will not allow the theory
of evolution to be taught, you go out and found the American
Civil Liberties Union as Roger Baldwin did. Or you concern
yourself with some purely local need—and form a playground
association or a parent-teacher group.

The enormous proliferation of special-interest association is,
from a sociologist's point of view, the distinguishing feature of
American life. Many of these associations are transitory—they
are born without labor and die without too much pain. Others
endure for decades or even centuries. In either case membership
is confined to no single group. Therefore the intricate network of
memberships ties people together in many groupings. This is
very different from the village society in which the whole group
works and plays and worships together, carrying on all its activities as an all-purpose organization. The civic-minded American enjoys a variety of associations, each one adapted to some
special interest or obligation. There has been a tendency of late
to idealize the *gemeinschaftliche* kind of community where all
functions are performed by the whole group working together.
But membership in a number of associations, each one directed
at a goal, is actually far more stimulating and productive of
results. The man and wife who sing in a community chorus,
serve on education and political committees, attend Rotary and
the Woman's Club, help get out the vote for the party and study

pending legislation through the League of Women Voters, are by any standard of culture at least as well off as the villager who follows the ways of his father no matter what the impact of changing times does to change his conditions of life.

But don't all these associations by their very number constitute a kind of disorganization? On this point Jesse Steiner says in *The American Community in Action:*

"The disorganization that grows out of the multiplicity of divisions within a community is in itself nothing to be disturbed about. The large variety of group relationships that have become so common in this country has resulted in opening up new worlds of activity to people who otherwise would have no escape from narrowness and provincialism. To attempt to avoid the confusion that grows out of diversity by placing restrictions on the right to organize is unthinkable."

The number of opportunities for group activity helps to keep us alert. For every interest we feel, there is a group of people somewhere waiting for us to join, pay our dues, and get to work. This rich complex of free associations is the fountainhead of liberal democracy. De Tocqueville understood this when he wrote:

"The most democratic country on the face of the earth is that in which men have in our time carried to the highest perfection the art of pursuing in common the object of their common desires, and have applied this new science to the greatest number of purposes. Is this the result of accident? Or is there in reality any necessary connection between the principle of association and that of equality?"

Amazed at the way Americans formed associations for every purpose of life—to give entertainments, found schools and hospitals, build inns and churches, circulate books and send missionaries to the antipodes, De Tocqueville noted that "wherever, at the head of some new undertaking, you see the Government in France, or a man of rank in England, in the United States you will be sure to find an association. . . . It is evident that [the

English] consider association as a powerful means of action, but [the Americans] seem to regard it as the only means they have of acting."

"What political power," De Tocqueville asks, "could ever carry on the vast multitude of lesser undertakings which the American citizens perform every day, with the assistance of the principle of association?"

Returning to the notion of free association as a "science," he remarks:

"In democratic countries the science of association is the mother of science; the progress of all the rest depends upon the progress it has made. Amongst the laws which rule human societies there is one which seems to be more precise and clear than all others. If men are to remain civilized, or to become so, the art of associating together must grow and improve in the same ratio in which equality of conditions is increased."

De Tocqueville might have added that the very number and variety of voluntary associations buttresses democracy by bringing into existence groups which cross "class" lines, by offering an outlet for creative energies, by giving all the participants a stake in the system and a determination to maintain it so that their lives may proceed undisturbed.

Associations in the United States generally have a great tolerance for differences of opinion and background within themselves. The Grange or the Farm Bureau manages to hold together members whose economic interests are in conflict, and even these differences would seem to be serious enough. Yet both groups have members not only among working, commercial farmers but among people who simply happen to be living in the country though they work in cities, or among industrial workers and other residents in rural and semirural areas. Clubs like Rotary make a special point of getting cross-representation of business, trade, professional and farm (though not labor) people.

❀　❀　❀

Most remarkable of all voluntary associations is the political party, which instead of trying to draw like-minded people together as our third parties have attempted to do, tries to hold within its expansive arms every variety and shade of political opinion. The third party has failed precisely because it has tried to be consistent.

Foreign visitors think our party system more than slightly insane, while we ourselves often complain that our parties ought to stand for something—that the Democrats, let us say, might as well *be* a liberal party, the Republicans conservative. Then a man could know what he was voting for, a party could have some idea how it was supposed to perform, and the executive could have some hope of putting through the measures promised in the platform.

But this is to overlook completely the important social role of the American political party, as of all our other voluntary associations.

From very early times Americans have dreamed and spoken of a classless society. Frontier conditions fostered the absence of class because even the preacher had to roll up his sleeves to get his church built. Americans have always regarded class as one of the things their ancestors left Europe to escape. One reason why Marxism has failed to attract more than a handful is its insistence on class struggle with its consequent emphasis on class difference. The American way has been to wipe out class difference by constantly raising the standards of the poor and chipping away at the incomes of the rich, while making it possible to pass easily from one status to another.

To iron out the differences between different economic, social, geographic, religious, ethnic and occupational groups has been one of the great goals of American society. The vastness and diversity of the land may have made this a necessity, though it is an interesting speculation what might have happened if France had held on to the North American continent, in view of the splinter parties which have all but destroyed her political effectiveness at home. Whatever the causes, it is apparent that

Americans are determined to be united, even though this involves some sacrifice of principles all around, a constant accommodation to the needs and interests of others, an unrelenting willingness and ability to compromise. We know that we must do this or we shall fall apart. One reason for the often-lamented lack of logical consistency and intellectual muscle tone in our political behavior is that we consider it more important to live at times illogically than to be logically and permanently dead.

Our political parties, therefore, are marvels of inconsistency consistently arrived at. Each party is a friend of the farmer, the laborer, the businessman—though sometimes only the small businessman, whose size seems to confer an unassailable virtue. Each party promises to raise incomes, lower taxes, increase benefits, decrease government spending, find more business for both exporter and importer, make the country stronger and do it with a smaller defense establishment, strengthen civil liberties and stamp out subversion, put an end to discrimination and protect states' rights. Since such a performance requires the services of a master magician, we elect as President the man who most successfully hypnotizes us into thinking that he can achieve the impossible. And when the hypnosis begins to wear off and we awake to reality again, we go to work through our organizations in order to bring pressure on the President and Congress to favor our side at the expense of the other. But since all the other sides are equally busy, what we achieve is a dynamic middle-of-the-road course.

The American system could be compared to the driver of a car with helpers seated on each side of him with their hands on the wheel and a car full of other helpers in the back seat. The driver—the President—tries to listen to all the voices from the rear. The front-seat helpers listen only to their backers, who hold contrary opinions. Since these two front-seat helpers exert a pretty constant pressure in opposite directions, the vehicle runs a fairly straight course down the middle of the road. But if a crisis arises the cries from the rear stimulate one helper to superhuman exertion, with the result that he nearly lands the vehicle in the ditch. Other cries stimulate the other helper, who obligingly heads the car for the other ditch. In this perilous situation, the riders raise their voices together, the helpers relax their grip, and the President is allowed to do the steering. With that hubbub still ringing in his ears, he tries to steer so as to arouse no one. But soon the performance starts all over again.

But the important point to notice is that the pressures which come from both sides are not divided according to party. Each party contains within itself a full variety of contrary pressures, which in turn are exerted upon the members of Congress in such a fashion that members of the same party will vote sometimes with the majority of their party, sometimes against, and in various combinations with members of both parties, depending on the issue. Each party is an association of men and women of varied backgrounds and interests. If their interests are to be represented, they must constantly be busy within the party. The result is illogical—but dynamic.

Again, the associations which act as pressure groups cannot afford to throw in their lot with one party alone. When they have tried it in the past, the results have usually been poor. Though they may attempt to be influential within the parties, from the local level on up, they must also exert pressure directly upon elected officials both in the legislative and executive branches—again at all levels. A further influence is exerted through appointed officials in friendly departments. The Farm Bureau has a recognized influence in the Department of Agriculture, business associations in Commerce, and a number of interests in the Department of the Interior. These arrangements are extra-legal, but they give practical recognition to the fact that American life is controlled by voluntary associations.

This interplay between government and voluntary associations goes on in any number of ways. When the Office of Defense Mobilization wanted to do something about employment of the handicapped, for instance, it called on the services of half a dozen voluntary welfare associations. The members of the

"Task Force" it set up included business and labor representation.

That strangely maligned government agency, TVA, which is looked upon abroad as America's outstanding achievement in the use and conservation of human and natural resources—TVA has shown how voluntary association on the local level can work with government. Instead of forcing a program upon hostile communities, TVA officials sought local understanding and co-operation. They went out to the farms, brought small groups of farmers together in the rural schools, explained what TVA could do for them and then waited patiently until suspicion and ignorance began to give way to hope and mutual aid.

TVA was the first major attempt to do what John Dewey had proposed—to use experimental methods in releasing the powers of human nature in the service of a freedom which is co-operative and a co-operation which is voluntary. It demonstrated the possibility of planning which was not imposed from the top, but rather worked out co-operatively with those involved. It took advantage of the American preference for voluntary association and showed people how to help themselves by helping each other. It made higher standards of living possible throughout a whole area, improved health, schooling, recreation facilities, revived industry, prevented flood and drought, added vastly to the power resources and thus to the wealth of the nation. Because it seemed to challenge business interests, its great social achievements have been ignored. But Palestine and India could see in it what many Americans failed to see—the best flowering and blending of two outstanding American traits—a genius for technology and a gift for voluntary association.

The reliance of government upon the voluntary activity of its citizens is deeply rooted. Since our first settlements were communities of choice, we have always looked at government as something we devised and should control and serve, rather than as something which should control us. The Constitution, by leaving with the states all the powers it did not specifically assume, and the states by leaving with the towns their ancient privileges, create an amount of political activity on all levels which involves a good many people in politics. The local, state and federal centers of political activity foster the formation of voluntary groups which can influence or direct political bodies. And this tendency to encourage group initiative helps to develop voluntary activity for other purposes.

As Frederick Lewis Allen has pointed out in *The Big Change:* "The moral and intellectual strength of the United States is based in considerable degree upon private organizations which are as consecrated to the idea of public duty as governmental ones should be, and in part perform services almost indistinguishable from governmental ones, but provide at the same time diversity and flexibility of approach, and vastly more interest, than could be harnessed in any other way."

The federal system itself, upon which our governmental structure is built, implies consent rather than constraint, with power held at local levels instead of being surrendered to one central body. Though we are now bound in one indissoluble union, we know that this union was originally based upon consent, even though on one occasion it had to be maintained by force. It is maintained by leaving great areas of power with the states and local communities, even when this division is very costly to us as a nation, as in the matter of racial discrimination.

Like government itself, our voluntary associations also follow the federal principle. The American Medical Association is a federation of state medical societies which in turn are built up from county societies. Grange, unions, women's clubs and service groups have a similar structure—not so very different, after all, from the way the Sons of Liberty worked things out. Federalism, like voluntary association, is an American habit. They go hand in hand.

*   *   *

We are familiar enough with the way voluntary associations influence and interact with the legislative and executive branches of government. Their relationship with the judicial—with the law itself—is less apparent. Yet it exists.

Judge Lester A. Drenk of Burlington County in New Jersey was disturbed by the youngsters who were brought into his court on one charge or another. His powers of jailing, threatening, putting on probation seemed entirely inadequate. What good were these ways of dealing with vagrancy brought on by brutal or ignorant parents or with delinquency arising out of broken or miserable homes?

While he was thinking about this problem, he heard of a system which had been used in Perth Amboy—a system of local juvenile courts made up of citizens. Judge Drenk asked John S. Conroy III, Deputy Attorney General, to get the service clubs throughout the county to assemble lists of civic-minded men and women who would be willing to serve on such courts. Wherever possible, these people were to be parents, and they were to represent every walk of life. The panels were given power to hold formal hearings, call witnesses and prescribe remedies. Their decisions were reviewed by the judge, but unless the case was an unusually serious one, he never saw the youngster involved.

Instead of trying to punish, these courts tried to understand. They heard the complaining witness first, then the child. Then they called in the parents and asked their opinion. Members of the panel went over the child's school record. Hearings were held in private and the decision of the court was given out only to those concerned.

One of their cases involved a boy of good family who got involved with two other boys in "borrowing" cars. One night they got hold of some wine, got drunk, broke into a church, smashed a stained glass window and threw the communion vessels in the river. Under the old system they would have been vigorously punished. But the juvenile court looked at all the facts, learned that the ringleader was in an unhappy home, and arranged for him to go into the Marines, which was what he wanted. Once away from home, he straightened out and was soon fighting and being decorated in Korea. The parents paid for the damage done. Instead of punishing the boy and leaving him embittered, the cause of his delinquency was removed.

Voluntary groups of citizens, knowing local conditions and personalities, can do what formal courts cannot.

Then there is the work of the American Arbitration Association, a voluntary organization which aims at solving problems before they reach the courts. Characteristically, arbitration in America is a voluntary activity, while in many countries it is controlled by government.

An actor in a Broadway mystery drama was wearing his own full dress suit when the revolver with which he was supposed to be shot came so close to him that a hole was burnt in his trousers. The actor demanded a new suit, the theater manager said the hole was in the trousers only, so why should he pay for a whole suit? An arbitrator, an expert on textiles, explained that it was practically impossible to make a proper match. So the actor got the suit.

From small matters like these to disputes between commercial interests half the world apart, the method of arbitration is now being used as a substitute for court action. A flexible process, it is not bound by the sometimes outdated and often time-consuming conventions of the courts. The disputants agree upon an umpire who is an expert in their field, and then agree to be bound by his decision. This is the essence of arbitration as compared with mediation or conciliation. Consent and equity are substituted for constraint and legality. Voluntary self-regulation takes the place of enforcement. Since arbitral awards are based upon contracts, they have the force of court decisions and can be filed in the appropriate court of record.

Over 90 per cent of American labor contracts today carry standard arbitration clauses which solve disputes before they occur. Yet hundreds of peaceful settlements go unnoticed while strikes get all the limelight.

In one case, a company brought in a new plant manager who promptly fired ten employees for loitering in the washroom. All of them had worked ten years or more for the company. The union claimed discrimination; management was determined to back up the new manager to prove his authority. With the workers on the point of striking, both sides sought arbitration. The arbitrator decided that while the men had been loitering, their previous records warranted reinstatement. There was no strike.

The American Arbitration Association has thirteen thousand arbitrators in sixteen thousand cities. Experts are available in every line of business. Disputants choose their own arbitrators (usually three), and settlement usually takes place within a week. Arbitration of commercial disputes between firms of different nations has saved thousands in court costs and more thousands in good will and future business. A system of world-wide arbitration is growing up which could in time become a powerful force for peace. Like the wagon train councils which settled each dispute as it arose, the arbitral system shows the same love of direct action, the same faith in the wisdom and ability of the citizen to handle his own affairs in association with other citizens.

*　*　*

This self-reliance is the mark of a society still optimistic about itself, possessing the self-confidence of youth together with its optimism and idealism. It is the mark of a society which welcomes change because within its experience change has always meant progress, even when it has been so rapid and radical as to seem revolutionary.

Such a society is held together, like the atom, by a constant tension and balance of forces. Not a fixed system, it is adaptable —able to benefit from changes in the environment, from technological advance. It is not static but dynamic, kept alert by a highly productive economy the fruits of which are continuously being extended.

This dynamism is maintained largely by voluntary associations. They provide the infinitely adaptable instrument by which changes are brought about—the political parties, pressure groups, welfare agencies, fraternal organizations, protest groups. They form, accomplish their work, and die. In their places come other associations which do the same. They make our culture lively, varied, zestful.

Yet they grew up in a period when philosophers glorified the individual and looked with suspicion at the group. Rousseau with his belief in the naturally good man who had been corrupted by society, Darwin with his emphasis on the struggle for survival which Spencer handily adapted to justify the predatory industrialist—these men prepared the platform for the doctrine of rugged individualism which in turn provided a philosophy for the "malefactors of great wealth." It has been fashionable to identify rugged individualism with the frontier, but we have seen that association in groups was a far more distinctive trait of frontier life, as of American life generally.

Along with the doctrine of individualism, Western civilization has developed the power state. These two ideas are not at all as incompatible as they may seem. The power state (at certain stages) is willing to accept the emphasis on individualism because an individual unsupported by any group is helpless whenever the state wants to limit his liberties.

The idea of society as consisting of morally autonomous individuals rather than as a constellation of groups is closely related to the idea of a society in which all authority is vested in the state. The theory of individualism therefore plays into the hands of authoritarianism. Without voluntary association, individuals become the pawns of the all-powerful state. Only as they associate freely can they acquire strength to resist the encroachments of the power state. Hitler knew this when he destroyed every kind of association from Boy Scouts to labor unions. Marx regarded all the traditional associations with hostility—the family, the neighborhood, the church, the voluntary associations. Any force within a democracy which attempts to stamp out voluntary association must be regarded as a danger.

The voluntary association is freedom exercising itself through group activity—the only way the individual can enjoy his freedom as a whole man.

Freedom with responsibility is the essence of democracy; in a democracy they are inseparable.

De Tocqueville noticed this when he said:

"The free institutions which the inhabitants of the United States possess, and the political rights of which they make so much use, remind every citizen, and in a thousand ways, that he lives in society. They every instant impress upon his mind the notion that it is the duty, as well as the interest of men, to make themselves useful to their fellow-creatures. . . . Men attend to the interests of the public, first by necessity, afterwards by choice: what was intentional becomes an instinct; and by dint of working for the good of one's fellow citizens, the habit and the taste for serving them is at length acquired."

From Plymouth on we have watched the intentional become instinctive, until the forming of an association "to do something about it" is now almost entirely instinctive with us. But behind the instinct lies the essentially moral idea that if men want to be free, they must serve each other, for no man is strong enough to be free by himself. Freedom in America has therefore not meant freedom from responsibilities—or when it has, we have been ashamed of it. It has meant freedom to develop the good life by service to the community—which in the end is the best kind of self-service.

In America this sense of the individual's responsibility for the public welfare is pretty much taken for granted, and we jealously guard the responsibility from a government which is always reaching out to take over. Because the essence of Americanism is the contract, the voluntary association, we are suspicious of assigning to a government bureau any function which can be handled by our multitudinous organizations. Within ourselves we have felt a personal responsibility to do as individuals what the socialist would hand over to the state.

*　*　*

Two currents of thought have run through the power network of American society—Puritanism and pragmatism.

Puritanism emphasized the importance of the individual soul, and the right of the individual to interpret the Bible for himself —Luther's "priesthood of all believers." It emphasized too the obligation of the individual to live a life of Christian service, to live therefore responsibly. Its firm belief in the dignity of man, in reason, and in the compact as the basis of the social order, were and are important contributions to American character.

Pragmatism is essentially the experimental method, the method of science—"Let's try it and see." This willingness to experiment and change is the essence of democracy, which is strengthened by change, not overthrown by it. For just as the scientific method is undamaged by developments which change scientific theories, so democracy is strengthened by its experiments. Authoritarian systems, on the other hand, cannot forsake the rigid assumptions on which they are founded, and therefore fear change and will resist it with whatever brutalities they consider necessary. But since they cannot either prevent change or adapt themselves to it, it will destroy them sooner or later.

While pragmatism—putting ideas to work and judging them by the results—is a fairly new word, it is an old habit. Inevitably it appealed to men who had to adjust themselves to a new environment. Ways of farming and building, relations with the Indians, the building up of institutions, communities, governments—all called for improvising and experimenting. The Declaration of Independence was a pragmatic act on the part of the signers, as was the Constitution.

Voluntarism combines the two. It is an open channel for the Puritan sense of individual responsibility and for the pragmatic method. Add to this the suspicion of authority which has always bedeviled American life, and voluntarism is the inevitable choice of citizens who want to acquire the services society needs without piling up government bureaus. It also helps to soak up the endless restlessness of the American who has more energy than he knows what to do with and a hunger for new horizons.

It offers a means of trying out ideas which may later gain government sponsorship, and thus prevents little errors from becoming big ones. The failure of a voluntary association can be positively advantageous where that of a government experiment might be disastrous.

Puritan and pragmatist, individualist and socially-conscious, traditionalist and experimentalist can all find common ground in the practice of voluntary association. Here if anywhere the conflict between the two aspects of life, individual and social, can be harmonized.

We ourselves, and much more those who look at us from outside, have mistaken pragmatism for materialism and Puritanism for intolerance. While we have been at our worst both materialistic and intolerant, these faults have actually been the by-products of our virtues, the defects of our qualities. A strong tone of idealism has run through American thought and history —an unwillingness to be satisfied with things as they are. This urge to change things has improved our material circumstances, but it has also raised health standards, built colleges and churches, poured out millions for the relief of suffering in far places, fostered adult education, supported symphony orchestras, museums and art galleries. Ours—not Marxism—is the authentic revolution.

Marxism, which claims to be revolutionary, is in fact more ruthless and exploitive than any capitalist system, and with its slave labor and police control of every aspect of life has already equaled Hitlerism and in some respects surpassed it. The Communist state is not revolutionary but reactionary.

The past hundred years have proven Marx wrong, not only in his falsification of the facts of the social order, but in every prediction as to the outcome of capitalism. There is no such thing as a cohesive "working class" whose interests are opposed to a non-working class. Rather, society is made up of many rather vaguely defined groups. Nor has Marx's "law of increasing misery of the working class" operated as he predicted. Instead, the rewards of technical progress have been shared among all groups while health, education and welfare standards have risen most rapidly in the countries that have industrialized most completely. Meanwhile the communist state, far from withering away as Marx predicted, has become a monstrous instrument of oppression, controlling the entire economy, the school system, the culture, and even requiring scientists to prostitute the experimental method to conclusions predetermined by Marxist theory.

Yet with every fact in our favor, communism is winning the battle for men's minds. It is winning largely by default, because it offers a simple program and a glittering future. The sick and the hungry cannot afford to worry about the prison camps, the slave labor, the lack of political freedom. Their need is urgent. Time is against them, and the communists promise a quick way out.

Perhaps we might have something to offer them, if we believed in what we have ourselves. But when they look toward America, what do they see? The fear of communism seems to occupy us more than anything else. We seem to put forward no positive program of our own, nothing they can grasp. In fact, we seem to be occupied with stamping out our own best heritage —our free associations. Congressional investigating committees make it a crime for a man to have associated with someone who may once have belonged to something called a communist front organization. Government employees are the objects of suspicion unless they can prove that they never associated with anything or anybody who in turn ever knew a communist or gave a dollar to a cause later determined to be pro-communist. The attack is actually against voluntary association itself, since any association by present standards of judgment may sooner or later be branded subversive.

De Tocqueville wrote: "If a certain moment in the existence of a nation be selected, it is easy to prove that political associations perturb the State, and paralyze productive industry; but take the whole life of a people, and it may perhaps be easy to demonstrate that freedom of association in political matters is favorable to the prosperity and even to the tranquility of the community." Wise words, prophetic in their application to our own times.

* * *

Men and women everywhere today seek emotional stability. They seek assurance that there is a way of life which can give them not only bread, but shared experience.

There are really only two ways of providing this. One is the patriarchal method, in which the citizen submits himself to the state as a child to a father, and depends upon the state to tell him what to do and give him what it thinks good for him. This is the way of absolute monarchy and dictatorship. It is currently the way of Soviet Russia.

The other way is fratriarchal. It assumes that all men are brothers, each with a vote as good as the next man's and entitled to the equal opportunity which permits every man to find his own level. Its pattern is horizontal rather than vertical. The state does not dictate to men; men determine what the powers of the state shall be. This is democracy.

Every society rests upon an emotional culture, and since emotions are formed upon childhood associations, a society must base its culture upon family relationships. A community is a social unit to which the family emotional culture has been extended, and every community has its symbols which establish that family feeling. So a college becomes alma mater, the church a mother, the nation a fatherland, the secret order a brotherhood.

In a democracy, voluntary association supplies these familial relationships. As the true family harmonizes authority with equality and growth, the democratic community must provide leadership without dictatorship, authority without authoritarianism. Every association gives its members a sense of belonging to a family-like group, and membership conveys a sense of fatherly guidance and mothering care. If every person in our democracy could be tied into the community by such membership, crime and delinquency would diminish.

Jesus in his life and teachings showed the importance of brotherly emotion in the working out of a common purpose. Where God had been thought of before as a patriarchal force, Jesus preached the brotherhood of all men—a proposition which in his day must have seemed absurd. Yet this idea was transformed into belief by emotionalizing it—clear proof of the power of the emotional culture. Christianity thus laid the emotional groundwork for democracy, whose basic propositions are that political authority lies not in a king but in the people; that intellectual authority lies not in custom and superstition but in reason; and that religious and moral authority lies in the individual conscience.

This was a great advance over absolute monarchy, mumbo-jumbo and superstition. It marked an advance in the emotional culture from patriarchal to fratriarchal—an advance which summarizes the whole march of mankind. To return to patriarchal forms is to retreat into absolutism, to lose all the gains humanity has made. This is what communism does.

"The manifest destiny of mankind," wrote Walter Lippmann in *The Good Society,* "is to become adult and to replace paternal authority with fraternal association."

Communism would reverse the trend. Yet to millions in search of bread and faith, communism seems preferable to the individualist materialism which America is thought to stand for, because the promise of a shared burden is emotionally preferable to the lonely road of individualism. They do not know that in America it is voluntarism—a free, dignified, unregimented working together toward social goals—that dominates our behavior.

The popular phrase for it is teamwork. In its origin, "team" means family. That comes pretty close to expressing the too-long-ignored yet traditional American ideal of men joined together in a common effort as closely as a family is bound. If we can make men *feel* that this is what we stand for, if we can find a way to let it into their hearts, we shall have provided an ideal to arouse those who now float apathetically in an eddy between the two tides of ruthless collectivism and selfish individualism.

It is the function of a democracy not to stifle free association, but to foster it; not to regiment but to encourage cultural diversity and the proliferation of associations which will represent all the interests of a mentally alert and morally responsible citizenry. Such a pluralism is the best defense against statism and dictatorship. Consciously or otherwise, those who attempt to inhibit associations by breeding fear are mentally oriented toward totalitarianism. It is time we stopped acting as if we were plunging into socialism or worse and realized that we have, as Frederick Lewis Allen says, found a way beyond socialism—a way to meet social needs without resorting to rigid state controls. That way is voluntarism.

Grave questions remain unsolved. How can we involve the many citizens who now stand outside the network of associations? How can this involvement be brought to the fluid populations in great cities who never stay long enough to grow roots? How can this cultural disintegration be halted? Is the Greenbelt kind of community an available solution? How can the pleasure and stimulation of group activity and community service be conveyed to those who have never tried it? How can the individual's responsibility for the group be made clear? How can our political parties become widely based voluntary associations, so that all of us will feel politically effective? How do we create the right emotional culture? How do we make life in a democracy exciting?

De Tocqueville speaks of the American genius for association as "a dangerous freedom." Americans, influenced by their English ancestors and by conditions peculiar to the new land, form associations for every possible purpose, managing their politics and all their civil affairs by this method. But such a freedom holds great danger, since it is dependent upon the moral fiber of the citizens. "It is by the enjoyment of a dangerous freedom that the Americans learn the art of rendering the dangers of freedom less formidable."

Could we capitalize upon the drama inherent in this danger

to attract men toward voluntary activity? Might we succeed in showing that the give and take, the reconnoitering, the struggle of opposing opinions, the ultimate victory involved in voluntary association are more fun than watching a horse opera or a prize fight—that it is always more fun to take part than to look on?

Somehow we must extend the beloved community to all our citizens. For the majority of Americans the village community is no longer available. But the warmth it generated can be recaptured through voluntary association, the unifying factor in our dynamic, diverse culture.

In the philosophy of Josiah Royce, the absolute assumes the form of a personified beloved community to which men are bound by a fervor of self-sacrifice and self-interest. That this is an authentic American vision is proved by the Mayflower Compact, the village republics, the devotion of dedicated people like Levi Coffin and Susan Anthony. They stand on the side of all the positive values we assert—democracy, freedom, brotherhood, creative activity, community. All these values assume an underlying base of voluntarism—the right to choose, the freedom to serve.

To enjoy such a freedom, as De Tocqueville observed, is dangerous. But not as dangerous as to lose it.

XIV

World Community and World Government

Voluntary association has worked for us, and worked well, at home. Has it anything to offer in an era when our major problems lie in the far parts of the world? Has it a part to play in the world struggle between freedom and totalitarianism?

In 1947 Elmore McKee went to the American Zone in Germany as head of mission for the American Friends Service Committee. His job was to develop self-help neighborhood centers in the bombed-out areas of Frankfort-am-Main and Berlin. After the Frankfort center had opened, McKee was at a meeting of its directors when the matter of opening a community laundry came up. The German directors had invited some laundry professionals to tell them how it should be done. McKee suggested that a committee of three be appointed which would include a laundry professional, a social worker and a neighborhood mother.

"In Germany we leave such matters to the experts," said one of the board members, a clergyman.

That evening McKee was having coffee with his friend Dr. Rudolf Prestel, one of the directors and also commissioner of welfare for Frankfort.

"The difference between your country and mine was demonstrated this afternoon," McKee told him.

"How is that?"

"In your country you tend to leave things to the experts. In America we believe that everyone concerned with an issue should have something to say about it. For instance, if we were going to open a community laundry, we would consult all the people who would be deeply concerned with it. We would try to get the complete horizontal human picture. In Germany you bow to the experts. The human element doesn't seem to enter in. The picture, in other words, is vertical, authoritarian. Between classifications—horizontally—there is no give and take, no cross-fertilization."

"Is that what you mean by democracy?" Prestel asked.

"Yes," said McKee, "the chance to plan and to execute and to be responsible. If people learn to face issues in one area, they will be ready to do the same elsewhere—in education, business, politics."

Prestel thought a while. Then he said: "I have been waiting a long time to find out what your government means by democracy. Now I begin to see. I can see too that this Germany very much needs. We shall try to make these centers places where this new thing can be tried."

The directors reconsidered their decision about the laundry. Gradually the Quaker centers became laboratories of democratic process. Because the American representatives of the Friends Service Committee lived in German homes and became part of the life, the people they worked with learned the methods of democracy more readily from them than from military government. Democracy became an experience, not merely a word or a theory.

This, Elmore McKee thought, was the test of freedom and democracy—not whether people pay lip service to the ideals but how they follow these principles in their daily lives. *Responsible shared action,* he concluded, was the heart of democracy. After helping to establish this practice in Germany, he returned home to set up an outstanding series of radio programs, "The People Act," which showed American communities engaging in just this kind of action. A number of these stories have been told in Chapter 1.

McKee's experience in Germany is paralleled by that of a

German social worker who came to America just before the second World War to escape Hitlerism and found a job with a youth organization in a Midwestern city. Though he had risked his life for democracy, he was surprised to find its principles being applied not only in politics but in such professional fields as his own, where he had assumed that the professional called the tune. Finally he attended a meeting of the Community Council on groupwork.

"Now I know what is so great about America," he said. "In Germany when there was something wrong in the community, we would say, 'Why doesn't the government do something about it?' Here, when something is wrong we say, 'Why don't *we* do something about it?' "

As in Europe, so in Asia the same self-help, do-it-ourselves attitude has been making headway. An American soldier who read an article of mine about voluntary association wrote from Tokyo:

"Several years ago a group of American women started a mass movement in favor of orphans. It was at Christmas time, and these women in their fur coats and stylish hats stood at the corners of the busy thoroughfares of Tokyo, with boxes in their hands, asking for donations. Their approach was startling, especially to the Japanese male. He had never before seen well-dressed women shoving a box in front of him asking for yen.

"One of the Japanese salesgirls in the PX said to me, 'But these are Army officers' wives, and they don't have to do that. They are doing it for children they don't even know.' The following year when the Japanese Red Feather drive was organized, thousands of housewives in kimono appeared on the street corners with red feathers for donors.

"Countless groups of servicemen and civilians year after year have collected funds for the orphans, painted churches and community centers and chipped in with all kinds of activities to help community projects. Thousands of men and women have braved cold, windowless schoolrooms to teach conversational English, to bring magazines to Economics teachers, and to help the teachers with their problems of English Conversation. Their work has helped convey to the Japanese the real thing behind the American scene."

When T/Sgt. Delbert Jenkins, at the age of seventy-one, returned from Japan with his wife, reporters asked him what he planned to do when he retired.

The sergeant announced that he was not expecting to retire, but to be reassigned. "We're not ready to retire to a rocking chair yet," he said, speaking also for his seventy-one-year-old wife who had joined him in Japan five years before. "I've still got a lot of mileage in me. With the world in such a precarious state, neither my wife nor I wants to sit on the sidelines." A veteran of the first World War, Sergeant Jenkins was sixty-one when World War II came. He enlisted, served in New Guinea and in the Philippines liberation, and went into Japan with the army of occupation.

From Japan he wrote to his wife that he wanted to stay there because "there's a big job to be done." Although they had sixteen grandchildren by this time (they had seven children of their own), Mrs. Jenkins decided she wanted to help with the big job too.

In Japan she came to be known as "the Mother of Yokohama." She organized discussion groups for Japanese young people. She formed the Council of Yokohama Women's Clubs. She organized Red Cross projects and, in her spare time, worked as a Gray Lady in Army hospitals.

"We feel," she said, "that in our little way, we've been doing our part in helping this troubled world."

Here, if anywhere, the real America speaks.

* * *

FOREIGN STUDENTS ENTERTAINED
HERE DURING HOLIDAYS

Eighteen foreign students and off-shore Americans studying at Montana State College in Bozeman arrived Wednesday night to spend the Thanksgiving holiday in various homes in the community and surrounding area. They were accompanied to Whitehall by the foreign student advisor, Paul Grieder and Mrs. Grieder. The students were received by a welcoming group including Mrs. William Curdy, Rev. George Reid, Rev. Ralph Gray, Rev. A. J. Harrington, Mrs. L. B. McBride and Mrs. Donald Powell. People who are hosts to the students came to the Borden hotel, met the other students and took their guests to their homes.

There will be a community party at 8 p. m., Nov. 28 at the Whitehall gym. Families of the community and surrounding area are invited to participate in and assist with this party. Each family is asked to bring either cookies or milk, whichever is more convenient.

Included in the program of music, singing and games will be special numbers by some of the students, a panel discussion on a proposed peace in Korea and a question and answer forum. It is hoped people who are interested and their families will attend.

Also, being planned for the students, their hosts and other families interested is a get-together at the Indiana Geology school on Sunday after church, about 1:30 p. m. Each family is to provide one covered dish, sandwiches or rolls for his own family and table service, silver, cups, etc.

This article might have come from any one of a hundred or more communities. It happens to come from the *Jefferson Valley News* of Whitehall, Montana.

❉ ❉ ❉

Bennington College in Vermont holds a six-week summer school for students who come to America from all over the world for a year's postgraduate study in medicine, the arts and sciences, agriculture and every field of learning. Eight or ten other colleges throughout the country run similar programs at the request of the Department of State. The purpose of the course is to make the visiting scholars feel at home in the new environment, to prepare them for the American academic system, to give them a chance to discuss common problems with Americans, and to let them see for themselves what an average American community is like.

An essential part of the Bennington program is the relationship which grows between the students and the surrounding community. Before they arrive a group of citizens has organized, picked a chairman, and made plans. The Council of Church Women helps out with transportation. Members of the committee are on hand to meet the buses. A welcoming party gives students and townspeople a chance to get acquainted. Thereafter the contacts are frequent, friendly and informal. Volunteers drive the student group on field trips to near-by industries, historic sites, community activities. Students get invited out for dinner, for rides, for family picnics. They spend a week living in homes where they can share the family life, taking part in the household chores of dish-washing and bed-making. Finally they give a party to which they invite all the friends they have made during their six-week stay.

Then they go off to the universities where they are to spend the academic year. But many of them come back as week-end guests, for Thanksgiving or Christmas holidays. Spontaneous and voluntary from the beginning, the relationships continue on a basis of personal exchange long after the summer school itself is over.

* * *

Owatonna, Minnesota, makes a specialty of welcoming displaced persons. Through the Lutheran Welfare Society its citizens guarantee a job and a home to homeless people in Europe. They guarantee that neither the job nor the home will displace Americans, and they guarantee that the new arrivals will not be a public charge for a period of one year.

Owatonna, a town of ten thousand, has opened its arms to the displaced—to an attractive blond Ukrainian girl whose home was overrun first by the Germans and then by the Russians, to Poles, Estonians, Czechs, Germans. The people of Owatonna not only find jobs and homes for the newcomers, but fix their houses up before they arrive, meet them at the railroad station, and give showers to supply the newly-arrived housewife with many of the things she needs.

What does life in Owatonna look like to the new arrivals?

"We are so amazed," says a German woman who still remembers seeing her friends shot down by the enemy at a railroad siding. "Just take a trip to the supermarket. You go with a wagon around and pick out whatever you want. At first, we couldn't read it. We bought what looked nice to us. We were sometimes surprised at what came out."

Even more wonderful, to one who had washed clothes by hand all her life until every wash day brought cracked, sore fingers, was the automatic washer. "You put it just in and stand and watch, and then the wringer goes automatically."

But how would the new people be accepted by their fellow workers? At the Josten Manufacturing Company, makers of class rings and trophies, an ex-Marine named Don Smith was working with Uldis Kampe from Latvia.

"I first came across Uldis Kampe when he came with us in February of last year," Smith said. "At first, it was a little difficult to understand him because, well, it was new to us to get used to the accent of Latvians. I'd rather work with him now, myself, than just about anybody else."

Had anyone taken exception to bringing in these new residents?

"There have been several people that have voiced objections," said Foreman Helmer Bartz, "but they are in the minority and their objections are not too sound. The main objection that I've heard is that if we get too many DP's over here they eventually will force out American labor, which, in my opinion, is not true. We need the DP persons just as much as they need us."

* * *

The voluntary associations which have grown up in America as a response to our new world position prove that the heartbeat of the American way is as strong as ever.

On a Sunday in the spring of 1951 Dr. John Peters of Oklahoma City University preached a sermon at St. Luke's Methodist Church. He said that if America wanted to win the battle for men's minds and for world peace, individual Americans must be willing to take an active part, by stretching out a helping hand to those who suffered from poverty, ignorance and disease. This—the unfolding of a spirit based upon Christian love and democratic friendliness—would stop communism cold.

The people of Oklahoma City talked about Dr. Peters' sermon. They decided to do something about it. But what?

Several businessmen got together and called a public meeting. An organization called World Assistance was formed. In a little more than a year it grew into a national movement known as World Neighbors, with headquarters at Columbus, Ohio. Soon it was operating two pilot stations in India, working by person-to-person contact with people in the villages. Its teams specialize in agriculture, hygiene, crafts, child care, nutrition, literacy. They are teaching the use of steel plows in place of crooked sticks, the use of cow dung for fertilizer instead of for fuel, the making of compost heaps, the control of disease-bearing insects.

They are spreading out through fifty villages, teaching midwifery, garment-making, spinning and weaving, animal husbandry, reading and writing. Each pilot station plans eventually to reach 250 villages, leaving behind teams of trained villagers who can carry on the work. Within five years World Neighbors plans to have 120 pilot stations operating throughout Asia, the Near East, and in Africa and South America. Skilled workers have already been recruited to go out as soon as the stations can be opened. Every World Neighbors project is developed co-operatively; no one is forced to take part.

Chapters of World Neighbors have been set up in Pittsburgh, Cincinnati, Indianapolis, St. Louis and eighteen other cities. Each chapter aims at sponsoring a pilot station somewhere in the world. Teams of businessmen are raising the $20,000 needed to start each pilot station and run it for a year.

Then there is C.A.R.E. (Cooperative for American Remittances to Everywhere) which works out ways to help people help themselves. It has developed a plow especially suited to

India. It has a package containing insecticides to check disease and crop blights. It has midwifery and farm tool kits. Through C.A.R.E. ten million Americans have voluntarily sent tangible evidence of their brotherly feeling to thirty countries—more than $150,000,000 worth.

Under the sponsorship of Point Four and World Literacy, Inc., Dr. Frank Laubach has carried to India his famous method of teaching adults to read. The purpose of the program is not reading for reading's sake, but to give people a tool with which they can learn to do things for themselves. As soon as they get to their second book, they begin to learn not to eat their big potatoes and plant the small ones, but to plant the large ones so that they will get good crops. They learn how to breed better cattle, how to raise chickens for meat and eggs, how to build their wells to avoid pollution.

The Experiment in International Living of Putney, Vermont, has been sending young Americans to Europe for two decades. Young Europeans also come to America, and in both cases the visitors live in homes and become members of the family. They return home to tell their friends and neighbors what they have seen. Thus Henry Borgese of Niagara Falls went to Holland on the Experiment's "Community Ambassador Program." He wasn't at all what his hostess Mrs. Olida Smit of Zeist expected a young American to be—no bow tie, crew cut or love for Coca-Cola. Mrs. Smit changed her ideas about Americans, as did Borgese about Hollanders. Since his return to Niagara Falls he has made 140 speeches about his experiences.

The National Committee for a Free Europe, Inc., is at work on various devices to carry the story of the free world behind the Iron Curtain. The Crusade for Freedom also helps out through its support of Radio Free Europe. The Foster Parents Plan for War Children gives Americans a chance to provide for children left uncared for by the horrors of war. Associations too numerous to mention are helping to care for the sick and homeless in devastated Korea, for children in poverty-stricken areas everywhere. There are the Christophers, a Catholic organization numbering a million members who believe that each individual by his own deeds can change the world. But it is interesting to note that an association is needed to bring this individual power into action. The Quaker work camps, the post-war educational reconstruction carried out by the American Council on Education in co-operation with a host of other voluntary agencies prove the vitality of voluntarism in the international field.

The American Association for the United Nations is made up of people who want to make sure that Americans get the true facts about the United Nations, believing that the strategy of truth is as good for us as it is for those we are trying to work with abroad. Outgrowth of the League of Nations Association founded in 1923, the A.A.U.N. has pioneered in bringing other organizations together to promote international understanding and order. Each year it assembles delegates from over a hundred national groups in a conference on U.S. Responsibility for World Leadership. Here the delegates listen to national leaders in government, business and labor, discuss and pass resolutions, and carry back home what they have learned at the conference. A.A.U.N. also spearheads the celebrations for U.N. Week throughout the country, runs a speaker's bureau, a guide service at U.N. headquarters, a Peoples Section which through discussion groups helps bring the U.N. and its problems to the individual citizen. Its college affiliate operates on more than three hundred campuses.

United World Federalists, a consolidation of five groups which stood for world peace through the establishment of a world federal government, has only been in existence since 1947, but its roots go back to the many plans for world peace and order which were being discussed on the eve of our entering the war. It is a member of the World Movement for World Federal Government, an association of groups from many nations. World Federalists believe that the United Nations charter should be strengthened in the interests of more effectively maintaining world peace.

In addition to all these voluntary associations whose sole

purpose is to tackle some phase of our relations with the rest of the world, most of the civic-minded farm, labor, professional, service and women's groups are doing something too. Farmers all over the country are hosts to young farmers from abroad who live and work with them for several months under an exchange program worked out by the Department of State. Labor unions are hosts to visiting workers. Rotary Clubs sponsor exchange students, invite them to speak at meetings, entertain them at family picnics. The League of Women Voters gets out a guide for community action to foster international co-operation. It gives specific answers to such problems as appearing on a program where other speakers or members of the audience are hostile, dealing with an anti-U.N. campaign or with a press which opposes the idea of international co-operation.

* * *

This rapid review is at least sufficient to show that Americans are tackling international problems in the same spirit and with the same instrument which has served them in meeting the problems of the frontier, of slavery, of community improvement. If from the beginning we had waited for government to sense and to satisfy our community needs, the United States would be a very different sort of place if indeed it existed at all. Yet in writing our history we have emphasized governmental and economic activity while ignoring the impact of voluntary associations.

Now we are doing the same thing in the sphere of international affairs. We seem to expect the United Nations, a political body, to do all the work. We judge it, criticize it, defend it, talking all the time as if it bore the responsibility for world peace. Meanwhile, however, we have given birth to all these lively groups which are doing for our time exactly what the Sons of Liberty, the lyceums, the anti-slavery societies did for theirs. The outpouring of gifts, of plows and medicines and foods, of technical advice and of friendly co-operation such as that given by many projects of the Friends Service Committee and other religious groups, has already become a mighty flood.

To the agencies already mentioned would have to be added the foundations, whose expenditures run every year into millions. Many of them are now active internationally as well as at home. They hardly qualify as voluntary associations, yet they are not governmental. Clearly enough they are an outgrowth of the habit of mind which looks at human welfare as a responsibility to be shared, not left in the hands of government. This is the same point of view which gave rise to voluntary groups.

Yet all this outpouring of effort and material has been overshadowed by the governmental program of technical assistance (Point Four), a program which nevertheless has been operating for an entire year at a cost less than that of equipping and maintaining one United States Army division. A government program, it has, however, stressed co-operation and self-help. Its purpose is to show men how by working together they can free themselves from the crushing burden of ignorance, disease and destitution.

When the International Development Advisory Board reported to Harold E. Stassen, Director of the Foreign Operations Administration, at the end of 1953, they stressed the fact that the United States was particularly well fitted to extend its hand to nations less developed—not because of our economic strength but because of our human history.

Only fifty years ago, they pointed out, our infant mortality rate was 162 per thousand. Now it is 29. Fifty years ago crop yields were half what they are today. Not so long ago we were an underdeveloped country. So it is not only the tools of technology, education and hygiene which we can pass on to our neighbors. It is the experience of self-development, the spirit of self-help—the habit of voluntary association.

"Technical Cooperation," they observed, "is but a catch name for the principles and techniques with which the immigrant from Europe built a new world in this country. Every frontier settlement was based on the sharing of knowledge and on helping one's neighbor. It practised self-improvement through using the knowledge accumulated in the settled areas, adapting it to new conditions, applying it to the point where the new settlement itself became capable of rendering technical assistance to yet newer settlements further on. Technical Cooperation is but another name for our unique history and our unique achievement. It has brought us to the point where, with but 6% of the world area and 7% of its population, we produce over 40% of the world's manufactured goods and are therefore in a position to project technical assistance beyond our own boundaries."

Point Four projects are jointly undertaken in a spirit of cooperation, not only between governments but between American technical experts and the communities they enter. Point Four does not by itself do something for a government or a people; it works with them to do it jointly. There is no compulsion. Voluntarism is its foundation.

The results are seen in a lake of lush green grass on the barren, sun-baked desert at Wafi Rukban in the Hashemite Kingdom of the Jordan, made possible by water-spreading techniques used in Wyoming. Or in Neghu Ram's fivefold increase in wheat harvest in India, or in the six thousand children of Isfahan, Iran, who were able to go to school for the first time. Or in the malaria control program in the Philippines which in some areas reduced school absences from 50 to 3 per cent.

United States technicians are now in thirty-eight countries, working with the officials and the people of the co-operating nations to show how resources can be put to work for human welfare and how the human mind and imagination can raise standards of living. The scope, the challenge, and the results of these programs can only be hinted at.

In Iran, for example, twenty-four extension agents who had been trained through farm demonstrations aided over twenty thousand farmers in eight hundred villages.

In India, where the democratic way of life may be undergoing its most crucial test as a nation tries to lift its millions to a higher level of living, village improvement is a major phase of the plan. India hopes to reach sixteen thousand villages with a combined population of eleven million people through its Community Development program. One hundred and twenty-four American technicians have been involved, more than half of them working directly with over a thousand Indian associates. By introducing better tools and techniques, building farm-to-market roads, digging wells and opening farm co-operatives, the technicians are making it possible for farmers to raise their food output and thus their living standards. In 1951 the three-way co-operation of American and Indian technicians with the farmers helped to beat off the scourge of locusts and pointed the way to a permanent control program in Iran, India and Pakistan.

Lebanon, a country with magnificent scenery, a healthy climate and a great history, looks gay and modern if seen from its capital, Beirut. But in the rural areas life is hard. The land is densely populated and intensively cultivated. Rugged mountains limit to 26 per cent the amount of land which is farmed. But modern methods could increase this another 11 per cent.

To accomplish this, deeply etched patterns of behavior must change. The heart of Lebanon is in the age-old village community. Yet illiteracy, poor health and underdeveloped agriculture threaten the village life. The plan jointly developed for Lebanon was therefore based on revitalizing the village community, enlisting its institutions in an active program of self-improvement.

The Kasmie Rural Improvement Project was the first to be launched. In the area of biblical Sidon and Tyre, it took in five villages. Safe drinking water, health services, agricultural productivity were among the area's chief needs. The value of co-operatives as a solution to many farm problems was demonstrated. Farmers were shown how by working together they could produce more and better crops, grade and market their products, buy and use machinery. Other co-operative services are spraying, milk-handling, and purchase of supplies and seed. Enthusiasm for this new way of working together was fostered by actual demonstrations. Much of Lebanon's farming has to be done on terraces. One demonstration showed how with modern tools the work of three years' terracing could be done in two months.

Since the root of a problem is often a need for new knowledge, many of the projects are basically educational. In Bolivia a teacher training center has been opened at Warisata, high in the Andes. American and Bolivian technicians are preparing young people to teach not only the three R's but health measures, agricultural methods, home improvement and crafts. Education will thus meet the needs of the people and the communities they live in. Thousands of children have also been organized into 4-S clubs—voluntary associations patterned on our 4-H Clubs.

The University of Arizona is co-operating with the agricultural college at Abu Gheraib in Iraq, helping to develop it as a center for agricultural research and extension work. Similarly, the Imperial College of Agriculture is being established in Ethiopia through the co-operation of the Oklahoma A. & M. College.

In its report to Mr. Stassen the International Development Advisory Board stressed the importance of American voluntary organizations. For over a century, they pointed out, American missions, foundations and other non-governmental groups have been carrying on voluntary programs of service abroad.

"The voluntary agency is an organizational representation of free action of individuals pursuing desired ends through organizations of their choice—a concept basic to democracy." After pointing out that technical missionaries were carrying health, educational and agricultural programs abroad long before the government entered the field, the Board recommended that the government assume a creative role in developing programs with private agencies and provide a high-level office for promoting private agency participation in foreign technical assistance. "Cooperative action of voluntary agencies through 'holding-company' devices should be encouraged," they reported. Funds from a foundation might be brought together with workers from another agency through co-ordination by government. This was actually done at Assuit in Egypt, where the Ford Foundation supplied funds and International Voluntary Services, Inc., supplied voluntary workers.

"Point Four," says the description of the program in Lebanon, "is the vehicle on which scientific knowledge, technical invention and material progress become traveling companions with American ideals, American hopes and American aspirations for achieving real brotherhood among men."

If democracy wins the contest against authoritarianism, it will be largely because the habit of voluntary association manages to take root quickly and firmly in many parts of the earth. Our government is working hard to bring this about. Even more hopefully, our people, through their many voluntary associations, are working too—working directly with other people in all parts of the world. This is the big story, the story that ought to be told. Twenty or a hundred years from now no one will remember much about the current rash of investigations. But they will wonder, if they look back at our papers, why we were so blind to the really significant thing that was happening—the slow, sturdy spread of the thing few people mentioned because they were so busy talking about communism: the slow, sturdy spread of the thing that would stop communism—voluntary association.

*　*　*

Voluntary associations in America may be huge affairs like the National Red Cross or the Republican Party or the American Federation of Labor. But they are rooted in the local chapter or the town committee or the union local. Voluntary association has kept our communities active and healthy. It has made it possible for an industrial age to keep the neighborly, face-to-face quality of village life. If it has not always done this as thoroughly as it should, this fault lies not with the instrument but with the hands that have failed to grasp it.

The ability of the voluntary association to preserve the group warmth of the small community is of vital importance today. Industrialization and urbanization tend to weaken and destroy the small-town or village culture. Yet the village is still the effective social unit in most parts of the world, as it has been throughout history. In China the village was a kind of informal democracy, an autonomous unit in which the members ran their own affairs. Whatever the community required, it supplied by voluntary association. "The Chinese village folks are most capable of self-organization and self-government," wrote Liang and Tao in their *Village and Town Life in China.* "Reform, should any be needed, must come from within, not from without."

Village life in India followed a similar pattern as far back as it can be traced. "It would appear that in the earliest times the village communities enjoyed a practically unlimited autonomy. . . . Each village had its own council or Sabha. . . . The local disputes were settled by this council of the village elders," writes Altekar in A *History of Village Communities in Western India.*

In the early English village the plowing, sowing and harvesting were done on a communal basis. Evidence could be drawn from many parts of the world to show that the village community is an ancient and practically universal institution, and that for many centuries it was the only form of social organization beyond the family. The New England village, the frontier settlement, the wagon trains all repeat the basic pattern of the self-organization of the face-to-face group.

Voluntary association, which arose out of the village unit, solved the problem of maintaining face-to-face groups against the huge impersonal organisms of nation-state, industrial empire, metropolis. In a world which tends toward the massive and the impersonal, it makes close personal relations possible.

The face which we have turned toward the world is that massive, impersonal one—assembly lines, standardized products, entertainment coming out of a film can by way of a machine, material goods. Though it is not entirely our fault that the world has been more impressed by this material glitter than by our social and spiritual achievements, the fact remains that our material progress has obscured our social progress. The villager in

India or South America has been estranged from us by the very impressiveness of our material accomplishment. While we use the material as a step, he regards it as our capstone. Our economic progress has been so great that it has separated us from the rest of the world. It is hard to feel love for the rich man in the lighted mansion on the hill if you are hungry and unhoused out in the rain and the mud. One of our great errors has been to throw this material well-being in the face of the world, as if it would bring us friends. We should have been talking about something quite different.

For over three hundred years we have been experimenting with the means by which the virtues and strengths of the small community could be put to work for the welfare of all. As the nation became urbanized and industrialized, we kept adapting our basic instrument to fit the changing times. It is no accident that we still cherish the idea of the home town. In our popular mythology even a metropolis like Brooklyn becomes a village where everyone knows everyone else. We still cherish farm life, rural sports, church socials. This fondness for the small community is not pure nostalgia. It is based on the knowledge that men and women need to work and play together in small groups in order to become whole people.

Our history has repeatedly proved to us that as individuals we should perish, but that as members of a group we may save ourselves, build our communities, open schools and hospitals and museums, live fuller, richer lives. We know instinctively that the nation will be no sounder than the communities out of which our leaders must rise and in which they must be developed. We know that the strength of our nation is in the thousands of associations we have formed, in the millions of volunteers who operate them, in the billions of hours of work freely given in the faith that this not only contributes to the community life or makes it better, but that it *is* life.

This is the bond by which we are bound to humanity—to the millions of intelligent, brave, suffering human beings throughout the underdeveloped, disease-ridden, poverty-ridden, ignorance-ridden world. We too were underdeveloped, disease-ridden, poverty-ridden and ignorance-ridden. We have a long way to go yet. But so far as we have gone, we have gone by the road of self-help, of voluntary co-operation. And that way, close in spirit to the universal village way, is the path in which we may walk side by side with the rest of the world, in neighborliness, in friendship. If we once fully understand this ourselves, we can help our friends and neighbors throughout the world to see it. They turn away from our material accomplishment even when their eyes are caught by the glitter of it. They turn away because they believe—and the communists keep telling them so—that it is the sign of a base materialism. Once they see it as the fruit of a way of human association closely allied to that of their own communities, they will be able to raise their own material standards by letting us share with them a way of doing things which is essentially small-town, co-operative, and rewarding.

We have faith in the power of the people to co-operate voluntarily for useful purposes, because we know that it was the Committees of Correspondence more than the state legislatures which brought on the Revolution, and that every important advance in our history has been brought about by the voluntary group action of our citizens. We have seen the beginning of an inspiring use of voluntary association in our overseas relations—in the World Neighbors plan, the technical assistance programs, the work of the Friends and other religious groups.

We know that our own government is shaped and sustained by the activity of hundreds of voluntary associations, and that these relationships give the dynamic quality to our polity and healthily involve us in the governmental process. So we can see that in time the United Nations—at present rather cold and formal because it has not yet aroused our emotions or commanded our allegiance as the nation-state does—in time the United Nations may gain strength through the support of the voluntary associations which have begun to rally individuals to its aid.

The U.N. is something like a huge circus tent, the Council and the Assembly and the member governments like the poles which hold it up. Without stakes and ropes to fix its shape it is nothing but a huge and dangerous pile of flopping canvas. Once pegged and roped all around, it becomes a serviceable thing, held in dynamic balance.

It is clear enough that men have progressed from smaller to larger social units. We are always forgetting that the nation-state is a fairly modern invention. In the middle ages it was the feudal lord to whom a man owed his allegiance, and in our own country the allegiance to the home state (as distinguished from the nation) was so deeply engraved that it is still an important consideration in national politics.

Some day the next step will be taken. As we have grown from village to feudal, then to a state and national allegiance, we shall some day own our allegiance to humanity. The old tribal prejudices will dissolve under the acids of science. We shall wonder how we could ever have pretended that one "race" is "better" than another, science already having established by such facts as the complicated foot structure and the universality of blood types that men are in fact brothers. When the time comes, it will have arrived largely through the activity of voluntary interchanges.

This is not to say that the small community will wither away. On the contrary, it will remain the focus of human activity. For as the world shrinks and the cities expand, men will more than ever need to sense their togetherness as one race through their activities in face-to-face groups.

As the growth of America went from highly localized groups to colonial and then intercolonial and then national relationships, so we may expect the associations of the future to involve the world. Each unit can remain manageably small, but in sum the associations will extend across national boundaries. We have the beginnings in the student exchange program, in the U.N. technical assistance teams which bring together experts of several countries, in the people who, with foundation or mission or voluntary agency support, join their lives with those of villagers in far places in order to help them help themselves.

Let us imagine that such interchanges, more and more of them, go on for twenty, thirty, fifty years. Is it not conceivable that the prejudices and hostilities which now keep people apart may dissolve as did the prejudices which kept us apart during the period of the Confederation? And is it not imaginable that in time this voluntary working together of peoples rather than merely of governments will produce associations capable of controlling and influencing the United Nations as our national associations now control and influence the government of the United States?

Both the opponents and the proponents of world government miss the point when they concern themselves with the formal organization of a world state. Government is an organism. It must grow. And if it is not to be authoritarian, it must grow through the support and influence of associations of its citizens. Instead of raising higher poles or patching holes in the canvas, those who want to see world peace assured through a world order should be busy about the pegs and ropes. When the people of the world, through better knowledge of each other, are convinced that the United Nations should become a federation of nations, as our states became federated, they can bring it about. But first they must shape the pegs and prepare the ropes.

It is a common error to think of government, international relations and public affairs as if they were determined by reason. But even reasonable men are motivated more by their passions than by logic. Emotion is really the basis of civilization, for society derives from the family and from the strong emotional ties established there. All government is but an extension of these relationships, patterned as we have seen upon the ties between and among parents and children. Even religion's highest reach is to a universal fatherhood and brotherhood. And so, until symbols are established which grab at men's hearts—until they feel a thrill run up their spines when a world flag goes by —the day of universal brotherhood will not have come. Yet these symbols—or the emotions they arouse—can be brought to life in a remarkably short time. In 1775 there was no American flag, but within a few months colonists north and south felt united in a common cause. In the last war strangers from distant nations were able to fight under a united command, and to risk their lives together as they would not have been willing to do even among close friends a few months before.

But must war be the only uniter?

Not if we make the fullest use of voluntary association on an international scale. Service such as that given by World Neighbors or International Voluntary Services may turn out to be that moral equivalent of war which William James was seeking.

For love is stronger than hate, and peace than war. It was fashionable in the nineteenth century, and even into the twentieth, to read into Darwinism the lesson that life was a matter of tooth and claw, that the survival of the fittest involved even man in the brutish business of pushing his neighbor to the wall. Hence rugged individualism.

In fact, however, it is love that is creation's final law. If this were not so, life by now would have been extinguished. Co-operation, not conflict, is the natural law of life. The scientific proof of this is abundant. Mutual aid among animals and co-operative altruism among men prove that physical and spiritual love are more powerful forces than hatred. The care and nurture of life transcend the struggle for survival.

Translated into politics, this means that the democratic way is stronger than the communistic way. Communism is irrevocably based upon the concept of life as hatred—as a struggle between antagonistic and irreconcilable classes. Democracy stands firmly upon faith in co-operation, brotherliness, love. Can there be any doubt as to the ultimate outcome of such a contest?

*   *   *

The word voluntary, as we have seen, encloses a paradox. Its freedom is a freedom to serve; its service is perfect freedom. The word association implies another paradox: people become better individuals by sinking part of their individuality in the group— by merging and becoming part of the group. These two paradoxes are firmly built into American experience and the American way of life. Our long experience with voluntary association has taught us a good many things. We know that association is based upon some form of contract—perhaps a formal constitution, perhaps only the willingness to be bound by the rules of the game, whatever the play may be. We know that there must be a real need for association, or the group will soon fall apart. We know something about the need of good leadership, intelligent planning, sound human and public relations, and most of all, faith and a goal.

We are beginning to understand something about the place the emotions play in human organization—how the symbol of fatherhood rests upon the leader and how the mother-warmth of the group brings satisfaction to the members. And we begin to understand how in our society the religious base—through the fatherhood of God, the brotherhood of man and the enfolding unity of the church group—has given us the pattern for all our voluntary activity, based as it is upon the two principles of freedom and contract. In the area of sports, teamwork and the rules of the game have given every child a notion of what freedom and contract mean. Teamwork and sportsmanship might well be used to popularize and give emotional content to the expansion of voluntary association which will be necessary if we are to help save humankind from the scourge of communism and authoritarianism.

We can be confident that we shall succeed in this if we stick firmly to our principles. Any attempt to restrict our voluntary associations will be a danger signal. For they have in them the universal germ of life which authoritarianism lacks. While we remain flexible, it must grow ever more rigid. While we embrace change, it must try to prevent change. Since change is inevitable, all totalitarian systems are doomed from the start, however they may flourish for a time. Only in a culture where men are free to work toward common goals can poverty and sickness and ignorance be overcome.

This free working together is what America has to offer. It is a way of working together for goals which we must determine for ourselves. It has universal roots, the most important of which in our history is the debt we owe to England. Accidents of history have given us the privilege of developing this way to a high point of achievement, and to the point where we now have the privilege of sharing and exchanging our knowledge with the rest of the world. Yet we have remained almost silent about this faith and practice which support our national life.

"If men are to remain civilized," De Tocqueville told us, "or to become so, the art of associating together must grow and improve in the same ratio in which equality of conditions is increased."

To develop and extend that art—this must be our central concern in the era which lies ahead. The future depends far less upon the actions of statesmen than upon the willingness of individuals everywhere in the free world and especially in America to live active lives of service in their own communities. From this base world service will develop naturally.

This is a time for greatness. Strangely enough, we have ignored the strong current in our history which can become the wave of the future, bearing us up as we ride through dangerous seas. But danger is a thing we are used to. Ours is a dangerous freedom, but what freedom is not? Since we know that life without freedom would not be worth living, we must accept the danger too. To our two paradoxes we must add a third: danger is in the end a safer thing than safety.

Sources

Chapter 1

Bloom, Murray Teigh. "Enlist the Teens." *The Rotarian,* Mar., 1953.

Commager, Henry S. "Is Freedom Really Necessary?" *Saturday Review,* Feb. 21, 1953.

Larrabee, Kent R. "New Residents and Old Meeting Houses." *Friends Intelligencer,* Third Month 14, 1953.

Magazine of Sigma Chi, Mar., 1953, p. 70, "He's President of 1952 All-American City."

May, Rollo. *Man's Search for Himself.* New York, 1953.

Newsweek, Nov. 5, 1951. (Brandywine)

"The People Act." A radio program sponsored by the Fund for Adult Education and the Twentieth Century Fund. (The stories of Arlington, New Sharon, Syracuse, Tin Top.)

Poston, Richard Waverly. *Small Town Renaissance.* New York, 1950.

Roche, Mary. "An Antibiotic for the Slum." *New York Times Magazine,* Oct. 25, 1953.

The Rotarian, Feb., 1953, "The Goshen, Indiana, Story."

Ruth, Kent. "Geary: Cash and Carry." *The Rotarian,* Feb., 1953.

Tocqueville, Alexis de. *Democracy in America.* New York, 1889.

Chapter 2

Smith, Bradford. *Bradford of Plymouth.* New York & Philadelphia, 1951.

Chapter 3

Andrews, Charles M. *The Beginnings of Connecticut.* New Haven (Tercentenary Commission), 1934.

———. "The Beginnings of the Connecticut Towns." *Annals of the American Academy of Political and Social Science,* I (1890), 171 et seq.

———. *Our Earliest Colonial Settlements.* New York, 1933.

———. *The River Towns of Connecticut.* Baltimore, 1889.

———. "The Theory of the Village Community." *American Historical Association Papers,* V (1891), 47–60.

Deming, Dorothy. *The Settlement of the Connecticut Towns.* New Haven (Tercentenary Commission), 1933.

Sly, John Fairfield. *Town Government in Massachusetts*. Cambridge Mass., 1930.

Tocqueville, Alexis de. *Democracy in America*.

Webster, Clarence M. *Town Meeting Country*. New York, 1945.

Chapter 4

Abbott, Wilbur C. *New York in the American Revolution*. New York, 1929.

Adams, James Truslow. *Revolutionary New England 1691–1776*. Boston, 1923.

Adams, John. *Works: Diary* (Vol. 2). Boston, 1850.

Anon. "The Sam Adams Regiments in the Town of Boston." *Atlantic Monthly*, IX (June, 1862), 701–20; X (Aug., 1862), 179–203; XII (Nov., 1863), 595–616.

Bancroft, George. *History of the United States of America*. New York, 1883.

Barck, Oscar T. *New York City during the War for Independence*. New York, 1931.

Becker, Carl Lotus. *The History of Political Parties in the Province of New York 1760–1776*. Madison, Wis., 1909.

———. "Growth of Revolutionary Parties." *American Historical Review*, VII (1902), 56–76.

Belknap Papers. Mss. in the Massachusetts Historical Society Library. Oct., 1745–Sept., 1776, Sons of Liberty Correspondence, sheets 109–29.

Boston Committee of Correspondence Minutes. Mss. in the New York Public Library.

Chase, Ellen. *The Beginnings of the American Revolution*. New York, 1910.

Collins, E. D. "Committees of Correspondence." *Annual Report of the American Historical Association*, I (1901), 245–71.

Commager, Henry S. *Documents of American History*. New York, 1944.

Davidson, Philip. *Propaganda and the American Revolution 1763–1783*. Chapel Hill, 1941.

Dawson, Henry B. *The Sons of Liberty in New York*. Poughkeepsie, 1859. (Disappointing, despite its title.)

Dillon, Dorothy Rita. *The New York Triumvirate*. New York, 1949.

Goodloe, Daniel R. *The Birth of the Republic*. Chicago & New York, 1889.

Gordon, William. *The History of the . . . Independence of the United States of America*. London, 1788.

Lamb Papers. Mss. in the New-York Historical Society Library. Letters to and from the Sons of Liberty in New York, 1766 and Mar. 2, 1770.

Leake, Isaac Q. *Memoir of the Life and Times of General John Lamb*. Albany, 1850.

Miller, John C. *Origins of the American Revolution*. Boston, 1943.

———. *Sam Adams*. Boston, 1936.

Montresor, John. *Journals*. New-York Historical Society Collections, New York, 1881.

Morais, Herbert M. "The Sons of Liberty in New York." *Era of the American Revolution, Studies Inscribed to Evarts Greene*. New York, 1939.

Morris, Richard B., ed. *The Era of the American Revolution*. New York, 1939.

New York Gazette or Weekly Post-Boy, Oct. 10, 1765–May 8, 1766.

New York Mercury, June 22 and July 6, 1767.

O'Callaghan, E. B. *Documents relative to the Colonial History . . . of New York*. Albany, 1856. Vols. 8, 10.

Trumbull, J. H. "Sons of Liberty in 1755." *New Englander*, XXXV, 299 ff.

Winsor, Justin. *Memorial History of Boston*. Boston, 1886.

Chapter 5

Atwater, Caleb. *A History of the State of Ohio*. Cincinnati, 1838.

Barber, Edward W. "The Vermontville Colony." *Michigan Pioneer & Historic Collections*, XXVIII, 197–287.

Backus, William W. *A Genealogical Memoir of the Backus Family*. Norwich, Conn., 1889.

Bond, Beverly W. *The Civilization of the Old Northwest*. New York, 1934.

Cutler, Manasseh. *Life, Journals and Correspondence*. Cincinnati, 1888.

Fairchild, James. *Oberlin, the Colony and the College*. Oberlin, 1883.

Fletcher, Robert Samuel. *A History of Oberlin College*. Oberlin, 1943.

French, J. H. *Historical and Statistical Gazeteer of New York*. 1860.

Fuller, George Newman. *Economic and Social Beginnings of Michigan*. Lansing, 1916.

Hall, Charles S. *Life and Letters of General Samuel Holden Parsons*. Binghamton, 1905.

Hildreth, Samuel P. *Biographical and Historical Memoirs of the Early Pioneer Settlers of Ohio*. Cincinnati, 1852.

Hotchkin, James H. *A History of the Purchase and Settlement of Western New York*. New York, 1848.

Hulbert, Archer B. *Records of the Original Proceedings of the Ohio Company*. Marietta, 1917.

Katkamier, A. B. *The History of the Township of Farmington*. Farmington, N.Y., 1897.

Mathews, Lois Kimball. *The Expansion of New England*. Boston & New York, 1909.

———. "The Mayflower Compact and its Descendants." *Missouri Valley Historical Association Proceedings*, VI (1912–13), 79–106.

Mau, Clayton. *The Development of Central and Western New York*. Rochester, 1944.

Paxson, Frederic L. *History of the American Frontier*. Boston, 1924.

Powell, Lyman W. *Historic Towns of the Western States*. New York, 1901. (Contains errors.)

Putnam, Rufus. *Memoirs*. Boston & New York, 1903.

Randall, Emilius, and Ryan, Daniel J. *History of Ohio*. New York, 1912.

Stewart, Alexander. "Sesquicentennial of Farmington, New York, 1789–1939." *Bulletin of the Friends Historical Association*, XXIX–XXX (1940–41), 37–43.

Stilwell, Lewis D. *Migration from Vermont*. Vermont Historical Society, Montpelier, 1948.

Turner, Frederick Jackson. *The Frontier in American History*. New York, 1920.

Turner, Orsamus. *History of the Pioneer Settlement of Phelps and Gorham's Purchase*. Rochester, 1851.

Vail, R. W. G. *The Voice of the Old Frontier*. Philadelphia, 1949.

The Belknap Papers at the Massachusetts Historical Society furnished a few items about the Marietta settlement. Search of the Phelps and Gorham mss. at the State Library in Albany failed to supply any information about early community organization. Percy Knapp at the Fifteenth Street Meeting House in New York and Oren B. Wilbur of Easton, New York, helped me in a search of Quaker records of the East Hoosuck Meeting, but no evidence was found to indicate that, as Turner says, the Friends who went west to Farmington were urged by their Meeting not to go.

Chapter 6
Bancroft Collection. Original mss. in the Bancroft Library at the University of California in Berkeley: Thomas D. Kaiser, "Narrative"; P. C. Kaiser, "Emigrant Road"; J. B. McClane, "First Wagon Train to Oregon"; J. W. Nesmith, "Recollections" and "Reminiscences."

Bancroft, Hubert Howe. *History of California.* San Francisco, 1884–90.

———. *History of Oregon.* San Francisco, 1886.

Bell, James Christy. *Opening a Highway to the Pacific 1838–1846.* New York, 1921.

Bidwell, John. "The First Emigrant Train to California." *Century,* XLI (1890), 106–30.

Branch, E. Douglas. *Westward.* New York, 1930.

Burnett, Peter H. *An Old California Pioneer.* Oakland, 1948 (a reprint of *Recollections of an Old Pioneer,* 1880).

Commager, Henry S., and Nevins, Allan, eds. *The Heritage of America.* Boston, 1939. (Reprints first-hand accounts of the American scene, including Applegate's "With the Cow Column on the Oregon Trail [A Day with the Cow Column]."

Geiger, Vincent, and Bryarly, Wakeman. *Trail to California.* New Haven, 1945.

Ghent, W. J. *The Road to Oregon.* New York, 1929.

Hastings, L. W. *Emigrants' Guide to Oregon and California.* Cincinnati, 1845.

Howe, Octavius Thorndike. *Argonauts of '49.* Cambridge, Mass., 1923.

Marcy, Randolph B. *The Prairie Traveler.* New York, 1859.

Monaghan, Jay. *The Overland Trail.* New York, 1947.

Nesmith, J. W. "Diary." *Oregon Historical Society Quarterly,* VII (1906), 329–59.

Oregon Historical Society Quarterly. Documents relating to emigrant companies, III, 390–2; IV, 278–80; XV, 286–92.

Page, Elizabeth. *Wagons West.* New York, 1930.

Palmer, Joel. *Journal of Travels over the Rocky Mountains.* Cincinnati, 1852. Reprinted as Vol. 30 in Reuben Gold Thwaites, *Early Western Travels.* Cleveland, 1906.

Steele, John. *Across the Plains in 1850.* Chicago, 1930.

Chapter 7
Buckmaster, Henrietta. *Let My People Go.* New York, 1941.

Coffin, Levi. *Reminiscences.* Cincinnati, 1876.

Garrison, William Lloyd. *William Lloyd Garrison* By his Children. Boston & New York, 1894.

Hart, Albert Bushnell. *Slavery and Abolition.* New York, 1906.
Macy, Jesse. *The Anti-Slavery Crusade.* New Haven, 1919.
Mordell, Albert. *Quaker Militant. John Greenleaf Whittier.* Boston & New York, 1933.
Preston, E. Delorus, Jr. "Genesis of the Underground Railroad." *Journal of Negro History,* XVIII (1933), 144–70.
Siebert, Wilbur H. *The Underground Railroad from Slavery to Freedom.* New York, 1898.

Chapter 8
Brooks, Van Wyck. *The Flowering of New England.* New York, 1936.
Burton, Katherine. *Paradise Planters.* New York, 1939.
Codman, John Thomas. *Brook Farm Historic and Personal Memoirs.* Boston, 1894.
Holloway, Mark. *Heavens on Earth.* New York, 1951.
Nordhoff, Charles. *The Communistic Societies of the United States.* New York, 1875.
Noyes, John Humphrey. *Bible Communism.* Oneida, N.Y., 1848.
Noyes, Pierrepont. *My Father's House.* New York, 1937.
Parker, Robert Allerton. *Yankee Saint.* New York, 1935. (A life of Noyes.)

Chapter 9
Brooks, Van Wyck. Cited above.
Dexter, Edwin Grant. *A History of Education in the United States.* New York, 1904.
Eddy, Sherwood, and Page, Kirby. *Makers of Freedom.* New York, 1926.
Ferguson, Charles W. *Fifty Million Brothers.* New York, 1937.
Hayes, Cecil B. *The American Lyceum.* Washington, 1932. Quotations on page 181 are from this book.
Holbrook, Stewart H. *The Yankee Exodus.* New York, 1950.
Hone, Philip. *Diary.* New York, 1936.
Hurlbut, Jesse Lyman. *The Story of Chautauqua.* New York, 1921.
Lutz, Alma. *Created Equal. A Biography of Elizabeth Cady Stanton.* New York, 1940.
MacLaren, Gay. *Morally We Roll Along.* Boston. 1938.
Stanton, Elizabeth Cady, and others. *History of Woman Suffrage.* New York, 1881.
Information was kindly supplied by the American Association of University Women, the General Federation of Women's Clubs and the League of Women Voters.

Chapter 10
Brooks, Robert R. R. *When Labor Organizes.* New Haven, 1942.
Chase, Stuart. *Roads to Agreement.* New York, 1951.
Galantiere, Lewis. "A Fresh Look at Our Economy." *Saturday Review,* Jan. 24, 1953.
Higgins, George G. *Voluntarism in Organized Labor in the United States 1930–1940.* Washington, 1944.

Hoffman, Paul. *Peace Can Be Won*. New York, 1951.
Lilienthal, David. *Big Business*. New York, 1953.
Millis, Harry A., and Montgomery, Royal E. *Organized Labor*. New York, 1945.
Powderly, Terence V. *The Path I Trod*. New York, 1940.
Ware, Norman J. *The Labor Movement in the United States 1860–1895*. New York, 1929.

Chapter 11
Buck, Solon J. *The Agrarian Crusade*. New Haven, 1920.
Gardner, Charles M. *The Grange—Friend of the Farmer*. Washington, 1949.
Truman, David B. *The Governmental Process*. New York, 1951.

Chapter 12
Bennington Evening Banner, April 14, 1953.
Community Chests and Councils of America. "Health and Welfare Planning in the Smaller Community." 1945.
———. "1952 Facts Book."
———. "Teamwork in Our Town." 1950.
———. "Youth and the Community." 1952.
Community Welfare Council of the Greater Sacramento Area. "Citizens in Action" (1952 Annual Report).
———. "The Oak Park Well Baby Clinic."
Council of Social Agencies, Shreveport, Louisiana. "The Shreveport Story." 1953.
Dillick, Sidney. *Community Organization*. New York, 1953.
Follett, Mary Parker. *The New State*. New York, 1918.
Ford, Lyman S. "Whither Federation?" *Survey Midmonthly*, Sept., 1948.
Morgan, Arthur E. *The Small Community*. New York, 1942.
Pennock, Clarice, and Robinson, Marion. "Why We Volunteer." *Survey Midmonthly*, Sept., 1948.
Red Cross. "Introduction to the Red Cross." American National Red Cross, 1951.
———. "Annual Report, 1952–3." Bennington County Chapter.
Warner, W. Lloyd, and Lunt, Paul S. *The Social Life of a Modern Community*. New Haven, 1941.
———. *The Status System of a Modern Community*. New Haven, 1942.
Welfare Association of Cleveland. "Area Councils." 1953.
———. "Neighbors in Action." 1952.
———. "Your Welfare Federation." 1948.
———. Several speeches by Edward D. Lynde, executive secretary.

Chapter 13
Allen, Frederick Lewis. *The Big Change*. New York, 1952.
Boulding, Kenneth E. *The Organizational Revolution*. New York, 1953.
Brewer, John M. *Wellsprings of Democracy*. New York, 1953. (How to run local voluntary groups.)
Brownell, Baker. *The Human Community*. New York, 1950.
Commager, Henry Steele. *The American Mind*. New York, 1950.
Curti, Merle. *The Growth of American Thought*. New York, 1943.
Denison, J. H. *Emotion as the Basis of Civilization*. New York, 1928.

Goldman, Eric F. *Rendezvous with Destiny*. New York, 1952.
Gray, Richard. "Are You Witch-Doctoring Delinquency?" *The Rotarian*, Feb., 1954.
Hird, Lewis A. "Arbitration—Growing Vine of Peace." *Ibid.*, Jan., 1954.
Homans, George C. *The Human Group*. New York, 1950.
Kluckhohn, Clyde. *Mirror for Man*. New York, 1949.
Lilienthal, David. *TVA: Democracy on the March*. New York, 1944.
Linton, Ralph. *The Study of Man*. New York, 1936.
Lippmann, Walter. *The Good Society*. Boston & New York, 1937.
Mumford, Lewis. *The Culture of Cities*. New York, 1938.
Nisbet, Robert A. *The Quest for Community*. New York, 1953.
Office of Defense Mobilization. "Report of the Task Force on the Handicapped." (Reprinted from the *Journal of Rehabilitation*, March–April, 1952.)
Smith, Bradford. "We're Selling America Short." *American Scholar*, Summer, 1952 and *Reader's Digest*, Dec., 1952.
Steiner, Jesse Frederick. *The American Community in Action*. New York, 1928.
Tocqueville, Alexis de. Cited above.

Chapter 14
Altekar, A. S. *A History of Village Communities in Western India*. Calcutta, 1927.
Boardman, Philip. *Patrick Geddes, Maker of the Future*. Chapel Hill, 1944.
Cowell, F. R. *History, Civilization and Culture*. Boston, 1952.
Department of State. *Fight for Food*. Publication 4534, April, 1952.
Ford, Mary Blackford. "The People Act." *Social Action*, April 15, 1951.
International Development Advisory Board. "Conclusions and Recommendations." Washington, Dec., 1953.
Jefferson Valley News, Nov. 27, 1952.
League of Women Voters. "Working Together for International Cooperation." Washington, Aug., 1953.
Liang, Y. K., and Tao, L. K. *Village and Town Life in China*. London, 1923.
Montagu, Ashley. *On Being Human*. New York, 1950.
Morgan, Arthur E. *The Small Community*. Cited above.
Mutual Security Agency. "Report to Congress on the Mutual Security Program." Washington, June 30, 1953.
New York Herald Tribune, Jan. 6, 1952.
"The People Act," Program 20, 1952. Owatonna, Minnesota.
Smith, Bradford. "We're Selling America Short." Cited above.
Snyder, Harold E. *When Peoples Speak to Peoples*. Washington, 1953.
U. S. Technical Cooperation Service for Lebanon. *Point 4 in Lebanon*. Beirut, n.d.
Whitman, Howard. "The War of Amazing Kindness." *This Week*, May 17, 1953.
Information was also supplied by the American Association for the United Nations, the United World Federalists, and World Neighbors, Inc.

The Columbia Encyclopedia, the *Dictionary of American Biography* and the *Encyclopaedia Britannica* were frequently useful.

Index

305